D0855913

'Taking the complexity of cutting edge research and mixing it with the insights from expert performers in elite sport, *The Best* stands out in offering a glimpse of the characteristics of greatness and highlighting the many factors that lead individuals to sporting triumph' David Colclough, Head of Coaching/Sports Science at The Professional Golfers' Association (The PGA)

'*The Best* provides a perfect balance between evidence-based and anecdotal writing. It is easy to read, yet insightful and thought-provoking. It provides a good framework to understand the multifactorial and random aspects involved in human talent. *The Best* is a great resource for anyone interested in skill learning, talent identification and expert performance in sport' Xavi Schelling, Director of Sports Science and Performance, San Antonio Spurs

'The authors have created a piece of work that encapsulates everything we *should* know about identifying and developing champions. This book is a must for any coach, Sporting Director, teacher or mentor; in fact, anyone involved in finding talent and creating opportunity for potential to become reality. In this one book, the authors cover the full spectrum of requirements for elite athletes to become the best they can be and provide the tools for others to help them.' Les Reed, Technical Director, The Football Association

'A must read for any coach who wants to optimize and facilitate athlete development. The book highlights how talent develops by creating realistic practice situations and empowering athletes. The book, amongst other things, has the athlete and sport at its core, while bestowing on the coach a crucial role as the facilitator of sporting greatness'. Isaac Guerrero, Head of Coaching at FC Barcelona

'*The Best* is simply an essential read. It takes us on a rollercoaster tour of the journeys of some of the world's most celebrated athletes and explains how they achieved sporting greatness.' Christopher Carling, Head of Performance, French Football Federation

'In *The Best*, the authors' vast scientific expertise and real-world experience from the trenches of elite sport results in a fascinating, informative, and immediately relevant read. I devoured it in a weekend and immediately shared it with my National Team coaches and performance staff.' Peter Vint, Chief of Sport, USA Volleyball

'A comprehensive book, which thoroughly covers, using science and interviews with successful athletes, the key factors that impact on a prosperous career in sport. For those involved in this domain, this is a very important read that helps improve understanding of the nuances that exist along the pathway to sporting excellence' Juninho Paulista, General Manager, Brazil National Football Team

The Best

How Elite Athletes are Made

A. MARK WILLIAMS
TIM WIGMORE

NICHOLAS BREALEY
PUBLISHING

London • Boston

First published in Great Britain in 2020 by Nicholas Brealey Publishing, an imprint of John Murray Press, a division of Hodder & Stoughton Ltd. An Hachette UK company.

British Library Cataloguing in Publication Data: a catalogue record for this title is available from the British Library.
Library of Congress Catalog Card Number: on file.

Hardback ISBN 978 1 529 30435 0
Trade paperback ISBN 978 1 529 30436 7
Ebook ISBN 978 1 529 30438 1

1

Typeset by Cenveo® Publisher Services.

Printed and bound in Great Britain by Clays Ltd, Elcograf S.p.A.

Hachette UK policy is to use papers that are natural, renewable and recyclable products and made from wood grown in sustainable forests. The logging and manufacturing processes are expected to conform to the environmental regulations of the country of origin.

Nicholas Brealey Publishing
Carmelite House
50 Victoria Embankment
London EC4Y 0DZ

Nicholas Brealey Publishing
Hachette Book Group
Market Place, Center 53, State Street
Boston, MA 02109, USA

www.nicholasbrealey.com

Contents

CONTENTS

About the authors

A. Mark Williams is an academic and one of the world's leading authorities on expertise and its acquisition in sport. He has published 18 books and written over 500 scientific articles on how people become skilled and achieve success in sport and across other professional domains. He has worked across the globe as a consultant with numerous Olympic and professional sports and has vast experience as a scientist, author and educator, and as an applied sports scientist.

Tim Wigmore is the author of *Cricket 2.0: Inside the T20 Revolution*, the winner of the Wisden Book of the Year award for 2020. He is a sports writer for *The Daily Telegraph*, and has also written regularly for *The New York Times, The Economist*, the *New Statesman* and *ESPNCricinfo*. He is a former winner of the Young Cricket Journalist of the Year award and has been shortlisted for the Cricket Writer of the Year award.

Acknowledgements

We would like to thank the following people for commenting on earlier drafts of chapters:

Genevieve Albouy, David Anderson, Joe Baker, Sian Beilock, Retief Broodryk, James Bunce, Geoffrey Burns, Rouwen Cañal-Bruland, Chris Carling, Joe Causer, Omar Chaudhuri, Steve Cobley, Israel Teoldo Da Costa, Dave Collins, Damien Conyngham-Hynes, Jean Côté, Stewart Cotterill, Edward Coughlan, Sean Cummings, Brady DeCouto, David Eccles, Mark Eys, Anders Ericsson, Jeff Fairbrother, Damian Farrow, Brad Fawver, Paul Ford, Dan Gallan, Claudia Gonzalez, Mark Guadagnoli, Daniel Gucciardi, Arne Güllich, Rob Gray, Isaac Guerro, David Hancock, Joe Harris, Chris Harwood, Nicola Hodges, Nick Holt, Nick Hoult, Robin Jackson, Chris Janelle, Ian Janssen, Ben Jones, Geir Jordet, Jarrod Kimber, Brad King, Tristan Lavalette, Amanda Lomas, Fay Lomas, Paul Lomas, Keith Lohse, Florian Loffing, Travis Maak, Joe Maguire, David Mann, David Martin, Jono McCrostie, Alistair McRobert, Daniel Memmert, Frode Moen, James Morton, Jamie North, Tim Olds, Les Podlog, Alun Powell, Matthew Reeves, Oliver Runswick, David Richardson, Andre Roca, Robin Russell, Jason Sherwin, Stig Arve Seather, Nick Smeeton, Alex Sword, Troy Taylor, Gershon Tenenbaum, Yannis Pitsiladis, Roel Vaeyens, Joan Vickers, Vince Walsh, Nick Wattie, Mark Wilson, David Whiteside, Ania Wigmore, Richard Wigmore, Stuart Willick, Zoe Wimhurst, David Wright and Gaby Wulf.

Our sincere apologies if we have inadvertently omitted anyone.

Particular thanks to Matthew Syed for setting up the collaboration between us, and to our literary agent, David Luxton, for his advice and support, and to Iain Campbell at Nicholas Brealey for his encouragement and enthusiasm.

We gratefully thank all the athletes that agreed to be interviewed and cited in the book. You remain a source of inspiration for our writing.

Mark would particularly like to thank his family – Sara, Tom, Matt and Alex – for their unstinting support on this project.

Tim would particularly like to thank his parents and partner, Fay, who probably wished this project hadn't occupied many of the months after their engagement.

Foreword

I think most of us, even those of us who are slightly obsessed with it, know that sport isn't the most consequential thing in the world. It may be fun and diverting, but it isn't life and death. As the great football manager Arrigo Sacchi put it, sport is "the most important of the unimportant things in life".

But sport has another role, too, beyond providing exercise and entertainment: it helps us to understand ourselves. It helps us to grasp why some people excel and others do not, why some strive while others fizzle out, why some cope with pressure and others fall apart.

This book is a cutting edge analysis of what we now call sports science, but is really a deconstruction about how we can all be the best we can be. From a starting discussion on why younger siblings tend to outperform older ones, we are taken on a journey into the rich terrain of the human body and mind.

I first came across Mark Williams when researching my first book, Bounce, because his academic papers stood out for their insight and clarity. I went to Liverpool John Moores University (his place of work at the time) to learn more about his research into perceptual intelligence in sport. This book is a timely way of bringing his research to a wider audience.

I first got to know Tim Wigmore while reading his fine and analytical articles in the popular media. He seemed like the perfect person to team up with Mark to write a book bringing together the different strands of sports science, in a way that might both help us to understand the construction of greatness, and offer practical tips on practice, parenting and performing.

It is interesting that sport, as a cultural institution, has grown beyond all expectation in recent decades. There are few nations on earth that are unmoved by the feats of the finest athletes, whether it is Usain Bolt powering down the track in an Olympic arena, Serena Williams powering her way to another grand slam title, or Roger Federer turning tennis into performance art. I have little doubt that sport will continue to grow, continue to inspire, continue to bring meaning both to the lives of those who watch it, and those who play it.

As I write these words, I am midway through watching The Last Dance, the ESPN documentary series about NBA giant, Michael Jordan. It is a thrilling narrative, chronicling the career of a sportsman who took a failing basketball franchise by the scruff of the neck and turned it into one of the greatest teams of all time. It is about strength of character, Jordan's refusal to brook anything other than excellence, and his willingness to set an example to all around him. Jordan could be difficult, perhaps even overbearing at times, but there is no disputing his relentless effectiveness.

I noticed on twitter one poster asking: "how do you become so good at something". Another asked: "How did he reach such incredible heights?". It is perhaps impossible to give a complete answer to a question so complex, almost mystical. But this book gives it a very good go.

Matthew Syed
May 2020

Prologue

Every day the best athletes are everywhere: on our television screens, on our social media feeds and in our newspapers. What are the odds of joining them? Actually, we know the answer. One US high-school player out of every 5,768 becomes a professional football player, one out of every 11,771 becomes a men's basketball player, and one out of every 13,015 becomes a professional women's basketball player.[1]

But this is just to become professional athletes. When it comes to being the best in their sport, naturally the odds increase markedly. There are 5.3 million female US basketball players[2] but only one Elena Delle Donne, who has the best free-throw percentage of any basketball player, male or female, in history. In South Africa, there are 460,000 rugby players – but, only one Siya Kolisi, who captained the Springboks to Rugby World Cup glory in 2019.[3] And in England only 180 of the 1.5 million players who play organized football each year become Premier League players – a success rate of 0.012 per cent.[4] This shows how remarkable Marcus Rashford's journey to scoring on his England debut aged 18 is.

Delle Donne, Kolisi and Rashford are three of the athletes that we interviewed to understand their journeys to the summit of professional sport. Jamie Carragher, Pete Sampras, Steph Curry, Dan Carter, Joey Votto, Ian Poulter, Annika Sorenstam, Mike Hussey, Ada Hegerberg, Helen Glover, Shane Battier, Kumar Sangakkara and Stephen Hendry were among those who also generously shared their insights.

The Best: How Elite Athletes are Made is the story of how athletes rise to the top. Combining cutting-edge sports science research with dozens of exclusive interviews with leading players and coaches, the book seeks answers to fundamental questions. What makes them stand out? What makes them the best at what they do? What separates them from those who fail to make the grade?

In the first chapters of the book we explore the luck of birth, and how this impacts who becomes the best athletes. It explains why younger siblings have a significantly greater chance of becoming elite athletes than older siblings. It explores what it takes to be the parent of future champions with the help of Judy Murray. It investigates the perfect type of town for athletes to be born in, and why mid-sized towns produce far more champions. We also go on a journey to the banlieues of Paris, the football hub of the world, to explore why the area produces more elite footballers than anywhere else – and what this reveals about the playgrounds of sporting greatness, and how environment and culture shape who rises to the summit of sport.

The book then explains how athletes perform their extraordinary feats. Athletes can process swathes of complex information instantaneously to decide on the appropriate action, often under intense pressure. As former Liverpool Football Club defender Jamie Carragher explains, reading the game is about the speed of players' minds, not their hands or feet. The best athletes, we'll discover, literally use their eyes differently than less successful ones. We decode how athletes think and read the game, and answer some essential questions: How do players really hit a baseball or cricket ball when it takes under 0.5 seconds to reach them? Why do underarm serves and grunts work in tennis? And why are left-handers overrepresented in elite sport? We also explore how Kolisi led South Africa to World Cup glory and what the story reveals about the science of teamwork in sport, why athletes choke, and why – like Ian Poulter in the Ryder Cup – some deliver their best under pressure. And we explain how to win a penalty shoot-out.

Finally, we explore how athletes practise and develop their skills to reach the next level. Delle Donne explores the training regime that helped her become the best ever free-throw shooter, and we explain what this shows about the type of practice necessary to attain greatness. The best athletes, we discover, have ownership over their practice, rather than simply being told what to do. We explore how coaches can enable greatness, encapsulated by the story of Danny Kerry, the former head coach of Great Britain hockey, who transformed his coaching based on research into skill acquisition, leading the country to its first ever hockey gold medal in the Olympics.

And we visit FC Barcelona, one of the foremost sports clubs in the world, to explore how they are using technology to improve their players further. Neuroscience and technology like virtual reality have the potential to push athletes to even greater heights.

Our focus is broadly on the most popular sports – so, while we cover Olympic sports, there is much football, basketball, cricket, tennis, golf, rugby union and baseball. The book combines world-leading sports science research with exclusive interviews with dozens of leading athletes and coaches. The range of athletes we interviewed illuminates the research and shows the many different routes that exist to reach the top. The focus of the book is mostly sociological and psychological – though, as we explore, physical and physiological factors do matter, too.

The result is, we hope, a genuine and compelling account of how the best athletes are really made – from their childhoods all the way up to how they train and how they think in the cauldron of competition. Naturally, this shows the messy complexity of reality – we have avoided the temptation to invent 'rules' which, while superficially attractive, conceal as much as they reveal.

We do not claim there is a simple template to becoming the best, or even maximizing your chances of becoming the best you can be – sport, like life, is altogether more complicated. Neither do we claim that everyone can become the best – leading athletes benefit from a complex, and interrelated, mixture of nature and nurture. But, as we explore, there are certain characteristics that are common in many of the best athletes during their childhoods and careers, and which shed light on what it takes to be an elite athlete. Players, parents, coaches and fans can, we believe, learn much from these stories.

Our aim in writing this book is not to provide a template for future would-be champions. It is, instead, to answer the two eternal questions of all watchers of great sport: Why them? And how do they do that?

We hope you enjoy finding out the answers as much as we did.

PART ONE

Nature, serendipity and the role of chance in making champions

For many parents, it would be an unpalatable test of their allegiances to see their children battle against each other in a public competition. Gjert Ingebrigtsen was used to it; he had spent much of the past 20 years seeing his children race each other. And so, when he settled in to watch the 2018 European Athletics Championships in Berlin, the sight was familiar.

To the rest of the world, though, what they witnessed on the nights of 10 and 11 August was altogether more arresting. In the 1500 metres track race on 10 August, 17-year-old Jakob Ingebrigtsen became the youngest ever athlete to win an event in the European Championships. After he did so, two of his elder brothers, Henrik and Filip, joined him in celebrating on the track at the Olympic Stadium.

In itself, there was nothing unusual about siblings celebrating with the new champion – except that both had just competed against him in the very same race. Filip, who punched the air, had finished only 12th; this was deeply disappointing, for he was the defending champion, after winning gold in the same event two years earlier. Henrik, who draped his arm around Jakob and pointed to him, had come fourth. He, too, knew what winning the 1500 metres gold medal felt like – six years earlier, he had done it himself. Now, all three brothers had won the European title, one of the marque events of the European Championships.[1]

Jakob and Henrik were celebrating together again just under 24 hours later at the Olympic Stadium. Jakob, remarkably, had won another gold medal – making him the first man in 84 years to win the 1500 and 5000 metres double at the European Championships, and all before he was old enough to be allowed to drive. As Jakob celebrated while holding the Norwegian flag, next to him was Henrik, who had finished the 5000 metres race just 1.7 seconds behind Jakob, to win the silver medal.

Younger … and better

When his girls Serena and Venus were three and four, Richard Williams hatched a plan: he would give them tennis rackets and train them both, setting them on a path to becoming champions. Even as Venus developed faster in their childhood years, Richard always said that Serena would go on to be the better player.

Richard Williams was right. Both Venus and Serena would become among the finest ever to play the sport. And, as her father had always predicted, Serena would go on to be the best Williams. With 23 singles Grand Slams and 39 Grand Slams in total, she is probably the finest women's player in history.[2]

This is the little sibling effect in action: younger siblings tend to outperform their older brothers and sisters. If you have a younger sibling, they are probably better at sport than you are.

On average, elite athletes have 1.04 older siblings, while those who are non-elite have only 0.6 older siblings, according to an analysis of Australian and Canadian athletes across 33 different sports.[3] In the study, elite athletes – who had reached senior international competition – and non-elite athletes – who had reached junior national or senior domestic level – on average had the same number of siblings overall. What mattered was whether they were younger or older.

Even when two siblings both reach professional level, the younger one retains salient advantages. In Major League Baseball, younger brothers outperform their older brothers.[3] Among pairs of brothers that played Test cricket – the five-day format considered the sport's pinnacle – younger brothers have had a more successful career twice as often as elder brothers.[3] On average, batters who played Test cricket for England between 2004 and 2019 had 1.2 older siblings, compared with 0.4 for county-level batters.[3]

Jakob is the fifth of the seven Ingebrigtsen siblings. And so he has been able to mimic the training techniques of his brothers Filip and Henrik, who are seven and nine years his senior. Even these two had the benefits of having an elder sibling – Filip is the second of the siblings, with an elder brother who also ran in his youth, while Henrik is the third born.

'I've been a professional runner since I was eight, nine, 10 years old,' Jakob said after his double triumph in Berlin. 'I've been training, dedicated and following a good structure – the same as my brothers – from an early age.

'It was a little crazy to get this medal, this is huge. But winning a second title in two days is the result of having done this my whole life.' From an early age, Jakob trained with his brothers, matching their intervals from the age of 16 or 17.[4]

While Jakob's victories in Berlin were extraordinary, surpassing his brothers was not. From the age of 15 onwards, Jakob achieved better results than his brothers at the same age in the 800 metres – and, from 16, in the 1500 metres.[4] Aged 16, he became the youngest ever athlete to break the four-minute mile.

As with the Ingebrigtsen clan, older siblings double as recruiters into a particular sport, with younger siblings often choosing, or being pushed, to play with their older siblings. Remarkably, after the 2019 Rugby World Cup, 46 sets of brothers had played for New Zealand; family ties have underpinned one of the most successful sports teams in history.

A trickle-down effect

'She would always drag me out to run or to kick balls,' Ada Hegerberg, the winner of football's 2018 Ballon d'Or Féminin for the best female player in the world, recalled of her sister Andrine, two years her elder. 'She was a leading figure for me.'

Ada is the youngest of the three children. 'If it hadn't been for my elder brother and older sister, I don't think I would have achieved what I have. I was a "hang-around" in the beginning, but slowly when I got to eight or nine years of age I was dragged into it and I couldn't stop playing football. So they had a huge impact.'

First-borns have to wait for their parents to play with them, or their parents to arrange play-dates; those with elder siblings do not. They are born with someone to play with – and if their elder siblings are ferried around to play sport, they will often be taken along with them, increasing their exposure to regular sport at a younger age.

'Older siblings play an important role in athlete development – they can act as socializing agents, introducing their younger siblings to sport, either through informal play at home, or by parents dragging younger siblings along to their older sibling's sporting commitments,' explained Melissa Hopwood, the co-author of the study into Australian and Canadian athletes. 'The older siblings then act as role models and coaches, teaching their younger siblings the rules and skills of the sport by observation or direct instruction.'

In team sports, younger siblings often play with their elder siblings – just as Ada Hegerberg did. Doing so, Hopwood said, can 'force the development of more advanced skills at a younger age in order to keep up with their teammates'.

The advantage multiplies in women's sports. A study of the US national football team – consistently the best country in the world, and the 2019 World Cup winners – found that fewer players in the squad were an only child than the national average. Only 20 per cent of national team players were the eldest sibling, but 74 per cent of players had an older sibling – three-quarters of these older siblings played football. Whether the older siblings were boys or girls made no difference.[5]

In many countries, having at least one elder brother increases a girl's chances of participating in sport. 'Older brothers are more likely to be engaged in sport and high levels of informal play, so this may normalize the activity for their younger siblings,' said Hopwood. 'For girls with older brothers there is likely going to be a greater physical discrepancy between the two siblings so the girls have to smarten up and toughen up.' Of the English women's football squad who reached the semi-final of the 2019 World Cup, 52 per cent had an elder brother, and two-thirds had an elder sibling.[5] All but one of England's cricket squad that lifted the Women's World Cup at Lord's in 2017 had at least one older brother who played cricket.

Sibling rivalry

The urge to keep up drives younger siblings. 'Everyone expects I will win and if I don't it will be a big disappointment,' Jakob said in a documentary following the Ingebrigtsen family before his professional career began.[6] 'My biggest dream is to be better than Henrik. I think when I am about 20 I will beat him.' He didn't even need that long.

Siblings develop different motivations and goals based on their birth order. First-borns develop a preference for mastery goals – those based on self-referenced standards of competence. Second-borns are more likely to prefer performance goals, which are based on other-referenced standards of competence. The contrast suggests that, in general, the goals of second-borns are better-suited to a career in professional sport.[7] A study comparing three groups of athletes – so-called super-champions, who reached the pinnacle of their sport, champions, and 'almosts', who didn't make it to the top despite promising junior careers – found that a desire to keep up with older siblings was a driving force for many who went on to be leading athletes.[8]

'You know I was always really very, very, very good,' recalled Venus Williams, who was born 15 months earlier than Serena. 'Serena, on the other hand, wasn't very good at all. She was small, really slim and the racket was way too big for her. Hopeless.'[9] Serena did not allow herself to be outclassed on the tennis court for long. As their mother recalled, 'With Serena, everything had to be perfect and she would get frustrated if it wasn't. She always had to win, no matter if it was a talent show, cards, she had to be the winner.'[10]

Some advantages enjoyed by younger siblings derive from how their parents treat them. Parents are notoriously more indulgent of later-born children, letting them go out at a younger age and engage in higher-risk activities.[3] Such effects permeate sport, too. Compared to older siblings, younger ones are 40 per cent more likely to play dangerous contact sports than their elder brothers and sisters – so they have more opportunity to make it to the top in these sports.[3]

In sport, and beyond, younger siblings are more likely to take an unorthodox, less conformist approach, and not feel confined to stick to the rules. First-borns take more conservative career options – earning more money at the start of their careers – and are more supportive of the political status quo. According to analysis done by Frank J. Sulloway,[11] later-born children are 'significantly more likely than first-borns to support radical political changes'. Sulloway has also shown that, remarkably, younger brothers are 10 times more likely than their older brothers to attempt to steal a base in baseball;[12] Jackie Robinson, acclaimed as the 'father of base stealing', had four elder siblings.

When competing against older siblings – and their friends – in informal games, younger siblings need cunning to make up for their physical disadvantages. Younger siblings often develop 'superior perceptual-cognitive skills, more creativity and highly refined technical skills' than older siblings, Hopwood explained.

As they have had less time to practise, and are less physically developed, younger siblings normally lose in family games. The experiences force children to become adept at dealing with failure, harnessing their competitiveness and mental resilience.

'They would try to intimidate me,' AB de Villiers, who was later ranked the number-one batsman in the world in both Test and one-day international cricket, recounted of childhood games with his two elder brothers, who were six and nine years older. 'My brothers were merciless. They were monsters. There were always a lot of tears – usually mine.'[13]

So perhaps Jakob's records will last only until his younger brother William – born in 2013 – turns professional. 'We have another brother who is turning five years old, and soon he can join the team,' said Henrik, after winning the silver medal in the 5000 metres race at the Olympic Stadium. 'There are no limits for us.'[4]

Learning together

Simply having a sibling at all increases a child's chances of becoming an elite athlete. Participation rates in sport tend to be higher among children with siblings. Worldwide, elite athletes' siblings are 2.3 times more likely to play sport regularly;[14] China's former one-child policy, then, does not seem conducive to producing champions.

'We are competitors, brothers and good friends,' Filip has said. 'We push each other during training.'[15] As with the Ingebrigtsen brothers, siblings can provide companionship, emotional support and drive.

'It is competitive between us in a healthy way,' Filip said in Berlin.[1] 'We try to train smart and push each other within the limits. But the psychological rivalry between us is one of the reasons why we are competing for medals every year.'

In 2017, Henrik recalled, 'I was injured and had to go through surgery. It was hard to start training for the 2018 season. When I could follow Filip and Jakob on the interval sessions during the spring 2018, I knew I was able to fight for a medal in the 2018 European Championship.'[15]

Working with siblings may accelerate learning. Two, or more, people working together to learn a particular task – dyadic learning – is more conducive to learning new skills.[16] Multiple people learning together leads to greater verbal interaction between learners, and greater motivation and feedback sharing. 'It's almost like getting a mirror on your own performance if you can watch someone who's similarly skilled make mistakes or gradually get better,' said Nicola Hodges, an expert in skill acquisition from the University of British Columbia. Such an environment benefits all learners, but especially younger siblings – younger children can learn more from their siblings than vice versa. 'I've learned a lot from watching Venus,' Serena said in 1998. 'Her results have encouraged me to work harder so that I can do well, too.'[17]

It is not only that younger children can learn from their siblings. Parents also learn from how they nurtured their elder children – retaining what worked best, but refining what did not to give their youngest children a better experience. This seems to have been the experience with the Williams sisters. 'It's almost like Venus, being the older sister, was the guinea pig on certain shots, and they got the technique better with Serena,' the former US tennis player Pam Shriver observed of the sisters.[2] Parents are 'more familiar with how to navigate the sporting system by the time their second child was involved,' Hopwood found in her study. 'They knew the good clubs, the good coaches, the commitment required, so they had a more informed, deliberate experience rather than flying blind.'

'Both Filip and him have learned from my mistakes,'[1] Henrik said after Jakob's first gold medal in Berlin. 'I have made a lot of mistakes!

'Every year we try to optimize our programme and all of our workouts and Jakob is starting his training with the perfect programmes, more or less ... My father, me and Filip [sic] have spent years optimizing the programme and making it perfect. Hopefully, we will tweak it and make it even better and let us take one gold more each.'

Jamie and Andy: a 'team family'

Growing up in Dunblane, a town of 9,000 people in central Scotland, Jamie and Andy Murray were a little like the Ingebrigtsens. They would play each other at everything – although, unlike the Ingebrigtsens, it normally involved a ball.

The local tennis club was a minute's walk away. The club was by a park, where the Murrays used to play football with friends, and a golf course. 'We'd just go and play – either together or with friends,' Jamie recalled. 'We'd just go and play and hit balls.' In the height of summer it is light till after 10 o'clock in Dunblane, 'so you could spend the whole day and evening playing sport'.

At home, the boys 'were always making up their own games, and their own scoring systems for all sorts of things', their mother Judy said. They wrestled, making belts out of cardboard and glue – Andy normally played as the Rock – played balloon tennis over the sofa, ping-pong over tables and golf putting competitions in the hall.

At home, Jamie remembered using junior trophies they had won as nets. 'We'd have these tiny rackets and a sponge ball – we would play for hours and just loved it. But that stuff was all teaching us feel and skill without us really noticing.'

While only children are more likely to be dependent on playing with their parents or in formal settings at schools or sports clubs, children with siblings of a similar age generally begin playing informally with other children at a younger age. 'We would always do the same stuff together,' Jamie recalled. The Murrays were an example of what Canadian sociologists have called a 'team family', with sport acting as the backdrop for the development of sibling relationships, creating an environment for practising skills, formal and informal instruction and shared identity and purpose.[18]

Informal games help develop movement skills and encourage players to think for themselves.[19, 20] Informal play exposes players to a far greater number of variables – and, therefore, new situations – than traditional formal training.

It didn't matter what the games were – they were fiercely contested in the Murray household. 'What helped Andy become that sort of uber-competitor was having an older brother who's a bit bigger and a bit stronger than him through most of his formative years,' Judy reflected. 'All he ever wanted to do was to beat Jamie.'

These childhood games shaped the tennis player that Andy became. 'The resilience of Andy is incredible. He has that real bloody-mindedness, Scottishness – so if you tell me I can't do something I will prove to you that I can.'

Success and sacrifice

Many elite athletes have risen from tremendous adversity to the summit. This creates the illusion that sporting talent can rise regardless of family background. Yet, even athletes who have experienced childhood trauma – like the death of a loved one or material hardship – tend to have benefited from crucial familial support.

'My whole family played a massive part in my life. Without them, you wouldn't even know me,' Raheem Sterling, the England and Manchester City footballer, wrote for *The Players' Tribune*.[21] At the core of the story of how Sterling became one of the world's best footballers is a tale of family sacrifice.

When Sterling was two, his father was murdered in Jamaica. His mother moved to London to work and study so she could provide for her children; Sterling remained in Kingston, Jamaica, with his grandmother, and then joined his mother in England aged five.

Sterling's mother was instrumental in his career development. 'My mum is a proper warrior. She knows how to make it in this world,' he wrote. When Sterling was approached to join Arsenal, his mother pushed him to join Queens Park Rangers instead – a far less prestigious club, but one that would give him more game time.

The journey to the club involved three buses. 'We'd leave at 3:15 and get home at 11 p.m. Every. Single. Day,' Sterling wrote. His elder sister always accompanied him. 'Imagine being 17 years old and doing that for your little brother. And I never once heard her say, "No, I don't want to take him."'

'My mum sacrificed her life to get me here. My sister sacrificed her life to get me here.

'My whole mission was to get a professional contract so that my mother and sister didn't have to stress anymore. The day that I bought my mum a house, that was probably the happiest I've ever been.'

Sterling's tale illustrates how central family support is to becoming an elite athlete. Children with an overall lack of parental or guardian involvement are less likely to succeed in any domain. The football development consultant Robin Russell observed that virtually every footballer, including those from the most deprived socioeconomic backgrounds, still typically had at least one crucial source of familial stability – at least one dependable, loving parent or surrogate parent or guardian, such as a grandparent or elder sibling – to help with their journey. So even in football, the most accessible and democratic sport in the world, the role of families is crucial. Positive family attitudes towards playing contribute to children's self-confidence and motivation to continue sport.

Parents need to ensure their children have access to appropriate facilities, opponents and coaches – through formal club structures, playing informally with friends or family, or kicking a ball around with their children themselves. In many sports, such support requires time and money.[22]

A big investment

When the Murray brothers started playing tennis, 'there were no coaches in our area, so I started to volunteer a couple of hours a week,' Judy recalled. She eventually became Scotland's national tennis coach in 1995, the year that Andy turned eight and Jamie nine. 'I had a £25,000 salary, and a £90,000 budget for the whole of Scotland, from age seven up through seniors, and that was to pay for courts, extra coaches, fitness training, and competitions.' She started small, with a group of 20 children, including her sons.

'You want to make things happen, you bring all the parents in, because nobody wants things to happen more for their kids than the parents. So, we created a car-share rota, people putting others up overnight. I taught them how to staff matches, how to run tournaments. And as a result of setting up this kind of family feel, everybody was in it together.

'It was like an adventure for them. We'd go off down to England sort of every second weekend in a minibus packed with kids, and they learned to fend for themselves and how to look after each other. Often I'd be driving the minibus, and it was just me and 16 kids – you wouldn't be allowed to do that now, but that was how it was. The older kids had to look after the younger ones. If I was going to do it again, I would do it exactly the same way, because it was fun, and it was normal.'

Judy and other parents ensured that players were exposed continually to new challenges. 'It's very easy in tennis to become a big fish in a small pond, and as soon as you become a big fish in a small pond you need to get out of the small pond and find a bigger pond. We got used to travelling long distances to find competition.'

As her boys developed – Jamie went to train in Paris, and Andy in Barcelona – so the demands on Judy increased. 'We couldn't afford to pay other people to do things, so I learned all sorts of things, including how to do the tax returns in four different countries. I did a massage course so I could do the "rub-downs" after the matches so we didn't have to pay. There were just loads of things that I had to learn to do, because it was a necessity. It's why so many parents travel with their kids on the tennis circuit – they can't afford to pay anybody else.

'When you play overseas in junior tennis there's no prize money – it's a bit like going on holiday every week. You're paying for the flights or trains and food and the hotels, restrings and the entry fees and the phone calls.

'It requires an awful lot of investment of time and money to grow a young tennis player,' Judy reflected. This isn't only true of tennis. In the USA, a study of the parents of women's youth national football teams found that 63 per cent of mothers volunteered in some role for their child's club, 56 per cent of fathers trained their daughters individually, and 50 per cent volunteered to coach their child's team.[23] The parents and other family members able to help their children in the right ways help to determine who morphs into elite athletes.

The dangers of 'helicopter parenting'

'They hover over and then rescue their children whenever trouble arises. They're forever running lunches, permission slips, band instruments, and homework assignments to school. They're always pulling their children out of jams.'

The child development researchers Foster Cline and Jim Fay first coined the term 'helicopter parenting' to describe parents who are obsessively involved in their children's lives, trying to solve all of their problems and protect them from danger.[24]

While parental involvement is often crucial for budding athletes, especially in individual sports, it must be the right type of involvement.

By taking responsibility away from children, helicopter parenting appears detrimental to their prospects of becoming elite athletes.

By micro-managing their children's lives, helicopter parents often prevent children from doing much informal play. The more that parents are hyper-engaged with their children, the less their children are likely to do physical activities – particularly unsupervised informal play, explained Ian Janssen, from Queen's University in Canada. So the greater the amount of helicopter parenting, the less informal play that children tend to do.[25] Rather than helicopter parenting, 'setting clear boundaries but allowing children freedom and independence within those boundaries are associated with positive outcomes in school and sport development,' explained Nicholas Holt, a specialist in sports development from the University of Alberta.[26]

Excessive parental pressure and expectations have been linked with higher anxiety, reduced self-esteem and self-confidence in young athletes, and even burnout and dropout. Helicopter parenting is associated with lower engagement in sport and physical activity among North American children.[27]

Ostensibly, Judy's involvement in her children's embryonic sports careers and her tennis pedigree may have encouraged her to be a helicopter parent. Yet she consciously eschewed helicopter parenting. 'I'm a huge believer in making kids think for themselves.' After they had played a match, and especially when they had struggled, Judy preferred to 'ask questions, rather than telling them what to do', she said.

'For the most part the more you ask them questions about what they think they should do in a match the better – what happened at certain points in the match, what could you have done differently if you played that match tomorrow, what do you want to work on? It was always about trying to understand what they took out of the match.

'It was really important for them to make their own decisions and choices, because if it's their decision they own that decision, they commit to that decision. And of course you jump in as a parent if you see them about to make a massive mistake, but I'm also a big believer in letting kids make mistakes and learning from their mistakes.'

Jamie recalled that his mum 'would always put the emphasis on us to talk about why things hadn't gone our way, or why did this not work, or what was your opponent doing to you that you were struggling with on that day that you couldn't adapt. Letting us talk rather than just be told "OK, your serve was poor today or your forehand was rubbish, you were hitting everything in the net." The emphasis was on us to take ownership for what we were doing out there, and take responsibility for what happened on the court, because ultimately it's up to us, right?'

As Judy also coached others, she was not solely focused on her children's tennis. 'It helped that I was the national coach and was responsible for loads of kids, which meant I didn't get so caught up in just my own kids, which I think for most parents is what it's like.'

Parenting can reinforce a child's development in sport – but it can also undermine it. 'The whole triangle between the parent, the athlete or the child, and the coach – it has to be a three-way thing,' Judy said. For instance, a coach trying to imbue a child with resilience is undermined 'if the kid is then being spoiled at home and treated like a little princess or prince … It's really important that the parents understand their role.'

The parents of budding athletes need to support the athlete, manage themselves and their wellbeing, and deal with the wider interactions in youth sport with other parents, coaches and administrators.[27] 'Parents need to develop and use effectively a range of intrapersonal, interpersonal, and organisational skills in order to best support their child,' explained Chris Harwood, a sports psychologist from Loughborough University.

Different jobs: parenting and training

Coaches often grumble about the need to create academies for the parents of prodigies, not just the children themselves. At the start of each intake of French football's famous Clairefontaine academy, there is a special address to parents. 'I have a meeting with all of the parents, and I say I do my job, and you do your job,' said Christian Bassila, the director of Clairefontaine. 'What is your job? Just to be parents, to be normal parents. Just stay parents, and it would be perfect.'

Bassila loathes parents who prematurely hype up their children. 'One father called me and said, "I have some journalist who wants to write an article about my son. Is it possible?" In my head I say "unbe-lievable". Your son is 14 years old. These parents dream too much. He cannot understand now, but it will have a big impact.'

Some children arrive at Clairefontaine with parents carrying 'everything' for them. With such special treatment 'you don't give them good values', Bassila reflected. 'Just take care of your son like a normal parent. Don't think, "Oh, my son is a very good football player."'

'The parents can be your secret weapon as a coach if you get them on side,' Judy Murray observed. 'They can really help you to develop the child as a professional – bringing a good attitude, being a great competitor, packing their own bag, getting their own snacks at the supermarket – understanding what their sport is about.' Travelling for junior tournaments, Judy readily encounters children who break strings in their rackets. When she tells them to get the racket restrung, they say, "My mum always gets it done for me. I'll call my mum. My mum will know." And I'm like, "It's not your mum's racket, it's your racket."'

Dave Collins, a sports psychologist, analysed what separated super champions – those with over 50 international caps or five or more world championship medals – from 'almosts', those who excelled at youth level but didn't make it beyond the second division or win any medals as an adult. The parents of 'almosts' seem far more consumed by their child's nascent sporting career.[8]

'Super champs would come home from school at 13, they'd just been training. Mum or Dad would go "How was that? Good. Now go and do your homework,"' Collins said. 'The mums and dads of the "almosts" were on the phone saying, "Why isn't my little soldier playing centre-forward?" "Let's get him some extra this, let's get him some extra that."'

'I see more helicopter parenting than I've ever seen before,' Judy Murray reflected. 'But it doesn't help you to produce fight-ers, competitors, warriors on the sports field if the parents are doing everything.

'You can't try and solve all your kid's problems – you can't protect them from everything. And that's actually bad for their chance of going on to become a top athlete.'

Unusually, the Murray brothers did not just both reach number one in the tennis rankings, they also reached the summit in completely different ways: Andy, a right-handed singles player renowned for his backcourt play, and Jamie, a left-handed doubles player who dominates the net.

'We've got a lefty, a righty, a singles player, a doubles player, one who loves all the flashy stuff around the net and the other one who runs around the baseline, never say die,' Judy said. 'They're completely different, but their game styles reflect their physicality and their personalities. And so they went completely different paths in tennis but they both ended up at the top of the game in different ways.

'It would have been much easier if they had gone down the same path,' she laughed. 'It shows you the importance of one size doesn't fit all.'

One school in the UK has produced an Olympic athlete in every summer games since 1956. Normally, a lot more than one – 26 pupils from Millfield School competed in the Summer Olympics between 2008 and 2016. In the 2016 Games, eight Olympians attended Millfield – more than the entire number of athletes representing Pakistan.[1] These Old Millfieldians won one gold and three silver medals between them – the same as Turkey. In the 2012 Games, ex-Millfield pupils won more gold medals than Mexico, India, Egypt and Belgium … combined.

Not that Millfield, nestled in rustic Somerset, solely serves as a training ground for future Olympians. Rugby players to emerge out of the school include: Wales legend Gareth Edwards, considered one of the greatest players ever; Chris Robshaw, England's captain at the 2015 World Cup; and prop Mako Vunipola, one of England's current stars. Four Old Millfieldians have played international cricket for England since 2000. In 2019, former Millfield pupil Tyrone Mings debuted for the England national football team.

An epicentre of sporting excellence

On a crisp December morning at the end of 2019, several hundred Millfield pupils, and a smattering of parents, crowd around the school's main rugby pitch to watch their annual game with Sedbergh, a private school in Cumbria which is an historic rival. For Millfield, this is one of the biggest days of the school year.

Based on the quality of players across the two sides, this match may well be the best game of schoolboy rugby in England this year. Both teams field four England, Scotland or Wales U-18 internationals. Sedbergh enters the game on a remarkable 46-man unbeaten run, but, buoyed by the boisterous chanting of their watching school friends, Millfield takes an early lead which they do not relinquish. This match is the showpiece event of the nine fixtures between Millfield and Sedbergh in men's rugby and girls' hockey on the day. The ritual is repeated at the same time each year.

That Millfield is able to host such a day attests to the school's extraordinary facilities: the first, and most obvious, explanation for the school's record of producing elite athletes. The school offers pupils 27 different sports, many of which use facilities that would be the envy of professional teams. To go with the three golf courses on site, the indoor golf centre includes six nets, an 81-square-metre putting green and a bespoke monitor that records the angle and speed of strokes. The indoor cricket centre offers a 4G grass area – fielders can dive indoors just as they would when fielding on grass – and nets that replicate conditions in Australia and India, helping players become accustomed to adapting.

The school employs 44 full-time sports coaches – including five who either competed or coached in the Olympic Games – supplemented by everything from psychologists to nutritionists and physiotherapists. The number of coaches allows training to be tailored to each individual's needs, a theme repeatedly mentioned by the school's most promising young athletes.

'It's very bespoke,' said Jami Schlueter, a 17-year-old aspiring Olympian in decathlon. 'There's a long-term plan, and Millfield support you the whole way through.' With his coach at the start of each year, 'we set our goals at the start of the season, we break them down into our process targets, then we break them down to how we're going to achieve the processes, how we can test them – and it helps keep us on track.'

Most pupils are boarders, which allows for particular flexibility in training. Schedules start as early as seven in the morning and finish as late as nine at night – enabling athletes to experiment with sessions that suit them best, as well as to get accustomed to training at unfamiliar times. The day before our interview, Lucy Matthews, a 17-year-old aspiring Olympian in hurdles, had an upper-body gym session at seven thirty in the morning, a personal gym session (when no more than four students train with a coach) during a free period, and then another gym session with the athletics squad after school finished at four o'clock. The schedule is intensive – 12–14 hours per week – but having facilities on site allows training sessions to be shorter and more focused, and spaced out during a day, so that athletes have a chance to recover between sessions. In netball, players normally have a court or gym session during the day and then full training from seven to nine at night.

The individualized attention coaches give extends to managing athletes' workloads meticulously. 'You have ready access to all of these facilities – it is quite easy to train too much,' Lucy said. 'I think the coaches recognize that, and they are really good at just holding you back when it is responsible to do so to make sure that you don't push it too far, to an injury.' The school manages all students' schedules to ensure they have a rest day a week.

During the sessions, coaches create a culture of players taking ownership for their own sport. At the start of the year, the coaches and athletes discuss their goals and how these may be achieved. Lucy's goal, for instance, is to win the world junior championships in hurdling. Al Richardson, Millfield's director of athletics, then set about challenging her about how to achieve these goals. He recounted their conversation.

'OK, so what time is it going to take? Homework piece number one. Anybody else who ran 12.8 seconds for 100 hurdles? What did they run for 60 hurdles? Don't know. OK, let's research it. So it was a little bit of task ownership, of starting to understand their sport, so they become more educated about their sport as well, and then they can start to ask the right questions.

'You start to develop a plan from a lot of questioning, and supporting them to get to the right answers, that they are driving the answers and they are driving the questions and they're driving their goals. Because ultimately they're their goals.'

How sport is embedded in the fabric of the school ensures that coaches get ample time with players. 'I've worked in a few schools and there aren't many that get the access and time with the players,' said Jenna Adamson, the head of netball. 'It makes a massive difference.' The abundant contact time creates 'the opportunity to fail' and then learn from these experiences, Richardson said.

It is not just that there is so much time; the time is structured in an optimal way to facilitate learning. At many schools, sport happens in a big block. The on-site facilities enable much of Millfield's coaching to take place in blocks of 45 minutes. 'The structure of the school allows us to coach little and often,' explained Richardson. 'More frequent, very small training blocks of high-quality work'. The facilities also allow children to play their preferred sports all year round – for instance, playing cricket in the nets during winter.

'Communities of practice'

Children who have moved from other schools to Millfield say that it is not only the facilities and coaching that help them improve but the power of internal competition. 'For the netball first team, there's quite a lot of defenders – which is the position I play – and it drives you to try and be better to just be on the team,' said Sophie Hamilton, a netball prodigy who was 15 when interviewed. 'At my old school there wasn't much competition, so there wasn't much drive to get a lot better.

'I've got structure, and I've got balance to my life, and as a result my academics and sport, neither one of them have to be compromised. I really feel that I can fulfil my potential in both areas of my life, and that's really important to me. So I'm much better off.'

Being around other aspiring athletes can create a culture that maximizes the prospects of any one of those athletes becoming elite. Such 'communities of practice' are pivotal in creating positive learning environments in sport, research from Diane Culver and Pierre Trudel, two academics at the University of Ottawa, has shown.[2] Such communities present substantive opportunities for informal and incidental learning outside of the traditional classroom setting, enabling athletes to learn from one another and improve at an accelerated rate.

'It's a bit of a hothouse approach,' said Mark Garraway, the school's director of cricket. 'You have elite cricketers, athletes, netball players, hockey players, swimmers, in the same houses, the same classes, the same social spaces.'

One aspiring athlete doesn't know what the competition does, or where they need to be in their sport. But a coterie of aspiring athletes – as there invariably is at Millfield – can always turn to each other to understand what the competition is doing. This sense of community, in turn, motivates them further, and means they cannot cruise to remain at the apex of their sport in the school.

'Competition helps me to become a better athlete,' explained Jami Schlueter, the aspiring decathlete. 'I train with lots of individual eventers, and I kind of see how they go about doing their individual events and what I can learn from them. Especially when it comes to something like 400 metre training – where you have to find something really deep within yourself to push hard – that's where I look at my partners and I see them speed up in the sessions, or really start pushing themselves, and they encourage me to do better.'

Aspiring athletes can also use each other for support. 'Lucy's had success internationally – I'd ask her lots of questions about what it's like being on the international stage, what it's like standing in front of the line. So when it actually comes to your day, and you're representing your country, you've kind of been told how it happens, how you behave, and it makes it seem less daunting. And especially being at a school like Millfield where our coaches, athletes, your training partners, your best friends, most of them have been at that kind of level. You're able to kind of learn from them.'

Success is self-perpetuating. From 2014 to 2019, 11 Millfield boys played U-19 cricket for England. As well as the internal competition, such a conveyor-belt of talent creates a constant dialogue between the school and professional teams, eager to ensure that they do not overlook any talent. These links mean that promising athletes at Millfield will generally get more chances to impress watching academy coaches, who regularly attend their games.

For these children, the notion of being a leading Olympian feels attainable, not some preposterous dream. That, in turn, encourages children to work harder to try to make it happen. 'Ambitious goals feel achievable here, and that's very empowering,' Lucy observed, declaring her ambitions to be Olympic champion and break the world record.

Millfield is an extreme example of the benefits of children going to leading sports schools; it has a fair claim to boasting the best combination of sports facilities and coaching of any school in the world. Going to the right school can profoundly transform a child's chances of becoming an elite athlete.

In the UK, around 7 per cent of the population attend private school. Yet, in 2016, 31 per cent of Team GB's Olympians attended private schools, according to the educational charity Sutton Trust.[3] Team GB came second in the medals table in Rio 2016, even with a team whose socioeconomic backgrounds were wholly unrepresentative of the nation as a whole.

The advantage of going to the right school is mirrored across other sports. All told, 55 per cent of players in the England rugby squad who reached the 2019 World Cup final attended private schools. This shows the extraordinary advantage of going to the right school – though some players had sports scholarships, covering some or all of their school fees.[3]

Similar dynamics are observed in other countries. Auckland Grammar School, the school that has produced more New Zealand rugby players than anywhere else, is a state school, but housing in the school's catchment area is notoriously expensive. In Australia, children who attend private schools are four times more likely to go on to play professional Australia rules football.[4] The resources devoted to school sport at private schools generally far exceed those in the state system, heightening children's chances of becoming elite athletes.[5, 6]

In all these sports, the opportunity to attend a private school – sometimes through scholarships, but overwhelmingly thanks to their family's wealth, with only 1 per cent of students at UK private schools having a full bursary or scholarship – transformed their prospects of becoming elite athletes. This fact is an instance of sport mirroring life: 65 per cent of senior judges, 52 per cent of diplomats and 48 per cent of British FTSE 350 CEOs attended private schools.[3]

In sport, the advantage is not uniform. In football, Britain's national sport – and, due to its popularity and the ease of playing, the one with the fewest barriers to entry – those from private schools are actually underrepresented in the professional game.[7] The same is true of professional footballers from Europe and South America and basketball players from the US.[8]

But in most sports, Millfield's advantage is two-pronged. For young aspiring British athletes, there is nowhere better to go to school to develop their talent. And there is nowhere better to go to ensure that whatever talent they have doesn't get missed.

Something in the water

Wagga Wagga, nestled in the Riverina region of New South Wales, is a sort of Australian Everytown. It is a mid-sized country city, with a population around 50,000, and equidistant between Melbourne and Sydney.

The local maxim has it that at precisely five o'clock each day, a wave flushes a secret nutrient into the Murrumbidgee River that flows through the city. This is how some locals explain Wagga Wagga's extraordinary propensity to produce elite athletes. Wagga Wagga has developed leading sportsmen and women across Australian rules football, rugby league, rugby union, golf, football, hockey and even triathlon. For a period in the 1990s, both Australia's Test match opening batsmen, Michael Slater and the captain, Mark Taylor, had grown up in Wagga Wagga. While Millfield illustrates the importance of where a child goes to school, Wagga Wagga shows the importance of another crucial factor in an athlete's journey: the type of area in which they grow up.

'I used to say when you're a baby you were held by the heels and dipped into the murky rivers of the Murrumbidgee like Achilles,' joked Geoff Lawson, who played 46 Test matches for Australia throughout the 1980s. Rather than the five o'clock wave, the real reasons for Wagga's sporting success are a little more prosaic. 'We had a combination of a town and rural existence.' For young athletes, Wagga Wagga combined both the best aspects of town and country life.

'Sport was a big part of what you did,' Lawson recalled. 'All the schools had major sporting teams, you had a strong school competition, you had a strong club competition, and we had lots of great teachers and mentors. Young people got exposed to excellent conditions to play, whether that was rugby league, Australian rules, rugby union, softball, football, basketball, all those sorts of things.'

In Australia, the Barassi Line divides the country in half: the northeast, including Sydney, where rugby league is the dominant football code, and the rest of the country, including Melbourne, where Australian rules is most popular. Wagga Wagga lies almost exactly on this line; many children play both rugby codes in winter – one on a Saturday and one on a Sunday. Such children may play more sport overall, increasing their athleticism and fitness. The most talented might also have a chance of making it as a professional in either rugby league or Australian rules, rather than just one – increasing their overall prospects of becoming a professional athlete. As the town plays both rugby league and Australian rules, children can find the sport that best aligns with their talent and interests. Wagga Wagga has produced both an abundance of Australian rules stars, including Paul Kelly – the former winner of the Brownlow Medal for the league's best player – and leading rugby league players, like the four Mortimer brothers – three of them played in grand finals, and two for Australia.

As Wagga Wagga is halfway between Melbourne and Sydney – about five hours from each, and only two and a half from Canberra – scouts from all three cities can attend matches easily. 'Not all mid-sized cities are the same,' said David Hancock from the Memorial University of Newfoundland. 'It appears that there might be a connection to distance from next largest city. Wagga Wagga is in an ideal location to have the benefits of a smaller community, but maintain a reasonable proximity to larger cities.'[9]

Steve Mortimer, the eldest of the Mortimer children, was born in Sydney, where he spent his first years. When he was five, he was diagnosed with asthma. 'The doctor said to Mum and Dad, "Get him out of Sydney, go to a rural region and he'll enjoy it a lot more – as will the brothers."'

The doctor was right. In Wagga Wagga the Mortimer brothers embraced the rural lifestyle, playing sport incessantly. 'It was just fantastic,' Steve recalled. 'We all played together.' Their father started a rugby league club. If he was not playing there, Steve was probably either playing cricket – his other great sporting love as a child – or tennis or doing short-distance athletics sprinting.

While Wagga Wagga has specific peculiarities, it is a microcosm of the small-town effect in sport. In Australia, Ballarat and Bendigo, in Victoria, and MacKay, in Queensland, are similar large country towns where the Wagga effect applies. These are all regional cities, with populations between 30,000 and 100,000, noted Damien Farrow, a sports scientist who previously worked at the Australia Institute of Sport. 'The Wagga Wagga effect is just the term that's been popularized here in Australia to describe the type of city where all those psychosocial factors come into play and produce elite sporting talent. Because they're that size, they've all got really good infrastructure – but you can get access to it. So it's not like a city where it's overcrowded. And there's enough elite coaches for the talent, and they can access them as they progress.'

Mid-sized hits the spot

In an age when big cities are resented for hoovering up the best opportunities and talent across society, smaller towns and cities actually produce a disproportionate number of elite athletes, and the biggest cities are underrepresented. In the UK, towns with a population of 10,000–30,000 produce a disproportionate number of male and female athletes compared with cities of over 500,000. In Germany, Olympians are overrepresented in areas with a population of 30,000–99,999.[10]

The same rule holds true across myriad sports in North America. Staggeringly, while only 1.1 per cent of the US population live in towns with 50,000–99,000 residents, 10–17 per cent of men's professional American football, baseball, men's basketball and men's golf players come from such towns. So, a boy born in a town with a population of between 50,000 and 99,000 has around 15 times more chance of becoming a professional athlete than the average child. In the USA, female professional football players born in cities with a population of fewer than 1,000,000 are overrepresented, as are female professional golfers born in cities with a population of fewer than 250,000.

A 'mid-sized city' is relative to a country's population – what is mid-sized in Finland is quite different from mid-sized in China. So Chinese cities in which athletes might benefit from a mid-sized effect would be too large for athletes to benefit from the effect in, say, Finland, explained Hancock.[11]

For burgeoning athletes, mid-sized towns are a sweet spot. They are big enough for children to be exposed to a good quality of competition and sporting infrastructure of a sort that is lacking in the very smallest communities; in Canada and Germany, Olympians are significantly underrepresented from areas with a population under 10,000.[11] But mid-sized towns are also small enough to ensure ease of access to facilities and sports clubs without too much travel – children can spend more time playing sport and less time being ferried between fixtures.

Wagga Wagga had the particular advantage of being bigger than surrounding towns – meaning that the best children from nearby towns would often come to play sport, boosting the standard, but those who grew up in Wagga Wagga seldom needed to travel elsewhere to play. 'The good thing about Wagga is we were probably the biggest town in the Riverina,' Steve Mortimer recalled. 'There would be Aussie rules teams in some of the little towns and also rugby league in some of the other little towns. So, it was really a mix but all the boys just played sport.'

The close-knit culture of Wagga Wagga makes parents happier for their children to play informally with friends, accelerating learning. 'It's generally regarded as safer so adults are more likely to let their children go out and play – less adult supervision, so more street sport which we know is a useful thing for kids to be engaging in on their path to excellence,' Farrow explained. For Mortimer, the rugby league ground was only half a mile away from the family house.

For Lawson, the nearest cricket nets were only 50 yards away. 'I used to spend three hours after school until it got dark bowling to my mate until my mum would literally yell out "It's dinner time". Your parents did have much more trust in what happened in those days.' At weekends, 'you either went from school to sports somewhere or someone's house or played something or your parents sent you out and said, "Don't come back till it's dark, or come back when it's dinnertime." So, you just went. Everyone knew everyone and you played all your sports.'

In the winter, Lawson played rugby league, football – soccer to the locals – hockey and some rugby union. In the summer, he played tennis, golf and squash along with cricket. On weekends, Lawson would play cricket from eight in the morning and then tennis in the evening; a local tennis club had floodlights, extending the hours when it was possible for him to play sport. 'I'd get back at 10 o'clock.'

Because there are fewer children than in large cities, children who are not early stars, or are wrongly overlooked for junior selection, are less often discouraged from playing; instead, they benefit from continued attention, and an environment far more conducive to late developers. A study of dropout rates in youth ice hockey in Canada found that players from cities with populations greater than 500,000 were 2.9 times more likely to quit the sport in any given year. Players in cities with populations in the range of 100,000–250,000 were most likely to remain engaged for the longest amount of time, and to play for at least six consecutive years.[11] Similarly, a study of Canadian swimmers found that children from cities with a population of over 500,000 were almost five times more likely to quit over a two-year period than those from towns and cities with a population between 15,000 and 500,000.[12] Such mid-sized towns are simply better at keeping talent engaged for longer, giving children the best chance of achieving their sporting potential: the big-fish–little-pond effect.

Mid-sized towns are likely to have more sports teams per head of population – encouraging children to stay involved, as there is more chance of them getting in the team. There may be more pride involved in representing a place where sport is intrinsic to the identity of the area – like Wagga Wagga. In smaller areas, talent is less likely to be overlooked. A study of Irish football by Laura Finnegan found that players from Dublin, the capital city and where one-quarter of people in the Republic of Ireland live, were 25 per cent less likely to make it to an Emerging Talent Programme centre than the national average.[13]

In Wagga Wagga, children did not lack for opportunities. From the age of 12, Lawson would play junior cricket in the morning – and then race home, get out of his shorts and into his longer cricket trousers, so he had the right attire to play senior cricket. 'You played where you were good enough to play. I remember being a 13-year-old playing against some seriously fast bowling. Playing against adults, you learn how to compete.

'You learn how to figure things out against bigger, stronger people. Particularly in a sport like cricket – you need to be able to think your way through a game and use the right tactics and the various aspects of the game to succeed. You don't have to be big in size to do that – you just have to be smart. It's not so much the physical challenge, it's the mental and creativity side when you play against adults. You've got to find a way to get it done and trying to do it every Saturday and every Sunday accelerates that learning.'

In bigger cities, where there are enough children to sustain age-group competition for longer, such advantages can be lost. 'We put them in the pigeonhole of their age-group sports these days and they don't get to compete against adults,' said Lawson, who became an international cricket coach. 'So they would tend to either fade away when they play against adults or it takes them a lot longer to mature.'

In Wagga Wagga today, a mural celebrates all the athletes that the town has produced. Children there can play cricket on a big complex with three ovals – one each named after Lawson, Taylor and Slater, the city's three Australia Test cricketers. Mortimer Field celebrates the contribution made by the entire Mortimer family to sport in Wagga Wagga.

Steve, the most famous of the lot, mused on how the misfortune of his childhood asthma helped his family achieve sporting greatness. 'You're so right,' he said when asked whether his family's sporting triumphs might not have been possible without the asthma that led to his family uprooting to Wagga Wagga. 'If I didn't have asthma, it would have been different, I don't know what would have happened there. But it was so wonderful playing sport in Wagga.'

The profound benefits of growing up in a mid-sized town are really a proxy for broader advantages. The size of the town where a young athlete grows up is not important for its own sake. It is important because small towns tend to offer the best balance of facilities, coaching, competition – enough to improve and be challenged at each stage of development, but not so much that children can't get a game – and a culture of informal play. This is why where you grow up matters.

How your country impacts your chances of being the best

In 1905, the story goes, Norway voted to break its union with Sweden. The son of Denmark's king was recruited to serve as monarch, and given advice by a Norwegian adventurer that, to win the hearts of his new people, he should learn to ski.[14] He did. The zest for skiing in Norway today is such that there are 1,100 ski clubs in the country – one for every 5,000 people. There are 149,000 members of ski clubs, and the amount of snow means that many of these can be used for much of the year.

The deep cultural affinity for playing, and being, outside has inspired the Norwegian concept of *friluftsliv* – which translates as 'open-air living' – popularized by a Norwegian poet in the 1850s.[15] These traditions continue to inform the nation's affinity, and aptitude, for skiing and winter sports. 'If you become a winter star, you do well in cross-country skiing or alpine skiing or biathlon, you're sort of the king,' said Eirik Myhr Nossum, head coach of the Norwegian men's national team.

Russia has a population of 145 million. Canada has a population of 37 million. Both have a climate ideally suited to winter sports. Yet Norway, with a similar climate and population of only 5.3 million, has won more medals than any nation in the history of the Winter Olympics. Remarkably, it has a smaller population than any of the top 20 most successful nations in the history of the Winter Games. To become a Winter Olympic champion, there is no better country in the world in which to be born – an emblem of how the country in which someone grows up impacts their chances of becoming an elite athlete.

In Ragnhild Haga's family home, there is a photograph of her as a tiny child. Wearing all red, she is standing up in boots, on a pair of very small children's skis, in the garden outside her house. It is a common sight in Norway in wintertime, even if there is one particularly distinguishing feature of this particular photograph: the picture was taken when she was only 13 months old. This photo is a snapshot of the vibrant skiing culture that continually produces Olympic champions like Haga, who won gold medals in both the 10 kilometre freestyle and 4 × 5 kilometre relay in the 2018 Winter Olympics in Pyeongchang, when Norway came top of the medal table. Again.

As a child, skiing was ubiquitous in Haga's life. Her father was a coach and passed on his enthusiasm for the sport. From as early as she could remember, Haga and her family – her parents and three younger brothers – would ski around the woods together on Sundays. 'I had a lot of fun with my brothers, trying to keep them behind me,' she laughed. Even 'playing cards, everyone hated to lose'.

In Holter, the village where she grew up, there was 'not so much to do'. The Hagas lived on a farm. 'We could play and go skiing outside our farm,' Ragnhild recalled. 'That's how Norwegian children learn to ski – we play, we practise downhills, and we do a lot of skiing.' Ragnhild's father used his tractor to clear land outside the house so the family could ski.

In winter, when there was enough snow, the children would some-times ski to school. At school, Ragnhild and other children would play with skis or figure skates in the playground. From the age of 11, Ragnhild attended a ski club twice a week, and entered cross-country skiing competitions. But most of her time on the slopes was out-side the club or formal competition. In Norway, there are no formal competitions for children before the age of six and no regional com-petitions before the age of 11. Until the age of 13, all children must receive a prize in a sports event if a prize is awarded, part of a culture that emphasizes mass participation in skiing from an early age and encouraging children to stay engaged with the sport.

'We learned when we were playing, and we looked at each other, and maybe on television, how other good skiers did things,' Haga recalled. 'So it was not like organized every day, no – some was organized and some was playing.'

Haga even used to ski by herself. When she was 13, 'I was kind of motivated, and wanted to try roller skis,' she recalled. 'I started roller skiing in summer outside my house on the road.'

Such broad experience skiing from a young age was essential to developing a feel for the slopes. 'Cross-country skiing is a very tech-nical sport. So, to get that ski feeling quite early, it's important. It's of course physical – you have to be fit and train a lot – but technique is something you have an advantage with if you learn very early, I think. It's hard to learn that when you are 20.'

Early exposure to skiing, and ease of getting to the slopes, is a common thread among winter sports champions. In the USA, 75 per cent of Olympic downhill skiers in the national ski team grow up within an hour of the slopes, with the majority first skiing before the age of three.[16]

In Holter, there were 'big traditions' of skiing, Haga recalled. 'We had some successful skiers before.' Her uncle represented Norway in cross-country skiing. Stories of local skiers who had made it to the top made Haga's dreams seem attainable.

'It was good to have some idols. It seemed like a long way up there, but as a kid I had big goals. I didn't have a goal to be in the Olympics, maybe, but I wanted to see how good I could become as a skier. So it was good to see that some had made it, and it was possible.'

Her experiences are typical of those of many young children elsewhere in Norway. Among Norwegian Olympians, those from smaller areas are overrepresented, Stig Arve Saether from the Norwegian University of Science and Technology has found.[17] Such areas show similar characteristics to the mid-sized town effect observed in Wagga Wagga. They typically have few competing leisure activities to skiing, close school relationships – with teachers often coaches at sports clubs and pivotal in the athlete's overall development – and most simply a vibrant skiing culture. This means 'we probably select the best talents from many, many children,' Haga said. 'So many people in Norway try skiing and different winter sports.'

There are eight regional departments within the Norwegian Olympic Sport Centre, so athletes throughout the country can benefit from both the expertise of qualified coaches and insights from sports science work that the Norwegian Olympic Sport Centre undertakes in collaboration with universities. The creation of the Olympiatoppen, which is responsible for training elite athletes, in 1988, introduced a more scientific approach to developing athletes.

'There is a culture in Norway, within winter sports, to exercise a lot with optimal quality, and you can find "cultural architects" – athletes who are at the international top level in their sports – in all winter sports,' explained Frode Moen from the Centre for Elite Sports Research at the Norwegian University of Science and Technology. 'Coaches and young athletes can observe what they do, compete against them, ask them questions about how to achieve different qualities, study them and so on.'

In some ways like Millfield, the sheer number of elite skiers in Norway is self-perpetuating. The competition between skiers is so ferocious that it drives them on to greater heights.

A year before the 2018 Winter Olympics, the Nordic World Ski Championships took place in Lahti. Haga qualified for only one event in the tournament, and did not come in the top three in that one – she finished fourth in the 30 kilometre freestyle, below three other Norwegians.

'When I started training for the 2018 season, my biggest motivation was to qualify for the Norwegian team in more races in the Olympics. I was so fed up with being outside the team in a championship. I was extra focused on my technique training, my nutrition and physical training that year.'

Without this extra internal competition, Haga believes that she would not have been spurred on to achieve double Olympic gold. The Norwegian culture does not just excel at producing fine skiers; the competition within it is also uniquely well suited to convert talent into medals.

'When I saw how my teammates trained more and probably smarter than me, and beat me in Lahti, I got really motivated to not only copy them but to do things even better. It was a bit all or nothing towards the Olympics. I don't think I would have improved so much after Lahti if I couldn't learn from the best in training camps or if I was the best in the team.

'The hard competition in the Norwegian team makes us better as a nation in championships.'

Even for a child going to Millfield, playing rugby league in Wagga Wagga or skiing in rural Norway, the odds of becoming an elite athlete are minute. Growing up somewhere with a culture for sport, an opportunity for abundant play and a system for identifying and nurturing the most talented is no guarantee of winning the sporting lottery – but it does buy a child a lot more tickets.

3
Timing is everything

The impact of relative age on success in sport

'I was in third grade and playing with seventh and eighth graders. They were obviously tough on me – they didn't want a little third grader coming in and showing them up, so I had to get knocked down, get back up, and it definitely toughened me up a lot.'

Elena Delle Donne, two-time winner of the NBA's Most Valuable Player award, on the benefits of playing with older children

The story goes that John McDermott, the former academy director at Tottenham Hotspur Football Club, turned to a colleague with a question: 'Who's the short little fat kid?' Richard Allen, the club's head of recruitment, is said to have replied, 'His name's Harry, he's got good feet. We think he'll be OK.'

The boy had already been released by Tottenham's arch-rival, Arsenal, aged eight. 'He was a bit chubby, he wasn't very athletic,' Arsenal's former academy director Liam Brady later said.[1]

Several years later, few thought much better of him. Aged 13, the boy recorded lower scores for agility, jumping and speed – and virtually every other metric – than with his contemporaries in the academy. McDermott called him 'the runt of the litter'.[1]

The boy would go on to become England captain, and 2018 World Cup top scorer, Harry Kane. He overcame two great barriers to make it to the top: being born late in the selection year – Kane was born on 28 July, so he had less time to accumulate practice than contemporaries in the same school year – and, even allowing for this disadvantage, he was a late developer biologically for his age. So he was both chronologically younger for his grouping, based on his month of birth, and biologically less developed, due to his small physical stature.

The relative age effect

In education, a child's date of birth is one of the biggest roadblocks to future success: those born at the start of the school year have 30 per cent more chance of attending Oxford or Cambridge University than those born at the end of the school year.[2] This phenomenon – the relative age effect – is as prevalent in sport – being first reported in 1985.[3] It is not the month of birth that is important per se, but rather where that month falls in the selection or academic year.

In sport, the selection year does not always align with the school year. The selection year for FIFA youth tournaments and generally across most of the world runs from January to December, but in the UK it runs September to August. Yet, whatever month the selection year begins, the relative age effect persists; those who are born earlier in the selection year have a far greater chance of being selected for youth teams or academies.

Late-born children are further disadvantaged if they are physically immature for their age. 'Players can vary as much as one year in age within an age group, but there is much more scope for variance in maturation,' explained Sean Cummings, an academic at the University of Bath who has worked with the English Premier League to reduce the relative age effect. 'Thirteen-year-old boys, and 11-year-old girls, can physically be two years younger or older for their age, a difference exacerbated by those who are born late in their year.'

'It's hard to tell at that age what the player is going to turn into,' Kane later said.[1] 'I was small for my age. I was a late maturer. So, look, it is hard to call a player at such a young age. I went to Spurs when I was 11. It wasn't like I then took off straight away, I still had to work hard.'

Thousands of footballers born late in the selection year have had their dreams of forging a professional career scuppered by the simple luck of when they were born in the year.[4] A leading English Premier League side recently analysed how long their academy boys stayed before the club released them. Players born from September to November stayed for an average of four years. Those born from June to August stayed for only a solitary year – a testament to the power of relative age. Steven Gerrard and Frank Lampard, two of the best England footballers of their generation, were both rejected by the Football Association's national academy at Lilleshall; Gerrard was born on 30 May, and Lampard on 20 June, both late in the selection year.

The worst time to be born

In the Northern Hemisphere, in sport and education alike, July is the worst time of all to be born if you aspire to be selected for an elite training programme.[1] There are twice as many English professional men's footballers born in September than in July;[5] the selection year in English football starts in September. Scientists have found the same effects across other major football leagues in Europe and South America: more players are born in the first quarter of the selection year.[6,7]

The same trend is evident for men across most major sports including basketball,[8] baseball[9] and ice hockey.[10] In these sports, 30–50 per cent of players in professional leagues are typically born in the first quarter of the selection year.[11]

The relative age effect permeates both rugby codes,[12, 13] tennis,[14] swimming,[15] handball,[16] volleyball[17] and alpine skiing,[18] among many other sports.[19] This systematic selection bias exists in virtually every sport where being bigger and stronger may offer an advantage; a notable exception is golf,[20] where players are not in direct physical contact with each other and club selection can reduce physical disadvantages. Generally, the more popular the sport, the greater the potency of the relative age effect – perhaps because the more young players that participate in a sport, the greater the perceived need to make selection decisions at earlier ages.[19]

Most researchers have focused on the relative age effect among male athletes, but indications are that the effect extends to women's sport. An analysis examining the relative age effect across 57 studies in 25 different sports, including football, tennis, volleyball, and track and field, found a generally small to moderate effect in favour of athletes from quarter one rather than quarter four, although the effect was not as pronounced compared with men. Unlike with males, the relative age effect was found in both pre-adolescent (11 or below) and adolescent (12–14) age groups, and at higher levels of competition. As in men's sports, in team-based sports the effects are more prominent than in individual ones, particularly in sports with high physiological and physical demands.[20]

The impact of the relative age effect is not the same across all positions.[21] The bias is strongest for goalkeepers and defenders in football – positions where being bigger confers a distinct advantage. In football, 46 per cent of central defenders, 53 per cent of strikers and 77 per cent of goalkeepers who represented England in men's World Cups from 1986 to 1998 were born in the first quarter of the selection year, compared with only 34 per cent of midfielders.[22]

When he was head of academies at England Rugby, Alun Powell noted that the relative age effect was particularly strong at youth level for second-row forwards, a position where senior elite players are typically at least 6 foot 4 inches. For scrum- and fly-halves, positions where tactical and technical acumen are more important than physicality, the effect is significantly diluted.

Powell led a study analysing 1,300 youth rugby players in England, which found that 71 per cent were born in the first six months of the selection year. This rose to 84 per cent for second-rowers, suggesting that the physical demands helped those born early in the selection year dominate these positions. In such positions, wasted talent – the players that could have made it but suffered from being relatively younger for their years – is particularly great.

The Matthew effect declares that small advantages accrue over time, and so the gap between groups of people – those who just pass and fail a school entrance exam, say – multiply over time. Perhaps this provides the best explanation for how the relative age effect distorts which talent ends up in professional sport.

Coaches are more likely to select players old for their year for school and club teams. In turn, coaches ask these players to do extra training, on the pitch and in the gym, and these athletes get to work with the best coaches and are exposed to the best – or biggest – players in their age group. Coaches tend to deny those young for their selection group these same opportunities, and so they fall progressively further behind their contemporaries. When taking into account their extra physical maturity, those selected may initially not really be more skilled or talented than those who are younger and narrowly miss out. Once selected, these older players benefit from extra training time and coaching, and the added motivation that comes from recognition.

From the earliest ages in grassroots sport, players and coaches alike suffer from warped incentives: they want to improve in the long-term, of course, but more important is the short-term need to win at all costs. Schools and clubs alike love parading their medals as vindication of what they are doing. For schools that offer sports scholarships – and the teachers and coaches that determine these – parents and their employers judge them on the number of trophies won. So incentives are warped; victories today are prioritized, inadvertently, over doing what is best for the athlete in the long-term.

'The growing, unquestioned, competitive culture within youth sport is expanding and making these issues more problematic,' said

Steve Cobley, a sports psychologist from the University of Sydney. 'The short-term myopia being created during a child's early years in education, schools and sports systems is fuelling the problem. The costs are multiple, including long-term health and participation in sport, and the development of potentially fewer high-quality athletes.'

Nick Levett, a former talent identification manager for the Football Association who worked with dozens of future internationals, analysed the ages of different teams in the Surrey youth leagues in the south of England – a total of 8,000 players. The findings were remarkable: the teams with an older average age were far more successful. There was a near perfect correlation between the ages of teams, relative to their selection group, and what division they were in; the teams with the oldest average age were in the top division, and those with the lowest average age were in division seven, the lowest. It was a window into a wider truth.

'Professional clubs are picking from a biased sample,' Levett said. 'The kid that might be 13 but physically 15 can hit a 40-yard crossfield pass because physically they can, they can cover more ground, and they can make more high-intensity sprints. That 13-year-old can do things that an 11-year-old can't do, simply because the younger player may not have the strength, stamina, power or speed yet. So who gets picked up by the scout who's watching that match? The best learner and the best player technically could be the little one, but just because physically they can't do it yet they're the one that misses out.'

Occasionally, the advantage accrues the other way – not to the oldest and brawniest but to the youngest and slightest. In artistic sports like gymnastics and figure skating,[23] lithe bodies help to increase flexibility and rotational speed. Younger-born athletes are overrepresented in these sports, particularly among females. The traditional advantages conferred to the eldest born are inverted;[24] partly because they tend to be smaller and lighter than their contemporaries, those young for their year are then invited to extra training, and the Matthew effect can then kick in. Yet this in no way amounts to an improvement on the normal relative age effect – it is equally unfair, just in the opposite way.

The underdog effect

For athletes who mature late physically and are young for their year, then, it is far harder to keep up. Yet for those able to defy these potential impediments and stay in the system – as Kane did – the rewards can be profound. The very difficulties of being physically immature for their selection year – and having to struggle to out-muscle or out-run opponents and rely on other qualities if they are to compete – are ideal preparation for professional sport.

'If you're a little kid, every single training session you have to think differently, you have to solve problems, you have to make decisions,' Levett observed. 'You have to try and get out of different things where you can't use a physical advantage. So you get brilliant learning as long as you stay in the system.'

Perhaps as important is how being physically immature can imbue players with essential psychological skills. Later developers must 'develop psychological skills that are crucial to successfully navigate player pathways and the inevitable challenges that lay ahead – like loss of form, injuries, being dropped,' Powell observed. The absence of physical prowess may drive them to develop technical and tactical skills.

This paradox of the relative age effect is termed the 'underdog effect'. Counter-intuitively, a higher share of the very best athletes are born later in their selection years; the relative age effect not only disappears but *reverses*. In men's football, baseball, ice hockey and Australian rules football, those winning Most Valuable Player awards are 1.2 times more likely to be born in the second than the first half of their selection year.[25] In England, 64 per cent of male Test cricketers with over 50 Tests are born in the second half of the school year, and 34 per cent in the last three months – even though there is a strong relative age effect in the domestic game.[26] The underdog effect has been found in the senior national squads of nine leading international cricket teams and 10 international rugby union teams globally.[13]

Malcolm Gladwell popularized the relative age effect with examples of Canadian ice hockey in his 2008 book *Outliers*.[27] But, even though a relative age effect remains detectable in professional ice hockey, only 17 per cent of the Canadian Olympic ice hockey team from 1998 to 2010 were born in the first three months of the year.[28, 29]

This finding reflects the broader success of players young for their year. An analysis of National Hockey League players in North America between 2008 and 2016 found that those born in the last quarter of the year (October–December) scored more points, and earned more on average, than those players born in the first quarter of the year. The gap became greater at the higher echelons of performance, with those born in the fourth quarter disproportionately represented among the 10 per cent highest point scorers and salary earners in the league.[30]

When players young for their year reach professional level, they tend to enjoy longer careers. Those born in the last quarter of the year who make it to the National Hockey League enjoy careers almost a year longer than those born in the first quarter; players born from October to December have an average of 7.8 years in the league, but those born from January to March last only 6.9 years.[28]

So professional ice hockey embodies the peculiarities of the relative age effect. When it comes to reaching professional level, those old for their year have a sizeable advantage – 58.2 per cent of all NHL players (excluding goalkeepers) are born in the first six months of the year, meaning that those born in the first six months have 40 per cent more chance of making the league.[30] Yet, those young for their year outperform those who are older by every conceivable metric, once selected. This is the paradox of the relative age effect; it is significantly harder for later-born children to reach professional level – but, if they can make it there, they have a higher chance of reaching the peak of their sport.

The curse of the early maturer

The underdog effect shows how early maturers can suffer from the vagaries of the talent development system, too. While it can be too hard for late-born athletes, it can be too easy for early-born ones. If their pace, strength and height are exceptional for their age, children will not be pushed to develop the full array of gifts they need to excel at adult level. The very existence of the underdog effect suggests a profound inefficiency in how coaches develop early-born players, especially those who are mature early.

While 45 per cent of players in men's Premier League academies have historically been born in the September–November window, compared with only 10 per cent from June–August, the imbalance is not as great in the Premier League at senior level.[30] Little relative age effect was found in an analysis of Premier League footballers by the football consultancy 21st Club conducted in 2019:[31] 56 per cent of players were born in the first six months of the selection year. The relative age effect was far stronger in lower levels of the game, again implying the underdog effect at work. Players old for their year in academies are far more likely to be released than younger ones – but the younger players find it far harder to get into the academies in the first place.

'Your return on investment is actually skewed,' explained James Bunce, a former youth coach at Southampton, who is now high performance director at US Soccer. 'You're putting less into quarter three and quarter four and getting more and more into quarter one and two and getting less back.

'While 25 per cent is roughly the output for each of the quarters, the question is how many players could we have developed better? Or how many players have we lost to the system because they didn't enjoy participation as a 10, 11, 12-year-old? Or they didn't ever hit their full potential as an 18, 19-year-old because they weren't challenged as a 13, 14-year-old?

'Are there other players who have not been discovered or developed? Have we had one of those quarter one players that coaches just did not push? Is there a quarter three or four player who wasn't recruited by a scout because they didn't look good in the game, and then lost interest and went to play another sport?'

That the relative age effect is far less marked at professional rather than youth level raises a deeper question. While being old for your age group remains a significant advantage, many players born earlier in the selection year are not challenged enough. An effective youth development system would imbue in those old for their year the same qualities that the system forces onto those young for their year in order to survive.

'The early maturer is not being pushed,' Bunce said. 'That player needs to be pushed up a year so they need to use their skills and tactics rather than just running with the ball past people.

'Why would we want to just create that challenging underdog environment for a late-maturing player? That's exactly what we should be providing for our early-maturing players to be the underdog as well. Because if those are the over-dogs – to coin a phrase – then they're never going to reach their full potential.'

Challenging the over-dogs

Bunce has been one of those preoccupied with how to create extra challenges for over-dogs – rebalancing youth development to provide appropriate challenges for children that mature both early and late.

Working at Southampton in the winter of 2006/07, Bunce observed a 13-year-old boy who stood out as unusually skinny and physically underdeveloped. 'His voice hadn't broken. He wasn't as big and muscular as the others.'

Bunce and Southampton's coaches decided to move the boy down a year, so that he could get more time on the ball and better develop his technical skills. After a growth spurt, the boy broke into Southampton's first team three years later, aged only 16. While Alex Oxlade-Chamberlain would excel as an all-action midfielder for England, Arsenal and Liverpool, perhaps his biggest impact has been on how teams develop talent.

The way Oxlade-Chamberlain forged a brilliant career from being a late developer was the 'lightbulb moment' in showing Bunce how young players physically develop at different rates, and need to be treated as unique, rather than simply lumped in with the rest of their year. The decision to move Oxlade-Chamberlain down a year was intuitive. But the success led Southampton to introduce more scientific rigour into the processes associated with how young players were grouped.

In 2010, Southampton adopted the Khamis–Roche method to determine children's maturity levels. This method takes into account height, weight and maturity to estimate a child's stage of development.[32] The method is not fool-proof, but its margins of error are small – it can predict a child's height from the ages of 4–17 with an average error of only 2.2 centimetres in boys and 1.8 centimetres in girls. This information helps teams allow late physical developers a fair chance to develop, reducing the chances of casting aside a player like Oxlade-Chamberlain prematurely. A number of Premier League clubs now routinely use the method in their academies. The aim is 'to create an environment specific to the demands of that one athlete,' Bunce said.

The process underpinning this approach is called 'biobanding'. This method involves grouping players together based on their height and weight, not year group. The concept can benefit early-maturing children just as much as late-maturing ones.

'All the players irrespective of maturity have a chance to develop the attributes that will be important should they become professional,' Bunce explained. 'You can be exposed to your age group but you can also train and play with different groups – and be exposed to a more physical game or a less physical game, a more technical game or a less technical game.

'Biobanding is for early maturers as well – so they're not in a comfort zone in the U-13s scoring 10 goals a week. In the long term that's a really bad and false environment for a player to develop. These players need to be pushed up a year so they need to use their skills, techniques and tactics rather than just getting the ball, running past people and scoring goals. When they're adult they won't have that physical advantage anymore – that's guaranteed. And if they haven't then spent their formative years developing technical skills to deal with situations, and tactical understanding and psychological resilience when they fail, when they reach adulthood they just drop off so significantly that they are lost to the game.'

By enabling greater equality in training and competition, and reducing the physical differences between players, biobanding can reduce injury risks. It means that training becomes less about physical size and more about skill.

The limitations of biobanding

Yet in junior football the relative age effect has stubbornly remained even since the adoption of biobanding. An analysis of a decade of the relative age effect – from 2001 to 2011 – across European football suggested that the problem was actually getting worse,[33] although awareness of the relative age effect has increased markedly. At the European U17 Championships in 2019, 47 per cent of all players were born in the first quarter of the selection year and only 6 per cent in the last quarter.[34]

Biobanding is not a panacea. The method actually brings risks of clubs making new mistakes if it is deployed clumsily and too rigidly. There are tales of clubs releasing young goalkeepers prematurely because the Khamis–Roche method – which, naturally, is not flawless in its accuracy – does not predict them to get to the optimal height for a goalkeeper, considered to be 6 feet 2 inches or taller. Even when this facet of the science is not fallible, the Khamis–Roche method is dangerous if it replaces human judgement. 'It doesn't take into account the whole child,' Levett explained. 'If they are technically great or psychologically really strong, yet a late physical maturer, playing them "down" because of a scientific method may not help them.'

Even when it does not bring these problems, biobanding is difficult to implement outside professional academies. These academies are themselves dealing with how talent has already been skewed by the relative age effect, from the very earliest years. 'Biobanding would not directly impact the players coming into the clubs unless it was applied at the grassroots level,' explained Cummings. 'As such, scouts are more likely to still bring in early- over late-developing players from 11 years on.'

When scouts see young players, they are already shaped by whether they are young or old for their year. Those old for their year won't enjoy just their transient physical advantages but the more permanent boon of having been exposed to better opponents, better coaching and – because the best tend to be singled out for extra training – simply having played more. The inequity in football academies, with the youngest for the school year staying only one-quarter as long as the oldest before being culled, is a symptom of the relative age effect as well as a cause.

In English football, even as awareness among coaches of the relative age effect has increased, 'nothing's really been addressed at grassroots level,' as Levett observed. 'We still have huge biases. Scouts are aware of the problem, but practically, limited changes have occurred. While there is more awareness of the relative age effect, the challenge is to really fight through people's biases to understand that performance today does not equal potential in the long term.'

Lessons from the All Blacks

The most prominent sport to be immune from the relative age effect, American football, provides some lessons for other sports.[35, 36] Unlike in most professional sports, in American football players are not placed into annual age groups and weight categories until late adolescence when maturation variability levels out, eliminating the selection bias. In the 2019, NFL draft, for instance, the birth dates of the players drafted showed no relative age effect at all – indeed, 27 per cent of players were born in the last quarter of the selection year, so they were actually slightly overrepresented.[37]

This finding attests to the enlightened way in which junior players are categorized in American football. Players are only eligible for the draft after they have been out of high school for three years – by which time the advantage accrued by the most physically mature in a selection year has dissipated. American football is a sport where late specialization is the norm, and it is mostly a North American sport, creating an internal monopoly. The same strategy may not work in sports like basketball and football, which are more global in appeal; in an effort to gain an advantage internationally, the norm is early engagement and selection into elite training academies, particularly for football.

So the sheer uniqueness of American football makes it difficult for other sports to implement the NFL model. Yet one essential lesson is that even if they do recruit talent before adolescence – a questionable policy, but one which would require concerted effort from the top of a sport to stop – sports teams must remain open to later routes into their pathway.

As well as biobanding, there are broader steps that can mitigate the relative age effect. New Zealand rugby was one of the first national sports teams to systematically divide players by weight, rather than age, at youth level. The All Blacks introduced the policy 'because Maori and Polynesian children tend to develop faster than their white counterparts', *The Guardian* noted.[38] The success of the All Blacks is a testament to the benefits of a more enlightened approach to developing young talent.

Boys aged 13–18 can play rugby in categories based on either their weight or age. 'You could choose to play in the U-15 age group category which is "open weight" or you could choose to play U-15 "restricted weight" – or you could also choose to play in a category where the maximum age is 18 years but the grade is governed by weight,' explained David Askew, the director of sports development at Auckland Grammar School. 'We want children to enjoy their rugby, which can be different things to different kids, so we make the effort to talk with them about their experiences and aim for making it better for them.' In a further sign of New Zealand's enlightened thinking, they have recently introduced a competition for players under 85 kilograms, to try to keep smaller players in the game.[43]

Alternative methods have been suggested to mitigate the relative age effect. Fixed quotas for athlete selection – around 25 per cent from each quarter – is a radical option; the Troendelag Regional Football Association in Norway has introduced a more tapered version where a minimum of 40 per cent of players must be born in the last six months of the playing year.[39] Other potential approaches include rotating cut-off dates from one year to the next so that each child in turn has the benefits of being in the first quarter, and increasing awareness of the potential disparity between chronological and biological age by noting a player's month of birth on the back of their playing uniform. These simple methods reduce selection bias.[40]

Another potential solution is to use corrective adjustments to dissipate the relative age effect. In sports like athletics and swimming, objective outcome measurements – centimetres, grams and seconds – determine individual performance. The influence of relative age can be quantified and accounted for by making adjustments to individual performances within age groups. In a study in 2015, scientists tested corrective adjustments in sprinting. With reference to a large data set of under -9s–15s sprinters, they calculated the expected performance differences from being one day to one year older in each annual age group, given an athlete's chronological age and date of participating in the sprint. Performance times were then adjusted to a standard reference point to provide a corrected sprint time. For almost all age groups, the potential relative age-related differences were reduced, with the effect absent in sprint performance categories.[41] Similarly, in swimming, scientists developed corrective adjustments to every swimming stroke and distance in youth competition. The methods have been implemented in youth swimming in Australia and appear to be removing relative age effects.[42]

Coaches can modify youth matches to be more advantageous to skill development. In football, playing on smaller pitches for longer, and not playing 11-a-side matches regularly until children are into their teens, can cultivate late-maturing players who would be unable to beat opponents through brute force. Coaches can apply the principle across a coterie of other sports – using small-sided games in rugby or smaller courts in basketball.

A simple reform Levett advocates is getting children to play sport based on their age, not their year group. So a child would play with other nine-year-olds when they were nine and then move up a year on their tenth birthday, giving them experience of being both the oldest player in their year and the youngest, as well as playing with a wider range of players and opponents. The principle is similar to biobanding, though the science is much simpler.

'They should be giving kids exposure to playing games above their level – so it's really hard and they fail,' Levett said. 'They should be giving kids exposure to playing games below their level – so that they can get loads of confidence and do really well. And they should have games at their level so it's really competitive.' Yet even this multidimensional approach involves a trade-off because it risks undermining the social structures on which much grassroots football depends.

In a similar way, Belgian football has been successful allowing players to move either up or down a year, depending on their physical development. This strategy has benefited late developers including Kevin De Bruyne and Thibaut Courtois. In Belgium, late-maturing children, particularly those born late in the selection year, can consult a specialized doctor, allowing them to play in a younger age group. Belgian football has also adopted other reforms – for instance, at FC Brugge second teams at U-8 and U-9 level now only include players born in the second half of the selection year, and the club organizes a separate recruitment day for those born in the second half of the selection year. Such steps have eroded the power of the relative age effect, but it has not been eliminated. 'The problem', said Roel Vaeyens, who is in charge of player recruitment at FC Brugge, 'is that the pool where we recruit from is likely already skewed due to the selection bias.'

Virat Kohli, who became the number-one Test batsman in the world, was born in November, in the first half of his school year. But Kohli was not confined to playing with his age group growing up. 'He had a lot of power for his age,' Rajkumar Sharma, his coach from the age of nine, recalled.[43] 'He had that ambition to play with the bigger boys and not in his age group. He always used to say, "Let me play with the elders", because in his age group nobody could get him out.' Even within the confines of their age group, coaches can stretch players in different ways. For instance, in net practice they can direct cricketers only to score on one side of the wicket, which may force them to develop new shots.

For future Women's NBA Most Valuable Player Elena Delle Donne, playing with older players was particularly important. Delle Donne was born on 5 September, putting her among the very oldest children for her year, and she was unusually tall for her age, ultimately reaching 6 feet 5 inches. In matches with older children, Delle Donne's height advantage was less pronounced, forcing her to develop broader skills and resilience.

'I was in third grade and I was playing with seventh and eighth graders,' she recalled. 'They were obviously tough on me – they didn't want a little third grader coming in and showing them up, so I had to get knocked down, get back up, and it definitely toughened me up a lot.'

Delle Donne was a natural over-dog. But by playing with far older players, she was effectively forced to develop the skills of an underdog, too. Aged 11, Delle Donne was routinely playing with 16-year-olds. 'It made me so much better, because I'm super-tall and was always really tall. And when I was playing in my age group it was just so easy. But when I played up and people were my same size and strength it challenged me to actually use skill to improve.'

Such tales illustrate how a smarter, more individualized approach to developing athletes can mitigate the relative age effect and ultimately improve the prospects of producing more elite athletes. Yet, no fool-proof system exists. Whatever is done to curb the relative age effect, 'there's always a trade-off,' Levett said.

An efficient talent system would have neither a relative age effect nor an underdog effect, but those from each age group represented equally and performing as well. That there are fewer late-born athletes in professional sport – especially because they then outperform earlier-born athletes – attests to an inefficiency in the talent identification process. It suggests what the prize could be for any system better able to grapple with the relative age effect and ensure more equal treatment for players born at all stages of the year: turning more short little fat kids into superstars.

4

Street spirit

How *ballon sur bitume* led Paris to become the football hub of the world

'In four- or five-a-side, the player will touch the ball every four seconds, whereas with 11 players, you can have a whole minute where you're not going to touch the ball.'

Mahamadou Gory, the coach of US Torcy U-16, where he used to coach Manchester United and France superstar Paul Pogba

Greater Paris is the football hub of the world. Sixty players who played in the past five men's World Cups were born here, 10 more than in Buenos Aires, the second best-represented metropolitan area, calculated the sociologist Darko Dukic.[1] Eight members of France's victorious 2018 World Cup squad came from the Paris region.

To understand why, take the RER train for 16 minutes north from the Gare du Nord. Then, you will arrive at Sarcelles.

Outside Garges-Sarcelles station, stallholders flog everything from jackets and scarves to fight off the winter chill to fried chicken. The centre of life in this community of 60,000, though, is not in this bustling weekend market. It is best observed a kilometre away, at AAS Sarcelles football club.

At weekends, AAS Sarcelles's two football pitches in the community sports complex – there are also rugby, tennis, swimming and archery facilities on site – routinely host three or four matches in the same day, one after the other on the synthetic pitches. The grounds stage everything from U-11 games to senior and over-55s football, all played out in front of crowds of enthusiasts and dreamers, wishing they themselves were out on the pitch.

Sarcelles is a deprived area, known for its tower blocks, high unemployment rates, a history of riots and occasional multicultural tensions. But, more happily, it is also renowned for its football. Of the 18 'notable people' Wikipedia considers to have emerged from Sarcelles, 12 – two-thirds – are men's footballers, including the Monaco and France forward Wissam Ben Yedder.[2] Six months older than Yedder is his childhood friend and teammate, the most famous Sarcelles native of the lot: Riyad Mahrez, a brilliant forward who has won two Premier League titles – the first Leicester City's 5,000-1 triumph in 2016, the second with Manchester City in 2019. France would have surely picked Mahrez, but he decided to play his international football for Algeria, helping them win the 2019 African Nations Cup. Yet, the competitiveness at Sarcelles was such that Mahrez, famously thin as a child, did not reach the first team for his age group until he was 17.

Just like Mahrez, the other professional footballers learned their game at AAS Sarcelles. But, even more than at the club, Mahrez and others like him learned to play football in the spaces between Sarcelles's ubiquitous tower blocks. It was here – in between trees, park benches, and in any space he could find – that Mahrez learned the dribbling, step-overs and dazzling ball control that would make Manchester City pay £60 million for him. Even after he had begun his professional career, Mahrez would still return to Sarcelles after his weekend matches for more games of street football – what locals call *ballon sur bitume*, which translates as 'concrete football'.

These games – which locals now play between the tower blocks in concrete cages which were not built when Mahrez was a child – are fiercely contested. They are generally pick-up matches of four- or five-a-side, played in tight spaces.

'Life is not easy in the city, but there is a lot of passion for football,' said Mohammad Coulibaly, the head coach and technical director of AAS Sarcelles. 'The hunger of the Sarcelles players comes from the environment … Young players have this rage to win.'

The games of *ballon sur bitume* are the playgrounds of champions. Since 1998 France has reached five World Cup and European Championship finals, two more than anyone else.

'Be strong and find a way'

With every passing year, the way that scouts identify and nurture the best young athletes becomes more structured and systematic. Paris – where there are believed to be more scouts than in any other city in the world, bar São Paulo – reflects this increasing professionalism. Yet Paris has been able to marry the science of modern-day talent identification programmes with a sense of spontaneity and street spirit better than anywhere else. Like Mahrez, the best Île-de-France players tend to play *ballon sur bitume* in the banlieues until well into their teens, even if they have already been spotted by academies.

'I think the Île-de-France players are the best in France,' said Ardhaoui Oualid, the assistant coach of AAS Sarcelles; like Coulibaly, he is a Sarcelles local. 'From when we are young we are always playing football in the street.

'The skills you get are dribbling, strength and a hunger to win. When you are young you don't want to lose because it's the street and you are going to see them every day. Those skills – we find them in Île-de-France more than in other places.

'You can see football everywhere … In Sarcelles you have players that have athletic qualities and are very good with their feet. In football, you've sometimes got players who just have athletic skills – they are big, they are strong. Others have just skills with the ball. Here in Sarcelles you can see players with both.

'They have great skills but they have something else – they are not afraid, they are creative.'

'When you're living in the housing estates, you play outside all the time,' Mahrez later explained.[3] 'Our parents aren't that strict and so they let us play and playing all day every day really helps you improve your dribbling and technique. I think that's why the best technical players come from the streets.'

So dedicated was Mahrez that he could often be glimpsed playing football well after dark, playing games lit by dim street lamps. 'Every night, even when there was no light left he would play,' recalled Coulibaly. 'He was obsessed.'

Mahrez's immigrant background – his father grew up in Algeria, and his mother is of Algerian and Moroccan descent – is typical of the players who thrive in Sarcelles, and in the banlieues more widely. 'It's a melting pot,' said Christian Bassila, the director of the National Institute in Clairefontaine, where the best young players from Île-de-France train. 'They come from everywhere, so it's a creativity, it's something in identity, it's difference, you know.'

'We have players of African origin, also players who might be of Asian origin,' said Mahamadou Gory, the coach of US Torcy U-16s, a club in the banlieues 35 kilometres south-east from Sarcelles where Paul Pogba used to play. 'So it's diversified. We have a mix of everything; lots of different characteristics.' The best of different football cultures come together in the banlieues, Gory said. An analysis of France, Belgium and England, three of the four World Cup semi-finalists in 2018, showed that those with migrant backgrounds were substantially over-represented in all the squads.[4]

Part of the magic of street football lies in simple mathematics. Because games are played in smaller areas, and the number of players per side is fewer, each player is more involved. Players get more time on the ball and more touches than in structured matches – though each time they get the ball they have only a few split seconds before needing to pass or dribble, as opponents charge towards them. In this way, *ballon sur bitume* is a perfect environment to accelerate skill development.

'In four- or five-a-side, the player will touch the ball every four seconds, whereas with 11 players, you can have a whole minute where you're not going to touch the ball,' explained Gory.

In *ballon sur bitume*, 'the ball, you touch it every five seconds. I pass to you, I run past you, the ball is going to come back to me straight away. That means that the ball, on average, you touch it every four or five seconds. Whereas with 11 players, you might touch the ball every 12, 15, 30 seconds, even one minute.

'When you're playing four- or five-a-side, you're already working on technical quality and above all on "one against one"' – when an attacker must try to go past a defender, and the defender must try to stop him.

Street football trains the body and the mind. As the number of players, the opponents and even the size of the pitch change constantly, players are always reacting to new information and having to make decisions off the cuff.[5, 6] 'The absence of direct instruction in street sport allows athletes the opportunity to seek out and perceive unexpected and possibly better alternative solutions to problems,' said Daniel Memmert, a scientist from the Sports University in Cologne.[7]

'You develop an independent intelligence, because you don't have a coach telling you "play there, play there",' Gory said. 'It's you who takes your own decisions.'

In *ballon sur bitume*, there are no rigid age categories. Who plays and when is simply determined by who is around, willing and able. 'In the street there is no age,' said Oualid from AAS Sarcelles. 'When I was about 10, I could play with people of 15 or 16. It makes you stronger.' Playing with older children effectively means that, even if they do not have older siblings themselves, young footballers in Sarcelles can enjoy the same benefits that younger siblings do in sport more broadly; the exposure to older players hastens skill acquisition.

The lack of age restrictions is particularly challenging for small children – as Mahrez was, until fleshing out a little around the age of

17. With no referees – free kicks are awarded for egregious fouls but seldom minor ones – he had to take care of himself in *ballon sur bitume*.

'Players like Mahrez learn in the street that nobody is going to give you something or treat you another way because you are not strong,' Oualid said. 'Sometimes you play a game, your area against another area. There is no referee. So you have to be strong and find a way.

'He can do what he wants with the ball. When you have no difficulty keeping the ball from one place to another one you don't need to be strong – you need to be efficient.'

Perhaps this is what street football prizes above all else – efficiency. It does not matter how players play. It just matters that they win.

The Brazilian way

It is not only the Paris banlieues that show the remarkable benefits of street sport.

Brazil remains the only nation to have won five men's football World Cups. Its success has come without a system that hoards pre-adolescent children into highly structured academies at an early age. There is little coach-led practice in Brazil before the age of 12, and sometimes even later.[8] Young players overwhelmingly play street or beach football – *pelada* – and *futsal*, a five-a-side game played on hard courts, instead. The Portuguese word *pelada* – which translates as 'nude' – has its origins in locals playing with bare feet and no shirt.

The best Brazilian players tend to spend as much time engaging in football activities in their formative years as those from other countries, but a far higher portion is through informal play. On average, Brazilian players before the age of 12 spend four to five hours per week engaging in informal play in football, a comparable figure to the time that leading European players spend in informal play.[9] But, as well as the four to five hours devoted to *pelada*, aspiring Brazilian players also tend to play *futsal* for a similar number of hours each week, effectively doubling the amount of time they spend in informal play activity in football compared with European children. While *futsal* is more formal than *pelada*, typically played on specific courts under formal rules, both are nurseries for children through the variability provided by informal, non-coach-led play activity.

Rather like *ballon sur bitume*, *pelada* and *futsal* matches are akin to more extreme versions of football – with players having to navigate their way out of a tight space and develop brilliant control, but getting more overall time on the ball over a match because of the smaller number of players.

'*Futsal* requires you to think and play fast. It makes everything easier when you later switch to football,' said Pelé, one of the greatest footballers of all time.[10] Other prominent players to have played *futsal* include Ronaldo, Ronaldinho, Robinho, Neymar, Luis Suarez, Lionel Messi and Cristiano Ronaldo, who played *futsal* during his childhood in Madeira. 'All we played was *futsal*,' Cristiano later said.[10] 'The small playing area helped me improve my close control, and whenever I played *futsal* I felt free. If it wasn't for *futsal*, I wouldn't be the player I am today.'

The dynamism and variability of *futsal* and *pelada* give players the flexibility to adapt to different situations. The *futsal* ball also bounces and feels very different from a regular size-five football, which scientists have shown transfers to improved performance with a standard-size football.[11]

Futsal cultivates 'game awareness and decision-making, as well as the technical skills of dribbling, passing and finishing,' said Israel Teoldo da Costa, an expert in street football from the Universidade Federal de Viçosa in Brazil. 'It also develops more motivation in the children to play the game, because it is smaller than 11-a-side and facilitates greater participation in the game.'

Play: the highest form of research

Germany's 2014 World Cup triumph was hailed as a victory for the transformation of the entire structure of the country's football after poor displays in World Cup 1998 and Euro 2000.[12] Undoubtedly, it owed much to enlightened reforms, which led to a surge in grassroots investment, transformed local facilities and made leading clubs far more involved in talent development. But, even in one of the wealthiest and most meticulously structured football nations in the world, it highlighted the value of street football.

Sports scientists analysed the development histories of members of the victorious German World Cup squad, in search of what helped differentiate them from other players in the Bundesliga and amateur players who played from the fourth to sixth tiers.[13] Strikingly, the World Cup winners had actually played less formal football all the way up to the age of 22. But the World Cup winners had played significantly more unstructured football in their teens than the other players. Similarly, women's German national team players had played more unstructured football than Bundesliga players.[14] So the world's best players learned more of their football themselves, rather than following instructions from coaches.

The Deutscher Fußball-Bund (DFB) has worked to ensure players learn street football qualities even in formal training. The DFB's reforms to German youth football after 2000 moulded resourceful, instinctive players – empowering them to learn implicitly, rather than just rely on coaches telling them what to do. Effectively, the aim was to develop street footballers artificially. A generation of creative players, infused with game intelligence to adapt to different situations, was created.

An analysis of Premier League academies in England reaffirmed the crucial role street sport can play in nurturing athletes.[15] A comparison of two groups of players who graduated through the academy structure – one group who were offered three-year scholarships aged 16 and another group released by their clubs at 16 – showed no difference in the number of hours of coach-led practice the two groups had accumulated in the academies. From this part of their developmental histories, there was no notable difference. But there was one salient difference away from the training ground. Players offered contracts had engaged in an average of nine hours each week of informal football play – street football with their friends in streets and parks – while those not offered contracts engaged in such informal play for only five hours a week.

'Everything I learned came from those small matches,' Wayne Rooney, who was forged playing games of street football and on a small tarmac pitch over the fence from his Croxteth estate in inner-city Liverpool, later said.[16] 'The tactical side of things comes later but 95 per cent of my game is from those days playing as a kid.

'Small-sided games see you get the ball in much tighter situations and you need to be able to get yourself out of them. You are used to getting the ball and immediately you are under pressure and therefore learn about how best to cope with that pressure. When the pitch opens up in 11-a-side games you seem to have all the space in the world.'

Paradoxically, what separates the players wanted by the best clubs from those discarded too early lies outside the academy grounds.[17] While informal street games throw up unpredictable, eclectic challenges, in academies, coaches tend to be overly prescriptive – providing constant instruction to players about what to do and when.[18] If structured coaching accounts for too high a proportion of a child's exposure to the sport, it can hinder development and players' ability to work through problems themselves. Players who play more unstructured football as children have been shown to possess superior game intelligence – essentially, the ability to anticipate and recognize situations during a game and make correct decisions under pressure.[21, 22]

More informal play doesn't just develop smarter players. Street sport may also inoculate players against burnout or dropout, which both become more likely in highly pressurized environments. In a study of groups of elite youth players in the UK, the hours accumulated in coach-led practice negatively correlated with levels of motivation, suggesting that overly pushy coaching was leading players to fall out of love with football.[23]

The benefits of street sport can also be seen in basketball. In 2018, the NBA commissioned a group of experts to make recommendations about youth development.[22] They noted that informal play exposes children to more variables – different roles and positions, varying rules, surfaces, court sizes and different numbers of players – which can accelerate skill development. Unlike normal drills, informal play 'involves the interaction of situation dynamics, perception, and motor solutions, and also provides extensive implicit skill learning'. Such ad-hoc games lead to 'smarter learners' used to adapting – the sort of players who can retain their equanimity when confronted with unforeseen problems during a play off game.

As talent identification becomes more industrialized, the ingenuity that is best learned in street sport has become more important than ever. In the cauldron of professional sport, those who can retain a sense of spontaneity, mischievousness and fun are more likely to shape a match than those who are merely relentlessly well-drilled.[23]

The chaos of unstructured youth matches gives players the tools to thrive when thrust into structured matches. Those elevated from street football in Paris to formal games have proper protection from the referee, smooth ground to run on, and more space; what should be a huge step-up might actually feel *easier.*

Street spirit is a common thread among the greatest talent hotspots in sport. South London has produced players including Jadon Sancho, Joe Gomez and Reiss Nelson in recent years. All are products of playing on concrete courts and in cage football – a culture of street football resembling that in the Parisian banlieues.[24] 'It's how we were brought up from the start – it's street football,' Sancho explained.[25] 'Everyone just expresses themselves and that's how people learn their skills. Street football means you fear no one because you have nothing to lose and you are just being yourself.'

In rugby, dynamism and self-knowledge are cultivated in the rural areas of New Zealand, before players often move to leading rugby schools. In basketball, many American inner cities breed players with spontaneity and individual brilliance. In 2019, 102 Major League Baseball players – 12 per cent of the total – were born in the Dominican Republic, where there is a vibrant culture of baseball games in streets and parks. In Twenty20 cricket, the greatest concentration of talent is in Trinidad and Tobago, where players learn the sport playing small-sided games with a plastic windball. The vitality and certain chaos of these informal environments imbue children with the skills, and spirit, needed to set them on their path to becoming elite. As Albert Einstein observed: 'Play is the highest form of research.'

Street spirit meets technical sophistication

The players who graduate from clubs like Sarcelles and Torcy to stardom are emphatically products of street football. But they are also products of one of the most sophisticated coaching systems in the world: there are an estimated 30,000 coaches in the Paris metropolitan area.[26] The growth of coach education, and scouting, in Île-de-France has coincided with the proportion of leading French players from the region soaring. The percentage of players born in Île-de-France in Ligue 1, France's top division, rose from 10 to 27 between 1996 and 2016, sociologists Bastien Drut and Richard Duhautois found.[27]

For coaches in the banlieues, their job, in essence, is to marry street spirit with the tactical sophistication needed in professional football. 'Generally when kids go outside, it's to go and play football,' said Gory, the coach of Torcy U-16s. 'Even before they're in the club, they develop a certain set of technical characteristics which means that individually, we already have good players. But we then have to get them to work collectively.

'When you do four-a-side or five-a-side, you don't develop the "collective", you develop only individuality.

'There are some players who dribble a lot, who are a bit "perso" – they really like playing by themselves.' Gory tells such players: 'You can dribble, but after dribbling, there has to be a pass or a shot. And that makes them more intelligent. That makes them make their technical skills work in the service of a collective.'

An abundance of players from the banlieues have outstanding technical skills. Those who become elite are those who learn to deploy these gifts most effectively, Gory said. 'Players who are going to be capable of solving problems that are in front of them with the solutions from their game intelligence – that's what we're looking for.'

At Sarcelles, young players train three times a week, for an hour and a half a time. A common training game is small-sided matches in which each player is allowed only two or three touches before they must pass the ball.

'You have to develop the way to think,' explained Oualid, the Sarcelles assistant coach. 'We are teaching them to play together. The ball has to run, not the players. Then you have to keep these skills when you are in the penalty zone but we need to develop those skills of playing fast, make the ball move.' At Sarcelles, the club judges youth coaches on how they develop players, not merely their results; coaches overly focused on winning at age-group level can damage long-term player development. 'The player that can put together his skills in small spaces and what he learns in the club can be a big, big player with athleticism and work.

'Each player is treated as individual but we put them in a collective. Each player is different. We have players that have creative skills, others have athletic skills, others have technical skills. Every player has his skills. Our job is to take all those skills and put them together.'

This is coaching perfectly tailored to the young players Sarcelles, and the other banlieues, specialize in producing. Mahrez's journey is not so much a tale of street football and raw ability triumphing over coaching, as it is sometimes presented, but of street football and raw ability triumphing when combined with high-quality coaching.

'He took his qualities as a street player – this creativity that you get in the street – and he took what we have been teaching him,' Oualid said. 'You cannot take a player who's only playing in the street and put him in the professional world. No. You have to learn real football – Riyad did that.

'When you put it all together you have the player we have today.'

Clairefontaine: where street football meets elite coaching

Nestled in a forest 50 kilometres south-west of central Paris lies the Château de Montjoye, a seventeenth-century mansion that has been renovated with five-star facilities. The 56-hectare site surrounding it includes 10 football pitches, a leading medical centre and stunning views of the forest. This is Clairefontaine, the French national training centre. It is also where, from the age of 13, the 23 best young players in Île-de-France go to train for two years. Across the five intakes from 2014 to 2019, there were five boys from AAS Sarcelles.

Displayed proudly on the walls of Clairefontaine are posters of the most famous alumni to graduate since the centre opened in 1988. These include Thierry Henry, Nicolas Anelka, Louis Saha, William Gallas and Blaise Matuidi, who all enjoyed long international careers.

But most striking is a handwritten note. 'Pour L'INF, merci pour ces deux années inoubliables' – For INF [Institut national du football – the French national football institute], thank you for two unforgettable years – it reads. The words were written by the most recent Clairefontaine graduate turned global superstar, Kylian Mbappé. In

2018, Mbappé's four goals led France to World Cup glory; he became only the second teenager, after Pelé, to score in a World Cup final.

The list of Clairefontaine alumni is stunning, especially considering that only 18 per cent of the French population lives in Île-de-France. Clairefontaine serves as inspiration for the next generation, and as a model for other national federations – in football and other sports – to scrutinize and try to replicate.

There is certainly much to admire in Clairefontaine. Selection for the academy is done during a six-month process, which whittles down about 2,500 of the best players in Île-de-France to the best 100, and finally the annual intake of 23. From their diets to medical facilities, those who make it here are supported in every way possible to maximize their talents. Simultaneously, the centre is designed not to give players a premature sense of entitlement – so, barring goalkeepers (who tend to be taller), all players share rooms.

Rather than overwhelming players with information, training is focused and sharp. From Monday to Friday, players train for an hour at 5.45 p.m. – apart from Wednesdays, when they play matches. During the day, players go to a local state school. 'If you are more smart in school, it will be the same on the pitch,' said Christian Bassila, the director of the National Institute. When they return home during weekends, players play another game for their clubs, so they remain in touch with their roots, and are exposed to different football challenges away from this rarefied complex.

The remarkable array of Clairefontaine graduates has not bred complacency. Coaches are encouraged to re-evaluate their methods constantly; for instance, in recent years there has been more emphasis on recruiting smaller players to combat the relative age effect. Players are challenged in unexpected ways, like being moved to a new position. 'You can understand the game better in different positions,' Bassila explained. 'The vision is not the same when you change position.'

Yet, however impressive the facilities, coaching and planning that Île-de-France's finest young footballers enjoy, there are no real secrets to Clairefontaine. What separates Clairefontaine from would-be imitators is not so much the training that players receive in these plush grounds as the wider culture in Île-de-France.

Just like the coaches at Sarcelles, those at Clairefontaine see their job as supplementing the street football that children have already played. 'It's the beginning of the education, street football, because you don't have a coach in the side saying play like this or play like this – you play like what you have in mind,' reflected Bassila, who grew up in the banlieues before his own professional career. 'That's why street football is very important for creativity.'

As a finishing school for the best teenagers from Île-de-France, Clairefontaine performs brilliantly. But it is largely the quality of the intake who come aged 13 that keeps the quality of those who graduate at 15 so high. Compared with other academies that have similarly brilliant facilities but do not produce the same calibre of players, 'the difference is you are in this area,' Bassila said. 'We have so much talent in Paris.'

Clairefontaine gives players the best possible chance to make good on their full potential. Yet, while the academy polishes and refines the gems, it does not make them. That work is done at clubs like Sarcelles – and, even more, in the *ballon sur bitume* played in the streets, cages and parks around them.

5

In search of excellence

Pathways to excellence in sport and why there is no
consensus

'We definitely encourage generalization over specialization. We
philosophically believe early specialization narrows long-term potential.'

*Dave Askew, director of sports development at Auckland
Grammar School, which has produced more All Blacks rugby
players than any other school*

'From eight to 16, I was playing junior tennis and had good competition
at the Jack Kramer club – tennis was my life, it was my focus. It was a
lot of hours. You talk about that 10,000 hours – those were my hours of
good technique, learning how to play and how to compete. Tennis was
my focus every day, every weekend, playing tournaments.'

*Peter Sampras, former World Number 1 and 14 times a
Grand Slam winner*

In spring 2007 Helen Glover's mum, Rachel, was reading the newspaper. Her daughter was in her last week at the University of Wales Institute in Cardiff, studying sport and exercise science. An advert for Sporting Giants captured Rachel's attention. This audacious scheme by UK Sport pledged to turn athletes with the right physical characteristics into Olympic winners in time for London 2012, notably in the sports of handball, rowing and volleyball. Those aged 16–25 could enter.

Helen, who had always been sporty, was intrigued by what her mum told her. In the days ahead, she did an online application, filling in details of previous athletic involvement, as well as basic facts like age, weight and height.

'I remember thinking this could be interesting. I'm quite competitive anyway so wanted to see how I would do,' she recalled. 'I didn't think a lot about the process.' Helen already had other plans; she was volunteering in Ghana and had been accepted on to a teacher training course for when she returned.

In Ghana, Helen got another phone call from her mum, telling her she had been invited to a testing day. Helen couldn't make the date, but switched to a later testing day – the final one in the first round. This event took place a few days after her return to the UK in Bisham Abbey, a national training centre in Berkshire.

'I remember walking out thinking I didn't see many people doing better than me – but I was significantly smaller than anyone else.' That wasn't surprising; when Glover hurriedly filled in the application form, she lied about her height. She was actually an inch and a half shorter than 5 feet 11 inches – the minimum required by the scheme. 'I remember thinking – argh, if anything's going to be the problem it's going to be this issue.' But after observing Glover and her athletic performance, a few centimetres ceased to matter.

Glover had thought that given her extensive experience playing hockey growing up – she captained her county team at age-group level – she might be selected for handball or volleyball. But when asked back for the final camp a few weeks later, it was to a rowing camp. Glover had never been in a rowing boat. 'I was quite surprised.'

In the next camp, Glover observed that several of the other women already rowed extensively – 'They didn't really look like I did.'

But Glover made it through to the final round, at Nottingham in the summer of 2007. Now, for the first time, she got into a rowing boat. 'What I was doing looked nothing like the rowing you see on television – it was like a different sport. Everything they make look so easy was just impossible.'

It turned out Glover had already made it onto the scheme.[1] One of the aims of the final camp was to be honest with the athletes about the extraordinary sacrifices the programme would entail. 'They actually wanted to make it very tough to give us an out. They didn't want people to quit jobs and leave loved ones behind only to drop out later.'

A few weeks later, Glover received a letter offering her a place as one of the 52 male and female athletes, out of 5,000, to be chosen for the scheme in any sport. If she accepted, she would have to move to Bath, in south-west England, to work with the coach Paul Stannard. By this point – it was now February 2008 – she had already moved to Plymouth on the south coast for her teacher training course. 'I came very close to saying "I can't." I've just left university in debt, I need to get a job, I'm 21, I don't know anything about rowing … When the phone call came, I genuinely didn't know whether I'd say yes or no.'

Glover began her journey with one outlandish aim in mind. 'I wouldn't have taken up the sport if I wasn't driven by the Olympics. Literally from day one the whole purpose of this wasn't enjoyment – it was getting to the Olympics.'

For two years, Glover lived a double life. In the day, she worked at Old Field School in Bath, where she got a job as a PE teacher. Before and after the school day, she did Olympic training. 'I'd get up around 4.30 in the morning to start at five on the rowing machine in the club. It's basically a shed – there were no toilets, no showers, nothing.' She would then walk up the hill to school. 'You get to the end of the day and have to do your hockey or gymnastic clubs. You'd be looking at your watch thinking, "This is eating into time I should be on the river."'

After school, Glover went back down the hill, ideally doing a full session on the water. The notion of a day off was a chimera. Glover spent Saturdays and Sundays doing three separate training sessions, with as many on the water as possible. 'The toughest thing was that you weren't recovering,' she remembered. 'I was absolutely shattered from working, but I was getting very close to getting on the coat-tails of some of the bottom girls of the team.' Glover trained for around 15 hours a week alongside her teaching.

At Easter, Team GB rowers did the most important trials of the year: time trials to decide who would make the team. To give herself the best chance, Glover quit her teaching job in February so she could train full-time for a few months before the trials; her parents covered her rent for a couple of months. 'It was a big leap of faith. If it didn't work, I didn't know what I'd do.'

Glover scraped onto the team. Her life was transformed instantly; from May 2010, Glover received full lottery funding from UK Sport – about £20,000 a year. Finally, she had one career rather than two.

Her weekly training time – on the water, on rowing machines or in the gym – doubled to 30 hours. The salient difference was not the amount of training but what came in between – 'the recovery, the downtime'. Her ascent when she turned professional was astounding: Glover won the silver medal in the pairs event at the World Rowing Championships in November 2010, with her partner, Heather Stanning, who only started rowing in 2006.[2] 'By November I was thinking I want to win the Olympics,' Glover recalled.

In the summer of 2012, Glover and Stanning won gold in the women's coxless pairs – Team GB's very first gold medal of the London Games. 'It felt like a bit of an out-of-body experience. It felt like it almost didn't belong to me – the whole story was almost too perfect.'

Against the 10,000 hours rule …

By the time she won silver in the World Championships in November 2010, Glover estimates, she had only been training and practising rowing for a total of 2,000 hours; by the time that she won gold in 2012, she had rowed in the region of 3,500 hours. She showed how, with a combination of the right physical characteristics – even if her height was less than Team GB's supposed minimum – extraordinary hard work and sagacious training it was possible to short-circuit the '10,000 hour rule' popularized by Malcolm Gladwell.[3] The 'rule' decreed that 10,000 hours of training – acquired over 10 years – were essential to acquiring expertise in any field. Glover got there in about one-third of the time.

While the pace of her advance was extraordinary, being able to get to the very top in substantively less than 10,000 hours of training is not unique. In some sports, athletes can rise to professional level after fewer than 10,000 hours of practice. Even in mass-participation sports like basketball it is not uncommon to acquire elite status in under 5,000 hours.[4,5] Yet, basketball may be something of an anomaly among the top four American sports due to the sheer importance of being tall and the fact that, physically, the game is difficult to play before a certain age due to the height of the basket and size of the ball.

The '10,000 hour rule' is seductive – especially for pushy parents, some of whom designed their children's entire schedules around reaching this hallowed number. But it is ludicrously simplistic, and such a broad guideline as to be of no use at all. Anders Ericsson, whose work provided the foundations for the 10,000 hour rule, has lamented that his work was misinterpreted.[6] The truth is that it was never a rule, but merely a rough guideline.

'I kind of debunk that,' Glover said of the 10,000 hours rule. 'On the face of it my speedy rise in the sport totally goes against that 10,000 hours rule. I was not practising 10,000 hours on really minute parts of the rowing stroke, but I had been taking part in various other sports at different levels literally from when I could walk. When I could toddle I was racing my brothers, I was playing catch in the field, my parents would take us to play hockey and basketball … Those hours add up and at school I was just playing sport.

'It's not exactly the case that I did not participate in sport and then suddenly became an Olympian in rowing because I was tall enough. It was a case of I'd done a lot of sport, hadn't quite found my sport and was incredibly lucky to have great coaches from day one of my rowing career. And then on top of that I worked so hard.'

When Glover discovered rowing, she went 'all in' on rowing. 'I was very much at one end of the spectrum on how much my life revolved around rowing. It's not what I'd suggest to everyone but for me it worked. I would go home and watch rowing videos and look up statistics on rowing and I would not drink and go to bed very early … If it had been my whole life, there's no way I'd recommend anyone live their life like that. It's just not sustainable and probably not very healthy over a long period.'

Glover's journey culminated four years after London, when she and Stanning defended their gold medals in Rio 2016. 'We were Olympic champions, defending champions and nothing else would do. We had to win.'

... And for

Just as the notion of a 10,000 hour rule needs contextualizing, so does Glover's achievement. While the swiftness of her rise is remarkable in any sport, rowing lends itself better to such a story than almost any other sport. Worldwide participation is comparatively small. Rowing is unusually dependent upon physical and physiological attributes. Late specialization – albeit seldom as late as for Glover – is the norm. And when Glover did specialize, she was exposed to UK Sport's training programme – arguably the best in the world. So, while Glover's story shows that 10,000 hours of practice are not always essential to reach the apex of your sport, there are limits to what can be drawn from her tale. For every tale similar to Glover's, there are counter-stories of players who have reached the top after a lifetime devoted to that sport.

Pete Sampras was given a tennis racket by his parents at age five or six. 'It was just how I fell into the sport,' he recalled, 'My parents did not play tennis; they had a racket in our basement and I used to just hit the ball against the wall. One thing led to another and I hit at the local park and took some lessons. For whatever reason, I was hooked and really enjoyed the sport. That's kind of how it all started.'

Around his seventh birthday, the Sampras family moved from Washington, DC to Palos Verdes in California. The young Sampras benefited from a climate conducive to playing throughout the year, a vibrant tennis culture and contemporaries who pushed him. He played sometimes with Andre Agassi, who was a year older and travelled for tournaments from Las Vegas, and regularly with Michael Chang, whose family also moved to California when he was a child. Sampras joined the Jack Kramer Club, a legendary club that also developed Grand Slam winners Tracy Austin and Lindsay Davenport.

'From eight to 16, I was playing junior tennis, and I had good competition at the Jack Kramer Club. Tennis was my life, it was my focus.'

Although Sampras did not completely specialize, he only dabbled in other sports. 'Tennis was my focus every day, every weekend, playing tournaments. I played recreationally some basketball, football and baseball just with friends and family but nothing serious, nothing organized. It was always tennis … It was a lot of hours.'

So many, indeed, that Sampras's rise to win 14 Grand Slams could have been a case study for the 10,000 hour rule. 'You talk about that 10,000 hours – those were my hours of good technique, learning how to play and how to compete.'

The big debate

The debate about specialization is grounded in the question of when an athlete should specialize in a particular sport. The debate is so polarized that academics have even struggled to agree upon a definition of what constitutes specialization.[7]

To generalize, there are at least three different pathways for sports engagement for children:

- *Specialization* – engaging predominantly in one sport, from an early age – often before adolescence – with training almost throughout the year.
- *Diversification* – engaging in a number of sports to an equal or similar extent until a child is in their teens.
- *Early engagement* – beginning engagement with their primary sport very young – generally before adolescence in the most popular sports worldwide – and spending the majority of time in that sport but still engaging to varying degrees in several others.

Naturally, the relative merits of these approaches – which exist on a continuum – vary across different sports. The challenge is coming up with clear guidelines as to what number of sports and hours of engagement would lead athletes to be grouped in one category or another.

If early specialization and rigid devotion to 10,000 hours were necessary to become an elite athlete, Glover's story would not have been possible. Neither would the tales of Mark Cueto, who did not play rugby union from the age of 10–17 but eventually played 55 times for the senior England team; Steve Nash, who did not play basketball until he was 13 but went on to win the NBA's MVP award twice; and Joel Embiid, who did not play basketball until he was 15. Three months later, Embiid was invited to a basketball camp – 'and the only reason was because I was like 6 foot 10', he later wrote.[8] The story encapsulates the notion that in some sports physical and physiological characteristics – Cueto had extraordinary speed, Nash was a powerful athlete[9] and Embiid was exceptionally tall – can help athletes overcome early practice deficits in their eventual sport.

These tales all show that it is possible to reach the top in some sports without specializing early. That much is not in doubt: pre-adolescent specialization is not always a requirement to become an elite athlete. The more interesting, and complex, question is whether someone's chances of reaching the top are greater if they specialize later or earlier.

The advantages of later specialization

A number of elite athletes have credited participating in other sports with imbuing them with distinctive, unusual skills in their ultimate sport of choice. Novak Djokovic has said that his flexibility on the tennis court – and his hallmark sliding slips to retrieve the ball – came from his time spent skiing in his youth. 'Skiing has helped the flexibility of my ankles and knees from a very early age,' Djokovic said.[10] Similarly, the footballer Zlatan Ibrahimović has attributed his astounding bicycle and scissor kicks to the balance he developed getting a taekwondo black belt aged 17;[11] England's Cricket World Cup winning star Jos Buttler has credited his ramp shot – hitting the ball over the wicketkeeper's head – to playing hockey.[12]

A report for the NBA in 2018 noted that a variable sporting childhood can accelerate skill development.[5] By specializing later, 'athletes acquire a multifaceted repertoire in terms of a wider and closer-meshed "network" of perceptual-motor skills, which facilitates the emergence of functional skill solutions.' It has also been suggested that engaging in a variety of sports helps children develop a broader range of movement competencies that may facilitate greater creativity and that, if athletes specialize too early, it can limit their motor skill development.

But while there is some evidence that tactical skills transfer across similar sports, particularly between invasion games,[13] there is not yet any empirical proof that technical skills transfer across sports. Even the evidence that physiological characteristics transfer is largely restricted to a level that may only be helpful during initial engagement in other sports.[14] The possibility of transfer is higher when two sports share common elements and processes,[15] yet no evidence exists to suggest the optimal number of sports in which to engage and the total hours needed in each sport to facilitate transfer. Similarly, while some athletes have credited other sports with developing psychological skills – the great Australian cricket batsman Steve Smith attributes his adaptability to tennis[16] – this notion hasn't been empirically tested.

If skill transfer between sports has yet to be proved, there are some unambiguous benefits to late specialization. Early specializers have over twice as much chance of picking up injuries due to overuse than those playing a range of sports.[17] Young tennis players are 1.5 times more likely to get injuries than those playing multiple sports; youth baseball pitchers who pitch in over 100 innings a year are 3.5 times more likely to be injured.[18]

As the pressure to specialize earlier intensifies, there has been a rise in overuse injuries in baseball, especially among teenage pitchers: children's bodies can only take so much strain before the risk of debilitating injury multiples. 'Early specialization and high training volumes will cause more injuries and loss of talent than later specialization and delayed volume of training in sport,' said Ross Tucker, a prominent sports scientist.

If they make it to professional level, those who specialize too early can still suffer physically from overuse, and have a greater risk of serious injury during their careers. In swimming, early specialists have shorter careers than later specializers.[19] Major League Baseball players who specialized before high school – normally the age of 14 – suffered more severe injuries during their professional careers than those who did not.[20]

Later specialization is also better for mental health. Early specializers are more likely to suffer burnout and quit their sport altogether,
overwhelmed by the relentless focus upon one sport and the lack of
equilibrium that comes when it becomes an all-consuming part of
childhood.[20]

So there is a powerful moral argument against forcing children to
specialize in a sport before they have even entered their teens. Even
those who seem precocious and are subjected to relentless training have only an infinitesimal chance of becoming elite. Of 35,000
young athletes selected to train in Russian sports schools – a notoriously single-minded environment – 99.86 per cent failed to reach
the elite level.[19]

In some sports, athletes do not need to excel at youth level to
have a chance of making it to the top. In athletics – a sport in which
capabilities can be precisely measured, rather than depending on
coaches' subjective opinions – just 9 per cent of men, and 13 per cent
of women, who ranked in the top 20 worldwide at senior level in
sprinting, throwing, jumping and middle-distance events had been in
the top 20 at U–13 level.[21]

Later specialization may mean there is more chance of children
picking the sport that is the best fit for them – not simply one that
suited their physical gifts better at a particular time or was their parents' favourite. At underage level, the best athletes in one sport tend
also to be among the very best in others, noted Tucker. 'Encouraging
diversification is good because it keeps their options open, potentially
making them better at the sport they eventually choose.' The earlier
children pick a sport to specialize in, the greater the risk of them
making the wrong choice.

Most strikingly of all, in many sports athletes who specialize later
simply have more chance of going on to become elite. A study analysed the developmental histories of 1000 UK athletes aged 16–18,
ranging from those who didn't play beyond their school level to those
who reached age-group international level aged 16–18. The study
looked at over 50 sports. In the five ages retrospectively measured – 7,
9, 11, 13, and 15 – athletes who later reached age-group international
level consistently played more sports and specialized later than those
of a lower standard. For instance, aged-15 national and representative

players were over twice as likely to engage in three or more sports compared to others; there was 'an increased likelihood of achieving a higher standard of competition when individuals participate in three competitive sports during the specializing years'.[22] So, in general, the more sports athletes played, the better they were at their best sport – a compelling case against early specialization, even if it does not provide evidence of causality and the study did not examine the total hours accumulated in other sports, only the number of sports in which they participated. German athletes who won Olympic medals specialized later than German athletes who almost won medals in the same sports, accumulated more practice in other sports and engaged in them for longer. The medallists also started their main sports an average of 18 months later – just before turning 12, rather than a few months after turning 10.[23]

A study of Danish athletes found that elite athletes – defined as those who had achieved a top 10 finish in world or Olympic events, or a top three one in European events – did significantly less weekly practice in their eventual professional sport than near-elite athletes until after they were 15.[24] At the age of nine, the near-elite group had accumulated 160 more hours in practice compared with those who would become elite. Between the ages of 9–12 and 12–15, the group who would become elite did two hours less training in a week than those who became near-elite. The near-elite group entered their first youth international competition two years earlier, aged 15 compared with 17, but this was a Pyrrhic victory – those who initially had less intensive regimes were setting themselves up better to make it to the top. It was only after turning 18 that the elite athletes started to do more training each week than the near-elite athletes, and then caught up on total training time in their main sport over their lifetimes.[24] A UK study in 47 Olympic sports showed much the same: super-elite athletes (medal winners at major events) underwent larger volumes of formal and informal play in other sports, started their main sport later and specialized in that sport later than those not as elite.[25] In these Olympic sports, as the Danish researchers wrote, 'the assumption that late specialization can lead to a delay in athletic development that cannot be made up at a later stage cannot be supported.'

A precocious start

Such studies show that early specialization is not always essential to reaching the top of professional sport. But saying that early specialization is not necessary is not the same as saying early engagement is not beneficial. In general, sports that are more competitive, and have more players worldwide, require engagement at an earlier age than less popular sports like rowing. Sports dependent upon high levels of tactical and technical skill also tend to require more hours compared with sports based more on physical and physiological factors.[7]

Aged seven, England football forward Marcus Rashford signed a youth contract with Manchester United – Liverpool and Everton were also interested.[26] Rashford continued to play other sports, too, but had a clear hierarchy of sports.

'I used to play quite a lot of different sports, with my friends – we always had a lot of energy and would take part in lots of different sports,' Rashford recalled. At school, 'we used to do everything – we used to play cricket, rounders, badminton, tennis.'

Rashford enjoyed a wide variety of sports, but football was the only one he ever remotely contemplated a career in, aligning with the early engagement model. Though he played a range of sports, we do not know the hours accumulated in each sport relative to those in football. 'Football was what we just enjoyed to do the most,' Rashford said. 'It's always been football.'

In the world's most popular sport, almost everyone who makes it to a high professional standard begins playing regularly at a very young age. They typically don't specialize completely at an early age – but, like Rashford, they generally play far more football than other sports. A study examining 328 of the best 16-year-old boys in the world, from Brazil, England, France, Ghana, Mexico, Portugal and Sweden, found that – despite the cultural differences between the countries – all these athletes had started playing football by the age of five.[27] Aged 5–11, they were involved in almost 10 hours of football-related activities – either practice, casual play or formal matches – a week, rising to nearly 15 hours at ages 11–16. By the age of 16, all elite players had accumulated around 5,000 hours in the sport. These players were not specializers per se – on average, they engaged in two or three other sports, but to a much lesser extent than football. In a sport as competitive as football, players generally need abundant practice: men's international players tend to have amassed over 6,000 hours of football-related activities by the age of 18, and Belgium international footballers were found to have accumulated 10,000 hours in football activities by their early to mid-twenties.[28]

Similar trends have been noted in women's football. A study analysing leading international teams, including England, Sweden, Australia and the USA – the 2019 World Cup winners – found that players tended to begin engaging with football aged five or six, with some minor to moderate involvement in an average of three other sports during childhood.[29] So while most future elite players are not early specializers, they are overwhelmingly very early engagers. There are no known examples of anything like Helen Glover's story in football.

Some sports demand that elite athletes have even more intensive training in their childhoods than those in football academies. Olympic gymnasts accumulate almost 19,000 hours in practice by the age of 16.[30] Because athletes tend to peak in their teens, gymnastics is a sport in which de facto specialization from before the age of 10 seems essential to any chances of reaching the top of the sport. In sports like artistic gymnastics, figure skating, platform diving and rhythmic gymnastics, which are all dominated by teenagers, super-elite athletes spend between three and seven times more time in training before the age of 10 than those in other Olympic sports: such children could be said to have specialized early.[31]

A study of elite alpine skiers in the USA found that, on average, skiers first engaged in the sport around the age of three, began supervised training aged six and competitive skiing aged seven. By the age of 19, elite skiers had accumulated around 8,500 hours in skiing-related activities as well as high hours in five to six other sports not directly related to skiing.[32] The best skiers tend to engage early with the sport.

A century ago, it was relatively common for athletes to win Olympic medals in disparate events: 24 athletes who first competed in the Games from 1920 to 1936 won medals in multiple disciplines. But only four athletes who began competing in the Games since 2000 have won medals in different sports. Two of those athletes triumphed in two very similar sports – alpine skiing and snowboarding; and speed skating and short track speed skating. That leaves only two athletes – the USA's Lauryn Williams, who won medals in athletics and bobsleigh; and Great Britain's Rebecca Romero, who won medals in cycling and rowing – who reached the podium in very different sports. Both of them specialized in one sport, then stopped competing in it before switching to the different one. Yet, these remarkable achievements were in sports with relatively low participation numbers, while all four sports may be viewed as being more reliant on physical and physiological attributes than technical and tactical ones.

These findings show that 'in your adult life, specialization's the only way you're going to survive,' said Timothy Olds, a sports scientist from the University of South Australia. 'Once you've got that sport, specialization's the only option. We just don't have poly-athletes anymore.'

A three-stage model

Some legends are embellished; others do not need embellishing. When he was 10 months old, Tiger Woods's father, Earl, said that he 'unstrapped him out of the high chair, allowed him to come over and play and he picked up a putter, put a ball down, waggled and hit a ball into the net. First time.'[33]

Woods first played a golf hole at the Navy Golf Club, the course that was a five-minute drive from his house, when he was 18 months old.[34] Aged two, Tiger used to call his father at his office and ask: "Daddy, can I practise with you today?' He appeared on television putting against comedian Bob Hope aged two, and carded a 48 for nine holes when he was three.[35] Before his record-breaking professional career, Woods won the Junior World Championships six times.

Yet, just as Woods and his lifelong immersion in a single sport is at one extreme, so Glover is at the other. As examples of the merits of specialization or diversification, neither is particularly useful.

Jean Côté, a prominent Canadian sports scientist, has devised a three-stage model for young athletes.[36, 37] Côté advocates that both to give themselves the best chance of being the best and for their wellbeing, young athletes should:

1 sample as many sports as possible until early adolescence;
2 focus on a few main sports in their early and mid-teens;
3 specialize in their mid- to late-teens.

The prevalence of this template in smaller towns, Côté believes, explains why they produce a disproportionate number of the best athletes. Following this model ensures that when athletes do pick the right sport, they have the energy left to commit to it wholeheartedly – in a way that had they specialized from before their teens may have been impossible without burnout.

Côté's model doubles as a description of rugby culture in New Zealand. 'We definitely encourage generalization over specialization,' explained Dave Askew, director of sports development at Auckland Grammar School. 'We still have "summer" and "winter" schedules for sport that do not allow the majority of people to play one sport all year round. We philosophically believe early specialization narrows long-term potential.' He believes that, besides a few sports – such as gymnastics – 'philosophically, the longer you delay specialization the better'.

In New Zealand, most boys engage with rugby from their very earliest years – similar to the early engagement model observed among the best footballers in the world – ensuring they amass sufficient practice. But they do so while playing other sports too, often having a clean break for several months from rugby during the height of the cricket season in the summer. This early engagement approach simultaneously ensures children get copious practice in a sport while allowing them to enjoy the benefits of being exposed to a wide array of sports.

Côté's model has a strong empirical basis, but it assumes that sports participation is ethically grounded. The danger with the approach lies in the practice deficit that athletes who play a diverse array of sports can accumulate. For instance, by the age of 15 a footballer who had avoided specializing may have played 2,000 to 3,000 hours less than one who had specialized aged 10. Even if this gap isn't insurmountable, it can be compounded by scouts viewing those from outside the academy system as less accomplished than those within it and, therefore, being reluctant to give players from outside the system a chance. Although some individual athletes may be better off specializing later, their chances of winning selection can be damaged if they try to keep up a range of sports for longer. 'At every stage where people identify talent they invariably shut the door behind them,' said Tucker.

Sports governing bodies working together – agreeing not to put pressure on multisport athletes to specialize until at least 13 or 14, say – would be one potential solution. In some countries, like the UK, awareness of the dangers of specialization has grown in recent years, and academy coaches have thought more holistically about athletes' development. But there is no sign of the broad cultural shift in youth sport that would be necessary to reverse the cult of earlier and earlier specialization in any meaningful way.

A hybrid approach: early engagement

Perhaps the early engagement model offers a prudent alternative to both early specialization and diversification.[38] In the early engagement model, players are actively encouraged to accumulate sufficient hours in their main sport or two, so as not to accumulate a large practice deficit relative to early specializers. But early engagers are also encouraged to continue playing as many other sports as they like. They accumulate sufficient practice hours to gain the necessary sport-specific skills, and have the opportunity to learn a broad range of physical and mental skills. Whether engaging in other sports leads to transfer or not is immaterial; early engagers develop a broader set of life skills, and reduce the risk of burnout and overuse injury in their primary sport. While there have been no empirical studies in sports like tennis, golf and ice hockey, all of which may be sports where early engagement is the norm, there is evidence that this is the prevailing model in men's and women's football and in alpine skiing.[28, 32, 39, 40]

Children who engage early still make profound commitments to their preferred sport, or sports – but the early engagement model is a far preferable and more rounded way of doing so than early specialization. The early engagement model both gives children a chance of becoming elite athletes and ensures they grow up in an environment that takes care of their physical and mental health. Sampling a large number of sports from a young age, children can then gradually ramp up engagement in their best sport, while being flexible enough to realize that their best sport could change over time.

In mass-participation sports the early engagement model may generally be the one that best marries the twin aims of maximizing a child's enjoyment in sport and their chances of becoming elite athletes. In lower-participation sports with greater importance of physical and physiological characteristics – like rowing – the diversification model may often be optimal.

'Some degree of sports specialization is necessary to develop elite-level skill development,' noted a group of academics.[4] 'However, for most sports, such intense training in a single sport to the exclusion of others should be delayed until late adolescence to optimize success while minimizing injury, psychological stress, and burnout.'

In different sports at varying times, athletes can rise to the top through either early specialization, late specialization or the hybrid early engagement approach. In different ways, all three of these approaches can work, depending on the context and the sport.

For most – but not all – athletes in the most popular sports, early and regular engagement seems almost essential to have a chance of becoming elite. But, within this framework of early engagement, athletes should have freedom to roam – especially for the good of their mental health and to prevent injuries.

Some athletes like Woods find their ideal sport in their formative years, and no more than dabble occasionally in others; others are best served by roaming around before settling on one. Some athletes credit other sports with helping them develop physical and mental skills; others simply say their skills are a product of years of dedicated practice in that sport. The point is that for all the temptation to say one particular path is a template for others to reach the pinnacle in a sport, all children are different and physically and mentally mature at different rates. Rather than have rigid rules, any sensible policy on specialization should have the wants and needs of the individual athlete at its very heart. Forcing children to specialize when they want to

6

The X factor

Why Freddy Adu didn't make it and how the UK went from one Olympic gold medal to 27 in 20 years – the art and science of identifying talent

'You can't teach a brick to float.'

Chelsea Warr, former director of performance, UK Sport

'Whom the gods wish to destroy they first call promising,' the writer Cyril Connolly famously observed.[1] Connolly was describing why he had failed to write a celebrated novel; his words could just as easily apply to sporting prodigies.

Predicting who will make it in sport is inherently hazardous. But, just occasionally, there are athletes whose qualities are so powerful that they leave scouts, the media, teammates and legendary former players in no doubt. The sport appears coded in their DNA.

'His left foot is fantastic,'[2] said Pelé, one of the most famous football players of all time. 'Mozart started when he was five years old. If you are good, you are good. God gave Freddy the gift to play soccer. If he is prepared mentally and physically, nobody will stop him.'

It was March 2004, and Pelé was speaking to the US magazine *Sports Illustrated* about a 14-year-old boy. His name was Freddy Adu.

Pelé was not alone in his enthusiasm. Aged 14, Adu was signed by D.C. United in Major League Soccer. His $500,000-a-year contract immediately made Adu the highest-paid player in the league. He was the youngest American man to sign a professional contract in any team sport. Before Adu made his MLS debut he had already been signed up by Nike for a $1 million endorsement deal; Nike chairman Phil Knight declared that Adu could be 'a superhero' and bigger than Michael Jordan, Tiger Woods and LeBron James. Adu had already starred in both the U-17 and U-20 World Championships – even though he was the youngest player on any side in both competitions. He 'didn't look out of place' training with the senior national team for the first time, the US head coach said.

'The resemblance between Adu and the teenage Pelé is almost eerie, from their open, innocent faces, unmarked by time, to their low-to-the-ground playing styles,' noted Grant Wahl, *Sports Illustrated*'s correspondent.

'It's pretty hard not to get caught up in it,' Adu said.[2]

Understanding talent

What is talent? In sport, talent is understood to be an individual who can stand out, and who has the potential to be high achieving. What distinguishes them is a combination of their genes and the practice they have done. Talent is 'the innate factors that affect the long-term development of skill, either directly – such as genetic factors affecting height and stature – or indirectly – such as when genetic factors affect rates and amounts of learning or adaptation,' said Joe Baker, a scientist from York University in Canada, and a specialist in talent identification. 'We like to think of talent as this stable, predictable thing but it's certainly more complex and nuanced than most people, even scientists, think.'

Talent identification is the process of identifying those who have the potential to become elite performers. As sport has become more professionalized, the age at which people are marked out as being talented or not has become ever younger; the battle between football academies for the most talented players under the age of 10 is notoriously brutal. In 2013, the Belgian football club FC Racing Boxberg signed a player who was only 20 months old; 'His ball control is incredible for somebody of his age,' the coach asserted.[3] In 2019, Manchester City launched their U-5 junior academy elite squad.[4]

One simple rule holds in talent identification: the younger the players, and the longer the time period between when they are recruited and when they are expected to peak, the lower the chances of them eventually becoming elite. There is simply less that is known about the athlete – and more that can go wrong over their journey.

It is sometimes said that talent brooks no argument. The stories of discarded players who have gone on to be elite – like Jamie Vardy, who was released from Sheffield Wednesday aged 16, and was still playing non-league football aged 25 and subsequently became one of the best Premier League strikers – suggest otherwise. Within professional sport, those considered the most accomplished at talent identification can have profoundly different views about which young talent to back. Scientists asked seven coaches and two scouts to group 13 ice hockey players into their top and bottom five based on watching video clips of these players in matches. Nine of the 13 players appeared in the bottom and top five lists, showing the lack of consensus about who are the athletes with the most potential.[5]

Adu became a nomad, moving within the USA, to Portugal, then to France, and then to Greece to try to develop his career. On and on

Adu's journey went – to Turkey, back to the USA, to Brazil, to Serbia, to Finland, and then back to the USA once again, but this time playing in the second-tier USL Championship, with no MLS teams wanting him. Even the 17 US caps that Adu earned along the way seemed more for the player that he was meant to have become rather than the one he actually was.

By the time he was 30, Adu had drifted out of professional football altogether. He later reflected: 'As a 14-, 15-, 16-year-old, you're young, you're immature, and you kind of get caught up in that a little bit.'[6]

Adu's story speaks to the difficulties of trying to identify talent. Adu stood out so much from his peers because he was physically more developed – not so much in his size, but in his speed. Children's development is non-linear – some develop far quicker than others, with the gap greatest before and during puberty – making predictions of future performance hazardous prior to this age.[7, 8] Adu, we can assume, was more physically and physiologically developed not just than his contemporaries but also than many of those older boys he played against in junior competitions.

'Growing up, I was always the best player,' Adu said when he turned 30.[9] 'Guys who were way below me at the time, you'd say right now had better careers than I did.'

Predicting success

Childhood performance is seldom a good predictor of future success – and is certainly not a precondition for success. In English Premier League academies, fewer than one in 200 players recruited before nine years of age go on to play for the club's first team.[10] In one study, scientists followed the development of over 500 players through the academy system over a 12-year period. At the age of 17–18 years, only 10 per cent of players remained in the system and almost 70 per cent of these were recruited at, or after, the age of 12 years.[11] In a study of British Olympic medal winners in 2018, two-thirds of the athletes that the authors described as 'super-elite' experienced no significant international success at junior level.[12]

Even when players are far older than when Nike gave Adu a $1 million contract, experts continue to flounder at identifying those who go on to achieve the most. Tom Brady – widely regarded as one of the greatest American football quarterbacks of all time – was the 199th pick in the NFL draft; this takes place when players are three years out of high school and are generally 21. Only 9 per cent of the variance in the number of games played in the NFL is predicted by the player's draft pick number, such is the ineffectiveness of franchises in identifying, and ranking, talent efficiently.[13]

The more complex a sport, the greater the number of attributes that can contribute to good performances, and the harder it is to identify talent. 'For almost any sport, identifying future success in a young athlete is extremely difficult and fraught with a lot of misguided efforts,' said John DiFiori, the director of sports medicine for the NBA. 'The data is pretty clear that talent identification has not worked in the past.'

The problem is particularly acute in sports that are tactical and skill-based – like baseball, cricket, football and tennis. You can excel in these sports in lots of different ways – in football, England's Peter Crouch is 6 feet 7 inches, whereas Argentina's Lionel Messi, arguably the greatest player of all time, is only 5 feet 7 inches. Both are strikers. To reach the summit of these sports, athletes need an extraordinary cocktail of psychological, physical, technical and tactical attributes, but these are so complex that right until players are adults, it can be almost impossible to distinguish those who will be the best from the rest.

The compensation phenomenon

The danger of being overly reliant on physiology to predict athletic performance is compounded by the compensation phenomenon.[14] This is the idea that an athlete deficient in a particular area – speed and agility, say – can go some way to overcoming this weakness by developing unusual strengths in other areas – tactical acumen and technical skill, for instance. In a sport like football, players can move to positions that negate their weaknesses and ameliorate their strengths. Claude Makélélé, a player who was both smaller and slower than virtually all his opponents, had such nous that he became one of the world's best defensive midfielders, winning the Champions League, two La Liga titles and two Premier Leagues. The best athletes do not always make the best players.

What matters also varies over time. Players unusually big or, in Adu's case, quick for their age group may be outstanding at one age group, because their physique stands out, but the same players may be less effective the higher up they advance. In sports like football, the relative importance of physical, physiological, psychological and sociological factors varies over time.[15] While physical and physiological factors are better predictors of progression early in development, psychological, technical and tactical factors are more important later on.[16] So at an early age athletes may be deselected based on measures that become less important in higher age groups and at senior levels.[16]

Arsène Wenger, the former Arsenal manager renowned for his talent-spotting abilities, told *Four Four Two* magazine about the difficulties of identifying young players with the right qualities to get to the top:

> I would say the first impression is vital and that takes 20 minutes. It does vary from player to player as some have obvious talent that you see quickly. Some more steady players who have less obvious skills need maybe six months before you realize they are the real thing. Lionel Messi at 13 years of age would have needed about one minute. I have seen tapes of him at 13. He gets the ball, dribbles past everyone and scores. He has talent. Some players – no, most players – aren't so obvious.
>
> At 14 to 16 you can detect if physically he will be able to cope with the demands of professional sport. And from 16 to 18 you can start to see if a player understands how to connect with other players. At 20 the mental side of things kicks in. How does he prepare? How does he cope with life's temptations and the sacrifices a top player must make? This is a job where you must be ready. If you get a chance, it has to be taken.[17]

The science concurs with Wenger. Decisions about who to select are largely intuitive, a study showed – based on a subjective evaluation of technical skills, game understanding, speed, personal characteristics like attitude and perceived 'coachability'.[18, 19]

Adu's physical qualities became less important the older he got; his genuine potential was probably never nearly as great as made out. He was, perhaps, profoundly unlucky to be cast as the saviour of men's football in the USA; the fact that the role needed to be filled did not make him the right man to do so.

While Adu's physical qualities became less salient, technical and tactical ability become more important as players age. Elite players show superior anticipation and decision-making too, with these differences emerging as early as eight years old.[20] But the extent to which such factors are stable, or developed over time, remains unclear. Technical ability is hard to measure, requiring the use of simple skills tests, data analytics from companies such as Opta, or subjective evaluation of match-play.[15] Scientists have not tracked the development of these factors over time, or tried to gauge how early success on these measures predicts later performance. While measures of technical and tactical ability differentiate age and skill groupings, the predictive use of these for talent identification remains unproven.

True grit

Psychology is at the core of elite performance. A study of Dutch footballers analysed questionnaires of psychological predictors – goal commitment, problem-focused coping, and seeking social support – taken 15 years earlier. In 72 per cent of cases, these scores successfully classified whether or not the players became elite.[21] The finding suggests that psychological characteristics – including grit, mental toughness, self-confidence, motivation and low fear of failure – are essential in professional sport. But the retrospective nature of the study makes it difficult to provide a template for those involved in talent identification. Whether children's scores on psychological tests predict what they will score on those same tests in the future is largely unknown, let alone how these measures relate to performance. Scientists report that 30–60 per cent of the variance in psychological characteristics is hereditary – so while athletes imbued with psychological skills are better suited to professional sport, these traits can be developed over time, and are not immutable.[16]

According to Adu himself, his greatest deficiency was in what Wenger termed 'the mental side of things'. That he moved between so many clubs suggests that he did not always fit in, could be difficult to manage and simply did not work hard enough on his game.

'I saw my game in a certain way,' Adu later reflected.[22] 'They saw it as, "You can give so much more to the team." And I wasn't doing that.

'When I see a kid who's really talented, clearly above the rest, and he's just coasting, trying to get away with his talent, I say, "No, no, no. That can't happen! You can't let that happen! They will surpass you." Because I was that kid.'

At the start of 2020, Adu should have been at his peak. Instead, he was without a professional football club, and recording short birthday messages on video for a website called Cameo. Each video cost $35.[23]

Talent identification: the Team GB turnaround

They were called the 'team of shame'. In the 1996 Summer Olympics in Atlanta, Great Britain won a paltry one gold medal. They finished 36th in the Olympic medal table, below Algeria, Kazakhstan and North Korea, and were regarded as a national joke.

In the same Games, Megan Still won a gold medal for Australia in the women's coxless pair event. Still was selected through a talent identification programme after having no previous involvement in rowing whatsoever.

Her success was one early example of how talent identification programmes can help achieve Olympic glory. And it was the inspiration for Chelsea Warr, a talent search manager from Queensland who relocated to England and took up a series of posts for UK Sport – the government agency responsible for investing in Olympic and Paralympic sport – in 2005. These methods helped turn Great Britain from Olympic dunces into a nation that routinely achieved the extraordinary. In the Rio Games in 2016, Britain won 27 gold medals – 26 more than in Atlanta two decades before – and came second in the medals table, eclipsed only by the USA. Britain won more gold medals in Rio than in six successive Olympics from 1976 to 1996 combined.

Talent identification may have much higher prospects in some sports. Such an approach may be easier in sports measured in 'centimetres, grams and seconds' – like running, jumping and rowing – in which physical capabilities are most important. In such events, the pool of athletes with the potential to reach the apex of the sport tends to be limited by physique – the odds of becoming an Olympic rower are much smaller if you are 5 feet 5 inches, whereas players could still be professional footballers at this height. In practice, this means that scouts can rule out vast swathes of athletes as potential Olympians in rowing because of their height and weight – even if, as Helen Glover's story shows, factors like height should not be used too dogmatically. An efficient talent identification programme can focus on those with the most likelihood of reaching the top.

After the humiliation of the 1996 Atlanta Games, the UK government opened up huge investment in Olympic sports, and prioritized the allocation of resources ruthlessly. But money alone is not sufficient to explain the metamorphosis in Team GB's Olympic performances; from lagging countries that spent less on the Games, the UK grew to outperform those that spent much more.

UK Sport deployed perhaps the most systematic talent identification of any country in Olympic history. In 2007, Sporting Giants was launched – a programme which aimed to turn athletes with the right physical characteristics into Olympic winners in handball, rowing or volleyball in 2012. Unsurprisingly, the posters put on trains around the UK prompted much guffawing.

Talent recycling

Talent transfer, as Warr calls it – or what may be best described as talent recycling – is the idea that athletes who are 'nearlies' in one sport, particularly sports with high participation numbers, may have the potential to reach elite status in another sport, especially those with lower global participation. Rather than assume that those who don't make it have fundamental limitations which mean they could never be champions in a sport, UK Sport regards many of the skills of near-elite athletes – physical skills and fitness, and resilience and training discipline – as potentially being transferable to other sports. These new sports may suit the athlete's physique better or, on an international scale, be less competitive, meaning that an athlete could still rise to the summit by pursuing the sport later in life; there are no major examples of talent being successfully transferred into football.

The principle is to 'find another place for those talents to be better utilized', said Warr. 'If you invest in a lot of athletes at the bottom of the ladder, the reality is most don't make the grade, so if you can be smart with that talent pool and shuffle it around you can maximize opportunities for young people to represent their country maybe in another sport that they've not even thought about.'

Glover, who took three years from getting in a rowing boat for the first time to winning the silver medal in the World Rowing Championships, and would win an Olympics gold medal two years later, was an extreme example of these ideas in practice. 'Her affinity with the water, her ability to feel the water as well as all of her other attributes, was just magical,' Warr recalled.

Yet Glover was not a one-off. Lizzy Yarnold, the UK's most decorated Winter Olympian, aspired to become a heptathlete. Yarnold didn't make it and, aged 19, entered UK Sport's Girls4Gold talent search scheme. She thought she might be identified as a potential jockey; instead, Yarnold was seen as possessing the right traits for skeleton. Within four years, Yarnold won a bronze medal in the World Championships; two years later, she won the first of her two Winter Olympics gold medals in the 2014 Games in Sochi.

The system to identify athletes whose talent can be recycled is one of 'design and not luck', Warr said. UK Sport's talent campaigns have assessed over 10,000 athletes since 2007. Those who went through talent identification or transfer programmes won 10 Olympic medals and 14 Paralympic medals between 2012 and 2018; the medallists were not known at the time to the sports in which they then went on to be successful and had minimal, or zero, prior experience in their sport.

When underpinned by the resources of a body like UK Sport, talent recycling can work for a variety of reasons, said sports scientist Timothy Olds. Some athletes may previously have been in sports that were not optimal for their talents – 'People may have chosen the wrong sport in the first place.' In sports with a shallower talent pool and less history of investment, talent recycling is more likely to work. The strategy has yielded better results in women's sports, Warr noted, because the infrastructure and participation numbers in many women's sports are not as developed as in the men's versions of each sport.

A transformation in grassroots sports or participation numbers, which have dwindled for many years, did not precede, or follow, the surge in the medals won by Team GB. The precision with which this talent was identified, recycled and developed was what changed, not the size of the talent pool.

This success reflects the scale of investment in British Olympic athletes. At the English Institute of Sport, a subsidiary of UK Sport that provides sports science support to athletes, 450 staff work on breaking down, understanding and quantifying elite sport – all in pursuit of a competitive advantage for the athletes themselves and in how these are identified. This work aims to bring previous intangibles out of the darkness and into the light. Swimming coaches once talked of an 'aquatic feel'; what was once an intangible can now be measured by distance per stoke in the water, which can help identify those most likely to win medals in swimming events, even if they are not the best in their age group at a particular time. Measuring and quantifying aquatic feel is simple enough, but only when underwater cameras are used – a small example of how UK Sport's resources helped identify the most talented athletes more efficiently than in comparatively penurious sports systems.

Mapping probable developments in sport means that UK Sport tries to judge prospective Olympians based not on what success in their sport looks like now but what it will look like in the years ahead, Warr explained. 'We call that a performance pathway, which is like this is what we're doing literally this week, what will medal winning times be in 2024 and 2028? We look back two years before that, four years before that, six years before that, eight years before that, and identify "what it takes to win", what are the characteristics, the profile – holistic, not just in one domain – that tells us these are really important at this stage and this is the evidence that we know these things are predictive.'

While such work emphasizes UK Sport's meticulousness, the transformation in the UK's Olympic record is best understood more as a triumph for talent development than talent identification. In the four Summer and Winter Olympic Games from 2012 to 2018, only 10 of Britain's 141 medals were won by those identified by national talent recruitment campaigns; 131 medals – 93 per cent – were won by those already in the system.[24] In the Paralympics over this time, 14 out of 147 of Britain's medals were won by those from recruitment campaigns, so 90 per cent were won by those already in the system.

The figures show that, despite the remarkable individual stories of talent being successfully identified late, Britain's Olympic success has owed far more to getting more out of those already in the system. The UK government's decision to prioritize winning medals – £69 million was spent on Olympic and Paralympic sports in the Sydney cycle, compared with £347 million in the Rio cycle running to 2016 – is crucial. This investment contributed to a 'winner-takes-all' culture that has been roundly criticized for damaging athletes' mental health, leading to a culture of bullying in many sports and taking away funding from sports like basketball which has high participation numbers but minuscule chances of winning Olympic medals.[25, 26]

But, for all these failings, such investment means that those already within the system have had the best possible chance to make good on their talent. When asked what she would do if starting out in her role as director of performance again, Warr would 'triple investment in coaches – they're the closest to the performer that can influence the outcome,' she said. 'Every sport and every system I ever look at where the biggest breakthroughs in performance come from, the quality of the coaching both in the pathway and at the elite level is futuristic and forward thinking.'

UK Sport's transformation shows the luck for athletes of being born in a country that was rich enough, and deemed sport important enough, to invest in both identifying and developing talent. For every talented athlete successfully recycled into a different sport in Britain, or galvanized to unlock their potential by the facilities and coaching they were exposed to, there may have been dozens more around the world – equally talented and equally hard working – who lacked access to a system that nurtured these gifts.

In elite sport, there will always be scope for unexpected rises, for athletes to surprise the most knowledgeable observers and even themselves and take a circuitous route to the top. But UK Sport attests to how marrying investment and meticulous planning can bring more order to the process, and ultimately increase the prospects of athletes becoming elite.

'I mean we beat China,' Warr laughed. 'I still can't quite believe that – sitting in the stands looking at my iPhone and going, "Take a photograph of that now, because actually we'll never see that again. Quick, just take it now."'

Nature and nurture

At the heart of discussions around the identification of talent is a simple question – how many people have the potential to be the best? A combination of nature and nurture is required to reach the top, with the balance between the two varying from sport to sport. Team GB's successes have been fostered by its precision in identifying the balance for different events – and then who has the right characteristics.

The ability to reach the pinnacle of sport is 'a very, very rare blend of a variety of aspects which could be physical, physiological, mental, and tactical', Warr said. 'In any prediction of talent it's never one thing or the other, it's a combination of things, and they come forward or they move back as you move through the pathway. What might be really important when you're 17 years of age will be quite different when you get to 19.

'There's got to be something about you that gets you above the rest of the population to start off with, and those things – no matter how hard you train them – won't shift. You've either got them or you haven't. And then there's a pile of things where you're like, right, now if we apply a stimulus some of those things will kick on as well.

'It's not always a physical thing – it can be a mental or technical issue. But there's something that gets you to the frequent flyer club, and then you've got to get into first class.'

Warr estimates that about 10 per cent of all people have the capacity – given the luck of when and where they're born, picking the right sport, parental support, good coaching, and avoiding injuries – to be high achievers in professional sport. It is impossible to assert such a figure with any scientific credence but Timothy Olds suggests that – with these caveats – 10 per cent is a reasonable estimate for the proportion of people with the potential to be a high achiever in one sport. For those with specific physical gifts the chances can be higher; about one in six American men aged 20–40 and 7 foot or higher are playing in the NBA, the writer David Epstein has calculated.[27]

Genes matter in sport and in trying to understand elite performance. 'Most researchers suggest that genetics contribute significantly to sports performance, but it's very hard to put a number on it,' said Olds. Studies of twins have shown that as much as 50 per cent of muscle strength is determined by genetic factors, and about the same for aerobic capacity.[28] This would mean 'you could explain 50 per cent of individual differences in athlete performance in marathon runners, for example, by genes. The rest is a matter of training and luck.' This suggests that nature and nurture are broadly of equal importance in the forging of elite athletes; naturally, both are intertwined and hard to disentangle.

The notion that exceptional performers at an early age are blessed with great genes is a significant overstatement. Genes develop unpredictably, in accordance with the environment to which someone is exposed. 'Genes aren't about inevitability,' wrote Robert Sapolsky, a biologist at Stanford University. 'Instead, they're about context-dependent tendencies, propensities, potentials, and vulnerabilities.'[29]

The way genes work can be changed by the physical and social environment, coaching and opportunity. The science of epigenetics studies how genes can be turned on or off, or up or down like a thermostat.[30, 31, 32, 33] The most contentious issue is the relative contribution of nature and nurture in the path to excellence. While people with the right genes are more likely to make the grade, many people who have the right genes never make it due to a lack of opportunity, desire, or interest to pursue such a path. Yet any conclusion is impacted by the nature of the sport, its popularity, whether early or late specialization is the norm, and the relative importance of technical, tactical, physical and psychological characteristics, as well as serendipity and environment.[31]

In some sports, predictors of athletic capability may be identified with reasonable precision from analysing someone's physique, physical fitness and their polygenic risk scores – a figure that predicts someone's likelihood to have particular qualities based on their genes. 'The easiest thing to predict would be someone who is going to be a good marathon runner,' Olds said. 'If you can find someone who's lean, a certain size – not too tall, not too short, not too muscular – and they've got aerobic fitness then we can steer them into running.' He suggested: 'You'd probably need to be in the top 1 per cent of polygenic risk scores for aerobic fitness to have any chance of becoming an elite marathon runner.'

Genes still matter in more multifaceted sports like cricket and football but these interact in a more complex way – technical and tactical skills are more crucial, and different athletes can thrive in completely different ways. If genetic differences alone explain around a half of the differences in performance among marathon runners, Olds suggested, they may explain substantially less variance in team sports such as cricket and football, where the impact of genes on technical and tactical skill development remains unclear. In general, a simple rule holds across talent identification in sport: the more multifaceted a sport, the harder it is to predict who will go on to become an elite athlete.

Yet even in sports in which genetic impact may be greatest, there are limits to where genes alone can get you – just as there are, conversely, limits to where hard work alone can get you. And the exact nature of the contribution of genes to success – especially in the most competitive sports – is impossible to discern.

'No genes have been discovered with any worthwhile predictive capacity, despite numerous publications in sports genetics,' wrote Yannis Pitsiladis, a leading sports geneticist in his study entitled 'Genomics of elite sporting performance'.[34]

This means that potential performance cannot currently be predicted with any reliability based on genetics alone. But this may change: so far, sports scientists have looked at 'less than 1 per cent' of the genome and mostly in non-elite athletes.

'A complex multifactorial phenotype such as sports performance will never be dependent on a single performance gene or even a handful of genes but most likely a complex interplay or algorithm of a very large number of genes – 100s or even 1000s,' Pitsiladis said. 'Until such genetic studies are conducted that interrogate the whole genome in elite athletes, the use of genetic technology will continue to have zero predictive capacity in terms of talent identification and should not be used.'

'You can't teach a brick to float.'

For all the hazards inherent in predicting sporting talent, as elite sport becomes more systematic, the athlete pool becomes more global, and the quality of performance rises accordingly, Olds and Pitsiladis both said that genes appear to be becoming more important in determining who the best athletes are.

'The evidence points towards the making of an elite athlete being very much genetically determined – obviously within the limits of the environment as well,' said Pitsiladis. 'As sport performance levels continue to rise, it excludes those individuals who don't have the genetics. So genes relating to physical prowess – size, power, endurance and so on – may be becoming more important.' A high VO_2 max is becoming more and more important in endurance sports as the level becomes more elite or performance records tumble. 'If you don't have a VO_2 max above 75, say, you can't run a competitive time. Forty years ago, you could.'

'Athletes in many sports have been getting taller and bigger over time; the rates of rise outstripping those of the secular trend,' Olds found in a paper he co-wrote.[35] The opposite effect seems to be at work in sports where being smaller is an advantage, such as gymnastics and horse racing. 'In some sports it is equally difficult to find athletes small enough to compete,' the authors of the paper wrote. The best female gymnasts are 6 inches shorter now than 30 years ago, Epstein noted.[27]

So both in sports that favour being larger and those that favour being smaller, the body types of elite athletes have become further removed from the overall population.

'Selection drives extremes in whatever characteristics are required for success in any given sport, whether those characteristics be physical, psychological or a combination,' Olds said. 'Throughout sport, professional athletes' physical and physiological characteristics are becoming more and more extreme.'

Athletes themselves are likely to be 'genetically much more similar now than they were 50 years ago, simply because, to succeed, you have to get people with the right genes,' Olds said.

'In elite sport, the demands are much greater, which means if you're really going to identify those top athletes, they have to not only have the best possible training but also you need to identify those who have the most potential at the start. Often, I think that's going to be genetic.

'Genes are likely much more important now. Previously you could have taken someone with good but not exceptional genetic equipment and with hard work, training and dedication they could have become a top athlete.' In this way, Olds joked, modern sport has become 'the opposite of the American dream – you can't become anything you want.'

Olds's argument has particular credence in sports where physical and physiological characteristics are strong predictors of performance. In sports where technical, tactical and psychological factors may be more crucial to performance it is much harder to evaluate whether the technical and tactical ability of athletes has improved. It is unknowable whether, say, Virgil van Dijk can read the game better than, say, Bobby Moore, or whether Serena Williams is mentally tougher than Martina Navratilova.

While those with the requisite talent to reach the top cannot be identified with any reliability at a young age, however hard they work at a particular sport, not everyone has the qualities to make it to the summit. As Warr observed, 'You can't teach a brick to float.'

'Everybody can be trained and improved,' Pitsiladis said. 'But if you're talking about getting to the very, very elite, for most people 10,000 hours or even 20,000 hours isn't going to be enough.'

PART TWO

Inside the minds of champions

7

How to hit a ball in under 0.5 seconds

Why 'Watch the ball!' is about the least helpful advice imaginable

'It honestly felt like a time warp. I saw the ball come out of the hand and then felt like I missed the middle bit and was either playing a shot, letting go or the ball was flying past my head. It was a bizarre, weird feeling. I didn't feel as though I had time to move my feet or even do anything really at that sort of pace.'

Australian cricket batsman Mike Hussey on facing deliveries at 100 miles per hour

Imagine standing by the service line on Centre Court at Wimbledon or the Arthur Ashe Court at the US Open. You know what is coming next – a serve at 140 miles per hour. You just don't know where it will land, how high the ball will bounce, or which way it will spin, if at all. And, after the ball is hit, you will have only 0.4 seconds to respond.

So the old trope 'Watch the ball!' is about the least helpful advice imaginable. Even for the best athletes in the world, it is physically impossible to wait for the serve to land inside the service box before reacting. There just isn't enough time to make a decision, align your movements and actually return the ball.

Over his 16-year professional tennis career, Michael Chang was one of the best players at dealing with this situation and returning the ball. His adroitness in reading serves helped Chang win the French Open and the Davis Cup, reach the finals of the Australian and US Opens, and climb to number two in the world.

Chang was only 5 feet 9 inches, unusually small for an elite tennis player. More than his physical gifts, Chang's brilliance in returning serves was rooted in the dexterity of his mind. From the age of eight, when he was growing up in California, Chang regularly played with Pete Sampras – who won 14 Grand Slam titles, and was perhaps the greatest server of all time. When they started meeting on the professional tour, Chang could decipher Sampras's serve as other rivals could not. He won his first five professional matches against Sampras.

At the start of his career, Sampras had very clear preferences for where he wanted to serve on the biggest points. 'My go to serve on the advantage side was up the middle,' Sampras explained. He tended to favour going down the middle on the biggest points on the deuce side, too.

Chang could 'read Pete Sampras's serve very well, in juniors and then maybe the first five times we played in professional tennis', he recalled. 'He had a great serve, no question – probably one of the best in the game – but I used to be able to read his serve very, very well. That's part of the reason why I beat him every single time early on in our careers.'

During the biggest points, Chang 'knew where he was going to serve. I knew his tendencies and because of that I knew that even if he hit that serve on the line I was there to cover it.'

And so Chang pushed Sampras into two unenviable choices. Sampras could either serve as he would normally do — but knowing that as Chang pre-empted such a serve, he would still have a strong chance of returning the ball. Or, Sampras could serve to the opposite side that Chang did not expect — into areas where his serve was less accurate and he preferred to avoid on the most high octane points.

'If he wasn't as comfortable hitting, the percentages for him to make it were lower,' Chang explained. 'When big serves came around I covered his best serve and forced him to serve the other way — serves that he wasn't comfortable hitting.'

Chang's hold lessened as Sampras developed serves that were previously weaker, making pre-empting one serve less advantageous. 'It became a little bit more difficult once he started being able to hit all the areas which he didn't used to like. Then it was a whole different ball game.'

But Chang's initial success against Sampras attests to how players can use context-specific information — deducing what a player is most likely to do, based on the score and circumstances — to their benefit. Against players he was less well acquainted with, Chang could lean on this information less. He relied on a second source of information: players' movements and postural orientation before and during their service motion.

Reaction, anticipation and prediction

There simply isn't enough time to react to a 140 mph serve, adjust your position and hit the ball. Players have to second-guess what will happen, using clues from the opponent's early movements and their own deep reservoirs of knowledge. Returners must anticipate the type of serve they will receive and where the ball will land before the opponent strikes the ball. For the best players, the information they gauge from ball flight adds to their judgements; less proficient players are entirely reliant on the ball flight, so they have less time to respond and execute their return.

Those about to return a serve also process tiny shifts in an opponent's ball toss, shoulders and torso, and use this information to deduce where the ball is likely to be served. What distinguishes the best returners is not that they can react faster; what matters is that they start to respond earlier, because their superior anticipation allows more time to line up a return. Elite tennis players spend significantly more time fixating on the head–shoulder and trunk–hip regions rather than the arm–hand and leg–foot regions and the ball itself, suggesting that they are trying to pick up early information from the body to read the serve. Less elite players spend more time fixating on the racket than any other area, followed by the ball, implying a more reactive rather than anticipative strategy.[1]

When Chang competed against some players, he could deduce what serves they were likely to perform – or, at least, which ones they certainly would not execute – from the start of their service motion. 'If they're changing their toss based upon how they want to hit a serve, I can absolutely read a serve before they've even struck the ball,' he said. 'If under certain circumstances they tend to toss the ball a little wide and they want to serve a wide serve, that's something that I can pick up. If they toss the ball behind their head, and that's the only way that they know how to hit a kicker serve, obviously I can read that.

'When a server tosses the ball way behind his head, most of the time he will be hitting a kick serve. In knowing that, I can move ahead of time to prepare to hit that return.'

The same applies to how players adjust during rallies. While players have longer to react to the ball from the baseline in a rally than a serve, the array of possibilities they confront is wider – the ball can be hit to any corner of the court, not merely the service box. As such, players must constantly scour their opponents for clues about what to expect.

'Understanding where a ball's going to go, it's understanding your opponent's position, it's understanding how their body's angled,' Chang reflected. 'If their body is angled in a certain way they're only in a position to be able to hit certain shots. That helps you to anticipate where a shot's going. Just because a player's in a position to hit a shot doesn't mean they can hit every single shot on all different parts of the court. It's not physically possible.'

Second-guessing shots before they are hit during a rally is rare. An analysis of over 3,000 rallies from male tennis players who were, or had been, in the world top 10 found that anticipation behaviours were observable on only 13.4 per cent of shots;[2] while anticipation can be pivotal, its use is highly selective. Mostly, the best players preferred to hedge their bets based on analysing the costs and benefits of getting the decision right or wrong. They tended to set up their position early before their opponents hit a shot, but in a way that gave them flexibility to adjust. Because they are so adroit at recognizing early cues before and as the ball is being hit, such as their opponent's position, the way they shape to hit the ball, and then the ball flight, players like Chang have far more time to adjust than less proficient ones. The more agile a player is, the later they can make their final decision about where to move to return the ball.[3]

'It's about understanding what are the high-percentage shots, what are the low-percentage shots – once you understand that you get a better perspective of where to move,' Chang explained. 'Sometimes guys are pulled so far out that their only option is really to lob it or hit it down the line because they're just not close enough to the ball where they're able to hit it cross-court. Or if they are able to hit it cross-court, you know it's not going to have much pace on the ball. In that instance you're automatically making sure that you absolutely cover down the line 100 per cent. Then you basically give him the short angle cross-court knowing that 99 out of 100 times there's no way that he's going to be able to hit that shot.'

Through the dexterity of their brains, elite players make the task of working out where the ball will be hit and then returning the ball less arduous. 'You don't have to cover 100 per cent of the court – you maybe only have to cover 70 per cent of the court because the other 30 per cent is impossible to hit.'

Elite tennis players can even anticipate opponents' strokes without any postural cues. A study in 2016 created animations of rallies, presenting the players as cylinders and removing all postural cues and information emanating from the racket, and the motion when players were in the process of hitting the ball – so players could only see where their opponents were and the court markings, nothing else. The most skilled players could still gauge where the ball would be hit far more accurately than less skilled counterparts.[4] The accuracy in judgement for less skilled players hovered below 50 per cent; the skilled group were over 70 per cent accurate in the animated conditions.

The relative movements of the players and ball, the shot sequencing, the angles between players and the position on the court all contribute to how players anticipate even with postural cues removed, or before an opponent has moved into position to play the shot.[5]

In the cauldron of matches, the game is stripped back for the best players, so automatic are their motions. 'I can't say that I'm necessarily so focused on the ball that I see it 100 per cent of the time,' Chang said. 'I know where the ball is and I know where my racket is so I will not actually necessarily watch the impact of the ball hitting the tennis racket.'

The most significant variation in visual search behaviours among players is after the server has hit the ball. As Chang observed, the most skilled players do not always track the ball during its flight. They move their eyes ahead of the ball to fixate on where the ball is expected to bounce, implying a more predictive strategy. Generally, while players may view the ball immediately after it bounces, in contrast to popular myth players do not track the ball on to the racket; the ball moves too quickly for the eyes.[6, 7] Instead, elite players tend to bring their eyes into the general vicinity of ball–racket contact and make a predictive movement towards where they will make contact with the ball.

'All I'm really thinking about is where I'm hitting the shot. I don't even really think about the mechanics anymore because I've trained the mechanics for so many years,' Chang explained. 'It's just a matter of OK I want to hit that ball down the line, I want to hit it cross-court, I want to hit it short, I want to hit it with angle, I want to hit it with top spin, I want to hit it with a higher trajectory, I want to hit it lower with slice.' Such mastery comes 'from having practised all of those shots and going out and executing them'.

Andre Agassi, codebreaker

Andre Agassi, a US contemporary of both Sampras and Chang who won eight Grand Slams, is regarded as one of the best returners of all time. Part of his brilliance lay in his acumen in assessing a server. 'Tennis is about problem-solving – it's really what it is. And you can't problem-solve unless you have the ability or the empathy to perceive all that's around you,' Agassi later said.

The first three times that Agassi played against Boris Becker, who had a ferocious serve, he lost. Before their fourth meeting, Agassi later recalled, he studied replays of Becker's serve. Watching replays, 'I started to realize he had this weird tick thing with his tongue.'

Just before Becker tossed the ball on his serve, he would stick his tongue out in the direction in which the ball would go. So when he was about to serve to the deuce side of the court, Becker moved his tongue to the left side of his mouth if he was serving out wide; it would stick out in the middle of his mouth if he was serving down the middle or into the body. Agassi could identify Becker's tell, like a poker player who knows when an opponent is bluffing.

Like the codebreakers who cracked the Enigma code, Agassi's difficulty was concealing his knowledge, and using it only when it mattered most. 'The hardest part was not letting him know that I knew his tell. So, I had to resist the temptation of reading his serve for the majority of the match and choose the moment when I was going to use that information.

'I didn't have a problem breaking his serve, I had a problem hiding the fact I could break it at will, I just didn't want him keeping that tongue in his mouth.'[8] After discovering Becker's tell, Agassi won 10 of his next 11 matches against him.

Do elite athletes have better vision?

Elite athletes seem like a breed apart. And so it is easy to develop myths about what makes them so good. Yet to understand what the best athletes possess, first understand what they do not have. The sight of Roger Federer whipping a cross-court winner from a 140-mile-per-hour serve with his balletic single-handed forehand, and able to win Grand Slam titles past the age of 35, seems a triumph for extraordinary reaction times. And yet reaction times for the best athletes are seldom much quicker than for others of the same age. Tests for basic visual reaction times – how fast someone can hit a button in response to a light – generally reveal that athletes and accountants alike can both complete the task in about 200 milliseconds.[9]

Perhaps the most pervasive idea is that elite athletes can literally see things more clearly than everyone else – that they appear to be able to see more because their eyes are better. In some ways, this is a comforting notion, a simple genetic explanation for why the best athletes can react in ways that we cannot. The idea of eyesight being critical is especially pervasive in cricket, where batsmen have to face bowlers delivering the ball at almost 100 miles per hour. But Don Bradman, who has the highest Test batting average of all time, had eyesight so poor that he was not allowed to serve in the Australian army during the Second World War. Tests show that most elite athletes possess only average levels of visual function. Many perform at extraordinary levels even with vision below average; throughout his career Denis Law, a great forward for Manchester United and Scotland, had a squint which severely affected his vision. Gordon Banks, England's World Cup-winning goalkeeper in 1966, remained formidable late in his career even after virtually losing sight in one eye. A survey of athletes at the Winter Olympics revealed that a large proportion had visual defects which had gone undetected.[10]

A group of scientists tested the batting performance of club cricketers against a bowling machine. The snag was that they were first tested while batting with unrestricted vision, and then using contact lenses that gave them progressively more blurred vision until only a rough outline of the ball could be seen. Initially, as vision was blurred, there was no decline in performance at all, which decreased only when vision blurred to the point where the batters could have been defined as legally blind.[11]

'We couldn't believe how much blur it took to decrease performance,' said David Mann, a co-author of the study. 'We would put the blurred contact lenses in the eyes of batters and they would be terrified. Vision was so bad that they were quite scared of batting. Yet basically everyone was amazed how well they could still bat with such poor vision.' Some batters even wanted to keep the blurred lenses, claiming 'it made them focus more on the ball and they felt as though they batted better with the lenses'.

In a separate study, the authors replaced the ball projection machine with real bowlers, providing extra information from their run-up and bowling action. Again, extremely high levels of blur were needed before any notable decline in batting performance.[12] Similarly, scientists tested 137 elite and sub-elite footballers in the UK using standard measures of sight, like those used in a local opticians. These measures – static and dynamic visual acuity, depth sensitivity and peripheral awareness – did not consistently discriminate between skill groups, explaining less than 5 per cent of the difference in anticipation; the remaining 95 per cent of variance was explained by cognitive factors.[13]

What sets athletes apart is not their eyes; it's their minds. Great athletes seldom have better reaction times or vision than the rest of us – but they have better perceptual-cognitive skills. Their enhanced perceptual and cognitive skills enable them to pick up and process information in an instant, and suss out what is the best course of action. The best sportsmen are like Agatha Christie's Poirot, picking up the most relevant clues to solve the problem before everyone else.

Split seconds

Twenty-two yards separate the stumps at either end of a cricket pitch. But there are only 20.7 yards from where a bowler is allowed to deliver the ball and the stumps at the other end. As batters have to stand in front of their stumps, there are fewer than 20 yards between where a bowler releases the ball and the batter. When bowlers deliver the ball at 90 miles per hour – as is common in men's international cricket, with a few balls recorded at 100 miles per hour – that leaves batters only about 0.6 seconds between the ball being released and it passing the bat. In that time they have to assess where the ball will pitch, how it will bounce after pitching, whether it will swing in the air before pitching, whether it will seam off the pitch after it lands, and then get in position to hit or leave the ball. Even when they hit it, batters have to try to find gaps between the bowler, the wicketkeeper and the nine other fielders who are there to stop runs being scored.

When facing bowling of express pace, Mike Hussey – one of Australia's finest ever Test batsmen – said that the ball was simply delivered too quickly to watch it all the way on to the bat. When facing bowlers like Brett Lee and Shoaib Akhtar – two of the three men ever to have been recorded bowling at over 100 miles per hour[14] – 'It honestly felt like a time warp. I saw the ball come out of the hand and then felt like I missed the middle bit and was either playing a shot, letting go or the ball was flying past my head … It was just a bizarre experience because you didn't have time to think or make up your mind on doing something. It had to just happen without thinking.

'I remember playing a pull shot and absolutely hammering it and thinking I don't even remember seeing that ball come out of the bowler's hand, I don't remember moving. It just happened completely on instinct. I don't know when I made the decision to hit the shot.'

Hussey's recollections align with the science of how a cricket ball is hit. Even the best batters need about 200 milliseconds to adjust their shots to the ball trajectory – the same amount of time that athletes and accountants alike need to complete basic visual reaction responses. So, as scientists Michael F. Land and Peter McLeod have found,[15] batters must commit to their shot 0.2 seconds before the ball reaches them – when the ball still has one-third of its journey to go. Whatever the ball does in the last third of its flight, batters can make only minute adjustments. And the margins of failure are infinitesimally small; to make effective contact, the batter must judge the ball's position to within 3 centimetres and the time it reaches them to within 3 milliseconds. If they fail to do so, they could edge the ball and be caught out, miss the ball and be bowled out, or miss the ball and be hit – including on the head. So it is in most ball sports: reaction times are simply too slow to allow players to react solely to the ball when served, bowled or pitched.

'If I'm clouding my mind too much about getting hit, getting hurt, getting out, they're all thoughts that are not going to be helping me pick the ball up really clearly and as early as I possibly can,' Hussey recalled. 'My plan was clear the mind, just see the ball and try and respond as well as possible. That gave me the best chance to play those bowlers. When you don't have time to think, you just see and react. It's amazing how well you actually play them.'

Hussey normally avoided premeditated shots, but still scoured for clues about what he might expect. 'You do get a bit of a feeling. There's lots of different cues – obviously there's the field they set that gives you a bit of an idea about what they're going to bowl. Also you get little cues as they're running in to bowl – so if they're running in harder or faster, quite often they're wanting more energy, it's more of an effort ball so it might be a bouncer.

'If a fast bowler's going to bowl a bouncer, obviously he delivers the ball later because he's got to bowl shorter. So if you're clear in your mind and you're watching the ball clearly out of the hand then you are very quickly and easily going to pick up that he's letting go of the ball later and it's going to be shorter. And you can start moving basically just as the ball's being bowled.'

Elite batters are more likely to use cues from the bowler's run-up, trunk, shoulders and bowling arm, before the ball is released, to anticipate what the ball will then do. Poorer players are not able to do so, and must react to the ball later, leaving them little time to get into position.[16] The best batters, Land and McLeod found, even adjust their eye movements depending on where the ball pitches. When the ball was pitched closer to them, they smoothed out the ways in which their eyes moved, to make their movements less jerky.

The researchers analysed three men's batters – a professional, a good amateur and a poor amateur – and found little difference in the way they approached deliveries after the ball had bounced. The salient contrast lay in how the professional pre-empted the ball's movement before it bounced. The best batters pick up more valuable information earlier in a ball's flight – so, after 100–150 milliseconds, a quarter of its flight, they can line up to hit the ball. This way, the best batters create the illusion they have copious time when facing bowlers over 90 miles per hour – so fast that they only have time to watch the ball for about half the time it travels. In simulations when they are given information about the state of the game and field placings, the most skilled batters can predict what delivery they will receive more accurately than less skilled batters.[17]

The role of the subconscious

The art of such anticipation is a combination of the conscious and subconscious brain. When at his best, Kumar Sangakkara – who scored 38 Test centuries, the fourth most in history, in an international career spanning from 2000 to 2015 – felt his subconscious taking over. Between balls, 'you make certain conscious decisions about when to attack a spinner, which fielders to take on,' he explained. But 'there's not a single time you should be thinking from the time the bowler runs in and delivers the ball. You think in between.'

Sangakkara's approach to building his innings was governed by a central idea. 'Reach that time when your mind shuts down – but you need to be still batting by then, when that happens. I didn't know how long it would take, but I immediately recognized when it did happen, because there are certain times when I'd hit a stroke, and it's just "How did that happen?" And then you realize that you're getting there.'

When he got there, Sangakkara could stay there: he converted 11 of his centuries into double centuries, the second most in history. 'Getting that first 100 was hard and getting my second 100 was not that hard, because then I was in that zone. I could tinker, I could change, I could be proactive, not just reactive.'

In limited overs cricket, when bowlers tend to try more variations than in Tests, Hussey excelled at predicting what would come next. 'I loved to try and get a feeling.' For instance, if Hussey sensed that the plan was to bowl yorkers wide on the off side, he would 'premeditate that they were going to bowl it and then ramp it … It's nice to toy around with the bowler, you can see what sort of plan he's trying to work to.'

One bowler – Kade Harvey, a state teammate whom he played against in club matches – bit his lip in his delivery stride whenever he would bowl a slower ball, so Hussey 'could basically call out his slower ball'. Other bowlers had subtler cues; the great spin bowler Muttiah Muralitharan initially tended to deliver his 'doosra', a ball that spun the opposite way to normal, slower than other deliveries.

'I would try and be completely still and clear of mind as he's about to let go,' Hussey said. 'Then you pick up those last little cues – whether it's a bite of a lip, letting go of the ball later for a shorter ball, a little bit more energy or expression in his face that might mean a quicker ball or a shorter ball, and then literally just try and react to whatever comes.'

The best batters do not consciously calculate all the variables that determine a ball's trajectory; instead, their subconscious and experience do it for them. When batting against new bowlers, or on an unusual pitch, batters act like computers constantly re-evaluating as they get more information. In unfamiliar situations, batters initially tend to prefer low-risk shots, helping them preserve their wickets. Tests have shown that as skilled batsmen face the same bowler over successive deliveries, they come to rely more on earlier information – cues from the bowler's run-up, shoulders and trunk, and the trajectory of the arm before ball release – and less on what the bowler does as the ball is released.[18]

By doing so, batsmen give themselves more time to prepare their shot. 'Facing any bowler, the longer you're facing them, the more comfortable you start to feel,' Hussey recalled. 'One, against the pace. Two, about what they're trying to do, how it's reacting off the surface and things.'

Second nature

When he was a baseball hitter at school, Joey Votto would do as the cliché advises: see ball, react and then hit ball. 'I could sit and read the ball as the guy was throwing 75 or 80 miles per hour.'

But as Votto moved up to higher levels of baseball, his old method swiftly became inadequate. 'When it started moving towards 85 and 90 miles per hour I was just so, so late.' In Major League Baseball, where he is a six-time MLB All-Star, and ranked twelfth in the league's all-time on-base percentage at the end of 2019, Votto learned to anticipate and read pitches. 'It's second nature.'

For Votto, the process of anticipating a pitch begins far away from the stadiums. Before matches, 'I try to know as much as I can about the pitcher, his tendencies.'

So Votto does much of his anticipating before he faces pitches. 'Even before I take the at-bat, the plan's already in my head so it's less reactionary and more just executing the plan. So if I'm looking for a slider in that particular swing and I get it, I better swing. If I don't, I'm upset with myself.'

In the split-seconds before facing pitches, Votto scours for final clues. 'Sometimes it's the catchers' tendency, something in the pitchers' body language, often it's situation-dependent,' he reflected. 'All my successes are a by-product of anticipating things and then executing them.'

The science of hitting a baseball is similar to that of hitting a cricket ball. One study recorded the gaze behaviours of expert and novice baseball batters when they could see the pitcher's motion. The novices moved their eyes earlier than experts, and looked at a much wider array of areas – including less relevant places like the pitcher's face and head. The experts fixated on fewer locations and maintained a steady gaze for longer, particularly on the pitching arm. Experts set their visual pivot on the pitcher's elbow and used peripheral vision to monitor the pitcher's motion, the moment of ball release and the ball trajectory.[19]

'There was a historical misconception that visual acuity reigned supreme in baseball,' explained David Whiteside, the director of performance science for the New York Yankees. 'Evidence coming to light in other interceptive sports is beginning to shift the focus to the predictive component of striking a moving object – the head and eye kinematics that comprise advance cue detection and dynamic object tracking as well as the contextual elements of anticipation. This is revolutionizing our approach to developing hitters and creating the next arms race in MLB.'

The very best baseball hitters, like the best cricket batters, cannot watch the ball all the way from it being delivered to reaching their bat because it moves too quickly to be tracked by the eyes. Instead, they need to use predictive or anticipative eye movements to work out where the ball will be and when it will arrive.

'We don't see it – it's a shocking stretch of time where we don't see it,' Votto explained. 'You see what you see and then you swing. Everything else is blind.' He estimated that MLB hitters see '60–80 per cent' of the ball's trip from the pitcher's hand, 'but sometimes it feels like less'.

Even Votto's figure is optimistic. For fastballs, hitters only have 400 milliseconds from the ball being released until it reaches them. But it takes at least 80 milliseconds between the eyes seeing something and the brain processing this information to fine tune an action, and at least 200 milliseconds to select a totally new action, leaving, at most, only 320 milliseconds to act.[20]

By the time of the last 150 milliseconds on the ball's journey, it is already too late. A study in Japan in 2016 made hitters wear glasses that impeded their vision at different stages of the pitch. Hitters did as well when their vision was impeded 150 milliseconds before the ball reaching them as they did when viewing the entire flight path, showing that 'seeing' the ball for the final 150 milliseconds does not help.[21] Add together those gaps at the start and end of the ball's journey and that leaves in the region of 170 milliseconds when batters can meaningfully see the ball. So they are effectively blind for 60 per cent of the ball's journey from the pitch to the plate.

Different neural structures in the brain are activated when hitters view different types of pitches. When a hitter is looking for a fastball, a horizontal deviation from that expected path – a slider – or a vertical deviation from that expected path – a curveball – activate different parts of the visual system that tracks movement. This finding implies that each pitch generates its own neural signature in hitters' brains, allowing them to adjust to each pitch early in its flight.[22] These adjustments can happen over the entire course of the pitch, allowing neuroscientists to use brain scanning methods to detect differences in neural activity lasting up to 700 milliseconds after the pitch is released. There are also neural differences between expert and novice hitters in the 200 milliseconds before the pitcher releases the ball. How hitters develop these interconnected neural structures drives how accurately and quickly they react to pitches.[23, 24, 25]

'The ability to anticipate in baseball hitting can even be parsed down to the approximate 170 milliseconds a hitter has to decide,' said Jason Sherwin, one of the authors of the study. 'This parsing is done using neural markers that evolve in space and time to tell what parts of the hitter's nervous system are materially driving their ability to anticipate.'

Votto's skill lies in being able to pick up cues as early as possible – both before the pitch is delivered and immediately after, when his brain has learned to recognize certain ways the ball moves in those first milliseconds after being released as a sign of what kind of pitch he will receive. 'You look at it coming through a really, really specific funnel – it's coming out and it looks very, very distinct and it matches a lot of the criteria you're looking for.'

8

Superintelligence

How elite athletes out-think the rest

'I'd rather have had a really good football brain rather than great pace, than have it the other way around. You know, the football brain is still the most important thing, even though the game is getting more athletic each season.'

Jamie Carragher, Liverpool and England central defender

It was an unfair contest. The fastest forwards in the world – Thierry Henry, Cristiano Ronaldo and Andriy Shevchenko – against a central defender who lumbered around at speeds typical of park footballers. He did not even have the usual benefit of being tall for his position. Often, those strikers he faced were taller, stronger and faster.

Originally, Jamie Carragher wanted to be a striker, too.

Carragher played as a centre-forward for much of his youth, until the age of 16 or 17. But as he got nearer the professional game, he was gradually moved back – first to central midfield, and then to centre-back – into positions in which his lack of pace wouldn't be so obvious.[1]

'I wasn't someone who was blessed with amazing physical attributes in terms of pace, height, strength. I was just average – on all of those, really,' he said.

Only, Carragher's speed came in another way: not from his limbs but from his mind. It did not matter if his opponents were taller, stronger and faster, for, on the football pitch, he was smarter. They could outrun him, but not out-think him.

To Carragher, a fast brain was worth more than fast feet. 'I had to be focused, always concentrating, and the reason I played at the top level is I had a really good understanding of the game. My reading of the game was very important, and that was something I had as a kid – an understanding of football.'

Other defenders could use their pace if they got into the wrong position; Carragher had no such insurance policy. But Carragher's brain turned a footballing everyman into a superman. He enjoyed a phenomenal 17-year career at his boyhood club, Liverpool, including winning the Champions League in 2005. In 2013, Liverpool fans voted Carragher the sixth best player in the club's history.[2]

Mind over matter

Carragher's career was a testament to how the power of the mind – the ability to understand the sport deeply and use this knowledge to anticipate or 'read the game' – can help players make up for relative deficiencies in the physical side of their game. In most sports, the correlation between who are the best pure athletes and those who are the best at their sports is far from perfect. The best players are not always the best athletes; but the best players nearly always have the best minds. Carragher attests to how a player's mind can elevate them from being an ordinary athlete to an extraordinary player on the pitch.

'One of my biggest strengths as a player was reading the game,' Carragher said. 'I was probably top level in terms of understanding the game, and would back myself against anyone of my era on this aspect, being able to read situations and understand what was going to happen in the game. And that was probably my biggest strength. I could see danger.'

The science of how Carragher could see that danger lies in how elite central defenders tend to look at specific areas on the field for less time and scan the overall field more broadly, taking in more information over a certain time span than less proficient players.[3] They take visual snapshots of play to create a picture in their mind of what is happening around them.

'With experience you don't think – it's almost like driving a car,' Carragher recalled. 'When the ball's in a certain position you know where you need to be.'

Carragher's brain was so supple that he could think not just what was the best thing for him to do to neuter the world's best forwards but what his teammates should do too. Effectively, he was many football brains in one.

'It's sort of autopilot. I was the organizer for the team, and I wouldn't just be thinking about my own position, I'd be thinking about everyone else's on the pitch. And I think that comes with experience, maturity.

'When you're in the position I was in, you're organizing the team. You're not just watching the ball, you're seeing where everyone else is, you're turning your head, seeing the bigger picture. I mean the top attacking players as well – they are always checking where defenders are. All top players have a great awareness of what is going on around them. But certainly as a defender you have to be aware – you're trying to organize other people and not just yourself. You have to be well aware what is around you.

'When you become a senior player, in some ways you take your own performance for granted, and you're actually more worried about what other people are doing. At times you'd be sitting at the back and thinking about whether the people in front of you are in the right position, whether one of the strikers is dropping back on the holding midfield player, where is your full back. So, you're actually organizing a lot of people, and if you do that – well, it saves you a lot of work.'

When the ball is not close to the penalty area, skilled defenders scan the field widely, but as the ball gets nearer the penalty area, they change the way they use their eyes. Faced with a player running directly towards them on the edge of the penalty area, skilled defenders fixate more on what is directly in front of them – the player with the ball – moving the head and eyes less frequently, and relying more on peripheral vision to monitor the positions and movements of other players off the ball.[4]

'When you can understand who you're playing against, what runs the strikers need to make, you're just trying to be one step ahead of them all the time,' Carragher explained. 'Being a centre-back, I think reading the game and understanding it is probably the most important attribute you need in that position, because it's not a lot of running or a lot of sprinting. It's just being in the right place at the right time.'

The football brain

From Carragher to Lucy Bronze and Virgil van Dijk, the best defenders know exactly where to look – fixating on the lower body of the player in possession of the ball, using the ball as a visual pivot point, while using peripheral vision to monitor for opponents' movements. They can fuse this information with auditory cues – calls made by teammates or opponents, or hearing players advancing towards them from outside their central vision – to anticipate what will happen next and the best position to be in either to make a tackle, intercept a pass or simply close down the opponent with the ball. The best players use a myriad of information – combining their visual and auditory senses with broader game awareness and specific knowledge of opponents and the match situation. They are masters of multitasking. 'You have to be aware of everything,' Carragher said.

As well as using the eyes more effectively to pick up relevant information, leading players are better at predicting what will happen next than weaker players. A study involved players watching footage of different match situations such as a goalkeeper throwing the ball out to a full back, and then asking the player to predict what the full back would attempt to do next.[5] Players highlighted the options available to the player with the ball and ranked these based on the level of threat posed to their team. Top players were better at identifying relevant options and ranking the likelihood of these occurring. The very best players develop a huge library of sport-specific patterns of play in their memory – based on the general situation, the match context and specific knowledge of their opponents – to subconsciously assign probabilities to the likelihood of each action occurring. This narrows down how players search for relevant information with their eyes, and the process of confirming or rejecting their initial prediction, enabling them to anticipate what will happen next.

'If it goes to Paul Scholes, the first thing he's going to do is look for a ball in behind you. He's got the killer pass,' Carragher explained. 'So, as soon as he gets it you need to be alive to that possibility.'

'If it's a winger – does he like to dribble or does he like to cross? The ball goes to [David] Beckham, and you're the centre-back, you've got to be ready for the cross straight away. If it goes to [Ryan] Giggs, well it might be a little bit different. He's going to run at his full back.'

So Carragher would adjust his position depending on which winger got the ball; if two players got the ball in an identical position, one would likely act very differently than the other. This knowledge meant that as Beckham whipped in a cross, Carragher would be waiting and expecting the ball. His legs got him there; his brain made his legs get there.

It is commonly thought that even central defenders with the brain-power of Carragher need a centre-back partner with more pace. Yet the most successful partnership of Carragher's career was with Sami Hyypia, who was even slower. The two played together for a decade, making up Liverpool's first choice central defensive pairing for several seasons, including in the Champions League victory in 2005.

'It wasn't the paciest of partnerships, but we both read the game very well,' Carragher explained. The two had contrasting strengths, helping them to be more than the sum of their parts.

'I wasn't the biggest centre-back. I'm just under six foot. He was six foot four, so he was the aerial lynchpin in some ways, and he was the dominant player – certainly defending set pieces.

'I was probably more aggressive on the front foot than Sami. He was better in the air. But I think the main thing was just the understanding of the game that we both had, and that's why we probably didn't get done for pace as often as maybe people thought we may have done.'

This partnership could easily be caricatured as a pairing of two tortoises. But to their opponents who could outrun them but not out-think them – and so were denied a chance to make their far greater pace tell – scoring against Carragher and Hyypia could seem impossible. For doing so meant trying to outsmart them.

'I'd rather have had a really good football brain than great pace, than have it the other way around,' Carragher reflected. 'You know, the football brain is still the most important thing, even though the game is getting more athletic each season.'

Super-scanners

'Those who see will get you wins. But not many players are able to see like this,' Arsenal manager Arsène Wenger once explained.[6] 'There are some special players who always find openings.'

Wenger used the statistic of 'scans per minute', which measured the number of times players checked their surroundings over a minute. It relates to how frequently a player moves the head in order to take in a different snapshot of the field. At one stage the top three players in the Premier League on this metric were Cesc Fàbregas, Frank Lampard and Steven Gerrard, who were widely regarded as the three best central midfielders in the league at the time. All averaged over 0.6 searches or scans of the field per second, using their eyes in a systematically different manner from less proficient players; almost like a scanner taking snapshots or pictures of play. The Barcelona midfielder Xavi averaged 0.83 scans per second – meaning that he took 50 different snapshots of the pitch every minute of a match; this was the highest figure ever collected in the research.[6] The best midfielders spend more time looking at opposing players and areas of space that may be exploited or defensive weaknesses that may be exposed; less skilled players spend more time fixating on the player with the ball or just ball-watching.[3]

Xavi, the king of scanning, was asked about why he scanned so much.[7] He explained:

> My brain works like a processor: it stores data, information. Turning my head helps me do it. And that's not only important, it's fundamental to master space-time. I think: my teammate is man-marked, so I turn my head to look for another solution. Behind me, an opponent says to himself: "I'm going to take the ball from him, he's turning his back, he does not see me." Except that I saw him.

> Football is a sport in which you have to watch what is going on around you to find the best possible solution. If you do not relate to others, you do not know anything and you cannot do anything. There is the space-time thing to apprehend in this game.

Perhaps the best distillation of scanning came in the most famous game of Xavi's career: the 2010 World Cup final. The match-winning goal was scored by Xavi's teammate – and another product of Barcelona – Andrés Iniesta.

In the 116th minute, with under five minutes to go before a penalty shoot-out, a Spanish player had broken into the Dutch half. The ball was intercepted and cleared to Iniesta. He took one swift touch to control the ball and then, without appearing to look, backheeled the ball to another teammate.

Iniesta did not need to look when he had the ball because he had been using his head to scan when his teammate had the ball and before it broke to him. By doing so, he had already created a picture of the pitch and the location of the other players before receiving the ball. Iniesta knew that there were Spanish teammates behind him who would be able to run onto a back heel before the Dutch players. And so what looked like an extravagant indulgence – a back heel at a critical moment in a World Cup final – was actually simply a pragmatic solution to help Spain advance with the ball. Thirteen seconds after his back heel, the ball was back with Iniesta, in front of the Netherlands goal. Once again, Iniesta had scanned constantly before receiving the ball, so he knew he could afford to take one touch to control the ball. Then, he smashed the ball into the bottom right-hand corner. For the first time in its history, Spain was the World Cup champion.

Iniesta's scanning before his backheel and the decisive goal are the favourite example of scanning used in presentations by Geir Jordet, a sport scientist at the Norwegian School of Sport Sciences. Before his backheel, 'you'll clearly see him scan his surroundings three times in that 5–6-second period, giving a frequency up there with the best,' Jordet explained. 'This behaviour is essential for performing that back-heel pass, which really opens up all that space towards the left, paving the way for the pass that ultimately ends up with Iniesta scoring.

'It just makes sense that to make good decisions on the pitch you need to know what's going on around you. In a game that's getting faster and faster, knowing what to do with the ball before you get it gives you an advantage.'

A study by scientists from Australia and Norway, including Jordet, in 2018 placed head-mounted sensors on semi-elite footballers during games, using these to examine the frequency of exploratory scanning movements of the head within 10 seconds of getting possession of the ball and their relationship to performance with the ball in match-play.[8] The scientists then used video analysis to document what the players did during games. When players turned their heads more frequently just before receiving the ball, they were more likely to turn with the ball, and to play an attacking pass rather than moving the ball sideways or backwards. Players classed as high frequency scanners completed 81 per cent of their passes, with 75 per cent of these being forward; those classed as low frequency scanners completed only 64 per cent of passes, with only 41 per cent of these being forward. Those who scanned the most could best identify passing opportunities and stay ahead of their opponents.

'We consistently see that elite players spend vast amounts of time looking at the areas of the field away from the ball,' said Jordet, who led the research. 'A very simplistic hypothesis would be that the best players in this game watch the game, whereas the not so good players watch the ball.'

Gaizka Mendieta was twice named UEFA's best midfielder as he led Valencia to consecutive Champions League finals in 2000 and 2001. He agreed with Jordet about looking at the game, not the ball.

'You shouldn't be watching the ball a lot, because you know where it is,' Mendieta said. 'You don't have to actually look at it to have a reference of where it is. Ideally, it's like a mechanism – your brain, your eyes, the ball and your body are all connected and you know where the ball is most the time. You have to look at options, you have to think of options, but it's all very fast so your brain has to act and react.'

Central and peripheral vision

Elite players are better at simultaneously using peripheral and central vision to pick up information during matches. While peripheral vision is more sensitive to movement, central vision is responsible for detailed vision.

These two types of vision interact dynamically when a player is trying to anticipate what opponents will do next. Skilled players use central vision more effectively when scanning for information; they fixate on more informative areas and move their eyes more efficiently.[9] Leading players are also better at using peripheral vision to extract information about opponents' movements 'off the ball'. 'You shouldn't be looking at the ball much,' Mendieta explained. 'You always have a peripheral view – the ball is always in that field of view.'

Some skilled players use 'visual pivot' points and anchors to fix their gaze on a central area such as the ball, while simultaneously using peripheral vision to monitor positions and movements of teammates and opponents.[4] The optimal use of central and peripheral vision depends on several factors, including the area of the pitch involved, the time available to respond and the number of players in close proximity.[10] Stressors like fatigue, workload and anxiety influence how central vision (the fovea) and peripheral vision interact in dynamic sport situations.[11, 12]

On the field, Mendieta twirled his head around constantly, moving his eyes, taking visual snapshots of the game around him and continuously refining exactly what the optimal position was for him to fit in among the other 21 players on the pitch. 'I always was looking around, where my teammates were, where my opposition was and what my options were by the time I received the ball.'

What Mendieta did when he received the ball was governed by who was around him. 'You have to have that first option – it's knowing where to put the ball on your first touch. But then you have maybe another idea so if I receive it on my own you turn and do something. It will depend on the situation. If I'm running to space, then I'm thinking of the next thing rather than getting rid of the ball. When I gain it in an area where there were a lot of players around I'm more likely to make a first touch or two touches. I'd always have options in my head.'

While scanning is crucial to performance, looking does not necessarily guarantee seeing. Two players can scan in the same manner but see different things. So the ability to scan must be coupled with the necessary knowledge to perceive and interpret the correct information at the right time. This awareness is honed through years of practice and match-play developing a vast library of knowledge.[13] The frequent repetition of similar situations, in which players have acted in a certain way, wires together the neurons in footballers' brains – so that they can automatically do the right thing without even needing conscious thought. This skill is thought to be based on a process called perceptual chunking: grouping positions and movements of players into meaningful chunks or patterns of play so that information can be processed more quickly.[14]

Rather like brilliant mathematicians seeing sequences where others see only a random series of numbers, the best players see teammates and opponents lined up in patterns. 'As a midfielder especially you need to always have awareness – where you are, where people are, what are the potential movements people might make, what you want to make those movements in order to be free or create something,' Mendieta said.

The ability to recognize patterns of play is deeply wired into players' brains. Scientists have conducted experiments in which video sequences of attacking actions are stripped down so that only white lines, reflecting the markings of the pitch, and coloured dots of light to represent the players on the two teams are visible. The best players are still able to recognize patterns and accurately predict what will

happen at the end of a sequence, far more accurately than less proficient players.[15] The findings attest to how expertly footballers' brains
have adapted to their needs.

An element of specialism exists in how defenders and attackers
scan during football matches – and, it is believed, in other invasive
team sports. Defenders must anticipate what will happen next; consequently, they have less control over the action that unfolds. This means
defenders scan the pitch more widely, trying to make themselves
aware of every possible option available to opponents attacking with
the ball. Their scan patterns are exhaustive; they avoid ball-watching for fear they will miss an opponent's crucial movement.[16] 'When
defending, you need to be aware of both where are your teammates
and your opponents,' Jordet said.

Forwards use their eyes differently. They scan the display more
selectively, looking for a teammate in a goal-scoring position or an
area of space to exploit; if they scan too extensively the opportunity
may be closed down by a defender and the moment lost. While players typically have both attacking and defensive roles in a team, the
game intelligence skills players develop are specific to their position.[16]

Mendieta's mastery liberated him to be spontaneous and instinctive
on the field. 'By playing and watching football, watching players –
that's how you learn to see where the mechanisms are in defenders,
midfielders, attackers. They're all different players and different personalities. By playing in a league or by watching the team you're playing against next weekend you know left-footer, tall, slow, fast, good in
the air, bad in the air, tackles – yes or no. All that information – you
have absorbed it and you have it stored in your brain. And you use it
as you need it on the pitch.'

The art of the quarterback

In American football, no position is more important than the quarterback. The quarterback is charged with dictating the entire team's
offence. The trouble is, he has only a few seconds between receiving
the ball and opponents descending upon him. Any indecision will be
fatal for the team – and incredibly painful.

When receiving the ball, 'what goes through your mind is a combination of things,' explained Kurt Warner, a former Super Bowl winner who enjoyed a 16-year NFL career and is rated the thirteenth best passer of all time.[17]

'We have a designed play that we're calling at each given time. So, the first thing that goes through your mind is all the different nuances and things that are going on with your play. And then the second thing is the ability to see and understand what the defence is doing. That's taking you to a particular player or two players on the field which you're focused on in – what we call "making your read".'

A good quarterback must 'decipher all that information, get to the right place at the right time to make that decision', Warner reflected. 'You want to get to the point where as much of that becomes innate and ingrained – it becomes less thinking and more reacting, in that three, four, five seconds that you have.'

American football is one of the most structured sports, with bespoke plays for every situation. But in the split seconds between receiving the ball and deciding where to throw it, a quarterback is still scouring the opposition defence for clues about the best place to throw their pass.

Quarterbacks 'allow the defence to tell you where to throw the ball,' Warner explained. 'I'm trying to decipher what the defence is doing, so I know which defender or which two defenders are going to dictate where, or if, I throw the ball. So, as soon as the ball is snapped I'm trying to get my eyes on the defence, because I should already know what my guys are doing.'

Warner would home in on the safeties – defensive backs regarded as the last line of defence – for the best clues about where to throw the ball. 'They've got to tell you, if it's on the snap of the ball, "What am I doing? Am I running to the middle of the field? Am I playing half of the field? Am I dropping down to help on the run, or down low in a passing game?"

'They kind of show – hey, if I'm going here then that means my other guys are going somewhere else. So, it starts by looking at the safeties, and then from there you bring your eyes down to different places.

'Who you're looking at all depends on the specific concept that you're reading on any given play. And so, on any given play, I could read anybody on the defence, or in the defensive backfield, just depending on where we're trying to attack.'

What Warner's eyes told him would then dictate what he actually did with the ball, and which training routine to put into action. 'My goal is to get my eyes on the defender, and allow the defender to tell me where to throw the ball. If he moves outside, I throw it inside. If he moves high, I throw it low. As soon as the ball is in my hands, I'm trying to keep my eyes on the defenders, and figure out where they're going so I can throw it the opposite way.'

In these split seconds, Warner leant upon his specific knowledge of the opposing team, honed over previous matches and pre-game video analysis. 'The whole goal was to try to figure out the tendencies of these teams in each and every situation. What did they do in third down? What did they do when we were inside the red zone? What do we do in third and long? If you can get those tendencies down, you can create plays to attack those tendencies.'

When faced with the opposing defence charging towards him, Warner's subconscious would be able to take over, enabling him to process a dazzling array of permutations, decide what he was going to do and then execute a pinpoint pass for his teammate to run onto in a few seconds. All the while, he knew that a minute mistake, or even a hesitation, would lead to him being 'sacked' by the opposing defence.

'You allow your arm to get away from you, you allow your feet to be in the wrong spot, you allow pressure to affect you – all those different things can force you to have bad technique. And, when you have bad technique, it just makes it harder to put the ball exactly where you want to put it.

'Once you recognize what the defence is doing, you have a sense of two or three different guys that you're going to throw the ball to. And it really depends on – over the course of that three or four seconds – how the defence reacts to your particular play. There's times that you would snap the ball and you think you're going to throw to one guy, and then by the time you throw it they've adjusted and done something different so you've got to react to that and throw it to somebody different. That happens all the time.

'We have what we call a pre-snap and a post-snap read. So the pre-snap read, before I snap the ball I've got a sense of "OK, I'm thinking they're

going to do this, so there's a good chance that I'm going to throw it here."
And then all of a sudden you snap the ball and then they do something
different, and now you've got to get a read on what they're doing after
the ball has been snapped. Then from there it's reading that one or two
guys to figure out exactly where you're going to throw the ball.'

Just like in football, leading NFL players develop their anticipation
through experience and how they store information – chunking. An
analysis of expert and non-expert American football players found
that when given diagrams of plays, experts could recall players' positions more accurately than non-experts.[18]

So, in those few seconds between getting and throwing the ball,
Warner could feel like he had far more time to find his teammates.
'When you know what you're seeing, you're getting the game to
slow down, and you're able to recognise what a defence is doing. It
makes it easier.'

A native language

In a very different way from quarterbacks, the best chess players are also
distinguished by foresight and the ability to plan ahead. 'In the opening
preparation sometimes you can go all the way to move 20 or 25 even,' said
Judit Polgar, widely regarded as the best female chess player of all time.

Later on in a game, it becomes harder to plan so far in advance. Deep
into a game, Polgar would generally plan only three to 10 moves in
advance. 'It really depends how concrete the position is or how strategi-
cal it is, how much is about the planning or the face of the game already.'

Polgar's mind was like a calculator constantly recalibrating the
optimal moves, and how each possible move would shift the moves
that were possible later in the match. 'Every move you calculate again
so it becomes like a tree with all the different branches,' she explained.
'You have a feeling of it. You see the movements, you see your opponents' strategies, you can analyse your opponents in advance when
you play on a top level.'

Chess grandmasters can recall with startling accuracy the positions
of pieces on a board after only a very brief glimpse. They can identify
board positions from earlier in a match with far more accuracy than

less accomplished players. As with footballers and American football-ers, this is due to chunking.[18]

'There are a lot of things which I take into consideration when I'm choosing a system,' Polgar explained. 'What is the most unpleasant system or ideas which can bother my opponent? What is the most uncomfortable situation he has to handle?

'You know the other rivals' strategy, their way of playing, their style, so because of this you can figure out many things in advance that you can expect from your opponents.'

On the board, Polgar's extensive preparation liberated her to be nimble, and have the flexibility to adjust her plans. 'If there are only one or two moves, it's steering the game in a completely different direction. You have to always be ready for changes.

'Sometimes you make the plans – what kind of strategic things and planning you want to do – but when it comes to concrete situations you have to calculate very well. You have to be sharp, you have to think how you use your time.' Polgar learned not to dwell on moves she had already made. 'You can easily get into time travel and that will affect your decisions.'

Athletes even adjust their decisions based on the specific circumstances of the game. During matches, athletes are unusually effective in assigning probabilities to potential event outcomes, scientists have shown.[5] Athletes use this ability to shape their decision-making; when a basketball team is losing, players are more likely to attempt threes (rather than twos), showing how athletes' actions are constantly driven by the match situation.[19] Basketball players marry their remarkable physical gifts with thinking like whizzes on the trading floor: not just working out probabilities, but also the average rates of return, of their different options – and whether, given the situation in the game, they need to adopt a riskier strategy and go for more threes.

Fast and slow thinking

In *Thinking: Fast and Slow*, Daniel Kahneman identified two routes to decision-making in the brain.[20] System one is fast thinking; here, decision-making is automatic or instinctive, with almost no effort involved. System two is slower, and more mentally draining, better suited to problem-solving and intense analysis. As Kahneman explains, system one is dominant in human beings most of the time, with system two called upon only when system one cannot – or thinks it cannot, oblivious to the biases that Kahneman documents – provide an answer.

While there is limited research on Kahneman's model in sport, it's likely that these two systems interact dynamically to facilitate quick and accurate decision-making on the pitch. In the heat of battle, players have only the time to engage system one; system two can be engaged in situations where the player has more time to reflect and consider. The best athletes sometimes have to be opportunistic gamblers; at other times, actuaries planning for the future and protecting themselves from loss.

'You know so many things unconsciously that it's all in your head,' Polgar explained. 'Sometimes a draw is enough for an opponent so you choose something else because you know he is not going to be very sharp – you are trying to avoid the very solid systems which can be easily drawn. So, you have to be aware when you're playing chess, from a sporting point of view. You have to take into account all the different elements when you're choosing your strategy, system and choices.

'It's like when you speak a language – it's natural that you can express yourself and talk right. This is what happens in your professional life, too. Chess is like a native language for me.'

9
The art of the con

Why grunting works and how to trick your way to victory

'You would never train to play against someone who was hitting an underarm serve. So he was taken by surprise and obviously after that it became not just a physical battle but a mental one too.'

Michael Chang on his famous underarm serve to Ivan Lendl in
1989 at the French Open Championship

As he walks up to the plate to throw a baseball pitch, Trevor Bauer has one aim in mind – how to deceive the batter standing 60 feet and 6 inches away, preparing to hit the ball. Bauer, a professional baseball pitcher for the Cincinnati Reds, cannot pitch at extreme speed. He can seldom beat a hitter for pace. Instead, he has to out-think Major League Baseball batters.

Bauer has honed six different pitch types – four-seam, two-seam, change-up, cutter, curveball and slider. His success depends upon how well he can use these variations.

'I like to have those different pitch types to be able to create maximum deception. If I can tunnel all of them, and locate them all for strikes, and where they're supposed to be located, I think that gives me the best opportunity to create the most deceptive mix for the hitter, and also be the least predictable.'

Bauer has studied the science of hitting relentlessly. 'The information that hitters actually use to anticipate the pitch is available before release – where they can tell if the pitcher slows down, or if his arm slot might change drastically, or the angle of his torso or something like that – and then really in the first 30 to 35 feet of ball flight, and after that the hitter's pretty much blind.' By denying the hitters cues about what they can expect, Bauer can shift the odds in his favour.

'No one actually knows for certain what the hitters see when the pitch is coming to the plate, or what they pick up from release point, or spin,' he explained. 'The best guess that we have is that if you can project all your pitches on the same initial trajectory and have them break different ways at different velocities, that's probably the best way to go about it.'

This concept is tunnelling. 'Pitch tunnelling is the idea that it can be effective for pitchers to focus on the early part of the pitch trajectory,' explained Rob Gray, a scientist at Arizona State University. 'If two pitches – say, a 90-miles-per-hour fastball and a 76-miles-per-hour curveball – can travel down the same initial trajectory long enough, batters won't be able to tell them apart before they need to start their swing. But the two will end up in very different locations. Hitting a 90-miles-per-hour fastball and a 76-miles-per-hour curveball requires completely different swing parameters, so if the batter can't tell which is which before they need to swing they are going to be in a pickle.'

A batter has around 400 milliseconds between a 90-miles-per-hour baseball leaving the pitcher's hand and it reaching the plate. A hitter must decide how to swing – and if they want to swing at all – shortly after the ball leaves the pitcher's hand, leaving around 200 milliseconds to process relevant visual information and a similar time period to execute the swing.[1] As the pitch approaches home plate, the velocity of eye movements required to track the ball exceeds the physiological limit of the human eye.[2] Expert batters possess superior ability to track fast-moving objects, using head and eye movements,[3] but the ball still moves too fast to track using the fovea – the central 1–2 degrees of the visual field. Because of the reaction time delay, batters may not be able to use visual information about the ball trajectory right before making contact. And so they must decide where to swing based on their prediction of the ball's trajectory early in its flight.[4]

Pitchers with fastballs are particularly well equipped to con batters. A study in 2014 showed that when batters failed to a hit a change-up pitch, this was normally because their movement patterns were too fast, and they failed to adjust to the slower speeds of change-ups. Most batters seemed to set themselves up for a fastball – expecting slower change-ups would leave them too little time to react to unexpected fastballs. So the greater speed a pitcher's fastball can reach, the greater their scope for fooling batters with slower change-ups.[5]

On average, when facing a fastball Major League batters have to make a decision when the ball is 23.8 feet away from home plate.[6] The art of successful tunnelling means passing this point with the hitter still oblivious to the type of pitch coming his way – forcing him to either anticipate or guess when, and how, to swing.

The core of Bauer's method borrows from Greg Maddux, one of the greatest baseball pitchers of all time and a 1995 World Series winner with the Atlanta Braves. Maddux may not have been aware of the science of tunnelling, but he still practised the art perfectly.

Maddux's main goal was to 'make all of my pitches look like a column of milk coming toward home plate', he later said. His approach entailed giving all his pitches 'the same release point, the same look, to all his pitches, so there was less way to know its speed', the *Washington Post* noted.[7] This way, hitters could not discern any physical cues, giving them less time to react. Maddux's ideal pitch lured hitters to commit to a swing, but left them so hoodwinked that they made poor contact with the ball.[8, 9]

Bauer has honed his pitching by conceiving of a hitter's options like a decision tree. 'Think about a tree with a bunch of branches, and you turn it on its side where the trunk is at the pitcher's end and the branches are at the hitter's end. All the pitches would travel down the trunk so they'd all look the same, and then they'd split off on the different branches of the tree as they got closer to the plate.

'Our best guess is that the better you are at channelling your pitches to make them all look the same for the initial phase before the ball leaves your hand, the more difficult it will be to the hitter, the harder it will be for him to square any of them up, and be on time.

'The tunnel gives you a roadmap on how to generate different types of outcomes, and deceive the hitter. And then you just have to read what the hitter's telling you in real time and know what pitch to throw out of that tunnel or to throw in the tunnel that can counter-act what the hitter is looking for.'

Sometimes, rather than shield his pitches, Bauer throws them in a way deliberately designed to deceive the hitter into thinking it is one kind of pitch when it is another. 'I can also go outside that tunnel and throw stuff that looks like a ball that ends up as a strike, or stuff that looks like a strike but ends up as a ball – so you can play around with getting hitters to take certain pitches or to swing at pitches that end up out of the zone.'

Deception and disguise

In sport, deception relates to the process of conveying false informa-tion to opponents to mislead them as to your true intentions. A side-step to the left in rugby before accelerating to the right or pretending to hit a tennis ball down the line before playing a cross-court winner are deceptive actions.

Disguise is closely related to deception. But with deception, ath-letes try to hide the information needed by the opponent until as late as possible in the action. In the tennis serve, for example, the initial actions may look similar for a serve delivered to the forehand or backhand side, making discrimination difficult. The best athletes use deception and disguise adroitly to gain the edge.[10]

A story about Bauer playing an intra-college game distils what he is attempting to do. 'I threw a right-handed hitter a first-pitch fastball up and in, and then a second-pitch slider down and away, and then a third-pitch curveball in the dirt – centred on the plate,' he recalled proudly. 'He swung and fouled off the fastball, he swung at the slider away and missed it, and then he swung at the curveball in the dirt and struck out.'

When Bauer mocked his teammate after the game, he replied, 'I don't know what I was supposed to do at a curveball that started off just like a fastball, broke like the slider and then dropped like the curve.

'That was the best encapsulation of what deception is about. He saw the initial trajectory as a fastball because that was the first pitch he had seen, and so when he saw the slider it looked like a fastball and then it broke like a slider. So after he had swung he processed it and said, "Oh, that was a slider", but to him it looked like a fastball so it was hard for him to distinguish the two. And then when I threw the curveball, the information that he had about the fastball and the slider looking the same – starting like a fastball and breaking like a slider – when the ball dropped more because it was a curveball, he saw the initial thing as a fastball or a slider, wasn't sure which one. Then it turned out to be a third pitch.'

This is an extreme example of what Bauer attempts to do every time he goes up to the plate – to deceive or disguise his intended pitch type and velocity to stop them anticipating effectively. For Bauer, the battle is not just one of skill, it is one of stealth and science, too.

Knowing the science, exploiting the stats

Certain pitches make a hitter more likely to make a mistake. A batter's average timing error for fast pitches is considerably higher when the fast pitch follows a sequence of slow pitches than when it follows fast pitches.[11] Batters, Gray has shown, begin to shift their coordination pattern for any given swing based on recent pitches.

Bauer, naturally, is aware of this finding. 'I know the science behind the process,' he explained. 'You don't want to throw the same pitch type too often because the hitter gets better at seeing it and hitting it the more you throw it.

'You don't want to throw to the same location too often because it's easier to hit it the more you see it in the same location. You don't want to throw the same speed, or the same pitch shape, but you want to make them all look kind of similar so that the hitter doesn't get an early indication that something's different and have more time to adjust.'

Other pitchers might not be aware of the science in the same way as Bauer. But, instinctively, they still act upon these findings. 'Whether they realize exactly why it works or not, they just know it works.'

How Bauer plans to con each hitter is subtly different. Some opponents react differently to cues, and so he uses both disguise and deception to trick batters into seeing the world differently from reality.

'There are certain hitters that will just sit on a specific pitch,' he said. 'It doesn't really matter what you throw them – they'll swing at it like it's whatever pitch they're looking for. A good example of that would be someone who just sits on fastballs. So if you throw them breaking balls that look like a fastball to start off, they'll swing and they'll miss the ball by 2 feet, and they'll look stupid. But if you happen to throw them a fastball, they'll hit it 400 feet or 500 feet.

'Other hitters are just kind of reactionary. They want to see the ball, and they're going to try to kind of defend everything that the pitcher's throwing at them.'

The hardest batters, Bauer said, are those who are unpredictable; whether or not they sit on or hit a pitch depends on the situation of the count. 'You never really know what they're looking for, and so it's very hard to sequence them and deceive them.'

Whoever he is pitching against, Bauer scours the opponent for clues. While he prefers not to watch too much footage of opponents before the game, he watches hitters on film mid-game. 'I try to see what they did against me in the first at-bat. Are they leaning out over the plate? Are they late on fastballs? I threw this breaking pitch that I thought he should have swung at, did he offer at it or did he just take it? And that gives me some information. And then also what pitch types that I've thrown this guy the first time or second time I've faced him, and how do I vary the pitch types while making them look the same for the second or third time through the order.'

Bauer's central craft – to disguise what he was doing – is embraced by other leading athletes. As a boy, Pete Sampras's junior coach used to yell 'wide', 'middle' or 'body' as Sampras was serving. This meant that Sampras was 'able to hit all my spots with the same ball toss', he said. 'What I used to talk about was having the same ball toss for every serve – that was something I did as a kid. So it disguised my serve.' Sampras's opponents could not read his serve from his physical movements, denying them a crucial source of information that could help them combat one of the most formidable serves in tennis history.

Why an underarm serve can be deadly

Michael Chang had cramp. He wasn't serving well. In the fourth round of the French Open in 1989, Chang – a 17-year-old playing in only his fifth Grand Slam – was deep into the fifth set against Ivan Lendl, the world number one. Chang edged into a 4–3 lead, with a break, in the fifth set, but was struggling to gain traction with his serve. In the eighth game, Chang slipped to 15–30 down, with Lendl poised to break back.

Then, Chang had an epiphany. 'I thought about it maybe two seconds before I hit it. I was really struggling with holding my serve and hitting my serve because I was cramping so bad so for me I was down 15–30, I was up 4–3 and it felt like I really needed to change things up because I was on the verge of losing my serve again. So without much thought I hit an underarm serve.'

Lendl was renowned as one of the most meticulous planners in the game. But here, at a high-octane moment, was a scenario for which he could never have prepared. The serve landed deep in the service box. Lendl returned the ball down the line, his momentum moving him so far forward that he had to charge to the net. Chang's passing shot clipped the top of the net, and Lendl missed his backhand volley.

'It was definitely a surprise,' Chang said. 'You can tell just by his reaction that he was not expecting that to happen. Ivan is the consummate professional. He prepares for just about every circumstance. But you would never train to play against someone who was cramping, you would never train to play against someone who was hitting an underarm serve. So he was taken by surprise and obviously after that it became not just a physical battle but a mental one too.'

With his underarm serve, Chang recovered to 30–30 in the eighth game. He then held serve, and broke Lendl immediately to complete one of the most sensational results in the tournament's history. A week later, Chang was the French Open champion.

Given how fast-paced their matches are, and how little time they have to react, elite tennis players must try to pre-empt what will happen next. The context of the situation, and their experience playing against the same opponent, leads them to assign probabilities to potential outcomes. Simultaneously, they try to pick up relevant information or clues from their opponents to confirm or reject their initial predictions. This need to predict what will happen next is what makes even elite athletes susceptible to cons.[12]

Why grunting works

For tennis, it is 'the issue that won't go away'. The sport is locked in an incessant debate over grunting – the noises that players, especially on the women's tour, emit as they hit the ball.

Many players hit the ball better when they grunt. Grunting can help players with their rhythm and to hit the ball harder without depleting their oxygen supplies[13] – skilled players hit the ball 4 per cent faster during rallies, and serve 7 per cent quicker[14] when they grunt as they hit the ball. But, most importantly, grunts can also deceive opponents.

Elite tennis players can judge a ball's trajectory partly from the sound when the ball is hit; the louder the contact between the racket and ball, the deeper in the court the ball is likely to reach. Grunting can obscure this crucial information, making it harder to judge where the ball is going.

Grunting when hitting the ball also means that opponents react 30 milliseconds later, when the ball has advanced about two feet more. After a grunt, the opponent's accuracy in deducing the shot direction decreases by 3–4 per cent. So players grunting can expect their opponent to be both slower at reacting to the ball and less accurate:

a double advantage that more than justifies any opprobrium they receive for their grunts.[13]

'If you grunt really loudly your opponent cannot hear how you hit the ball,' Caroline Wozniacki, the former women's number-one player, once explained.[14] 'Because the grunt is so loud, you think the ball is coming fast and suddenly the ball just goes slowly.'

When players grunt at a higher intensity, opponents predict the ball will land nearer the baseline than when a lower-intensity grunt is used.[15] A player could manipulate this instinctive reaction by grunting loudest, which would lead to their opponents preparing for a shot hit deep, when playing drop shots and suppressing their grunts when hitting more powerful strokes. In this way, they could use opponents' anticipatory reactions to their advantage, turning them into a weapon to be used against them.

'Tennis players could fake their grunts to their advantage – thereby deceiving their opponents just like a side step or feint in rugby,' suggested Rouwen Cañal-Bruland, a scientist at the University of Jena in Germany. 'A smart solution might be to use both fake and non-fake grunts so that opponents cannot use the grunting noise as a reliable source of information.'

Grunting can even hinder the best players in the world. In a Wimbledon match against Monica Seles in 1992, Martina Navratilova complained to the umpire that grunting prevented her from hearing the ball.[16] Navratilova once called grunting 'cheating, pure and simple'.

Grunting can aggravate opponents. 'When he goes for a big shot, his grunt is much harder, like he thinks he's a winner,' Ivan Lendl complained of Andre Agassi. 'It throws off your timing.'[17] In 2018, Wozniacki complained to the match referee about her opponent Monica Niculescu's grunting. 'She'll hit the ball and two seconds later when the ball is on my side and I'm right about to hit, she'll start grunting,' Wozniacki said.[18]

Legendary tennis coach Nick Bollettieri, who worked with 10 players who reached world number one in the men's or women's game – including Agassi – was accused of making his players grunt.[17] Maria Sharapova, who was enrolled at Bollettieri's famed academy for many years, reached 101 decibels with her grunts.[17] 'I've done this ever since I started playing tennis and I'm not going to change,' she once said.[17] Sharapova's grunts were said to be mysteriously absent on the practice court.[18]

It doesn't matter where they get the idea. Tennis players grunt because it works.

Tricks, fakes and feints

Kurt Warner, a Super Bowl-winning quarterback who was named the NFL's Most Valuable Player on two occasions, knew that opposing defenders would look at his eyes for clues about where he would throw the ball. So Warner sought to use his eyes as a weapon to deceive opponents.

'Looking a guy off' was a wheeze favoured by Warner. This process entailed looking in one direction and then throwing the opposite way. 'If I want to throw to left I may look to the right as I'm first starting to drop back.'

He also used other tricks to deceive defenders. 'I may move my body to the outside to try to draw him or make him go that direction, and so I can throw it to the inside of him. There's always times where you're trying to manipulate guys with your eyes, or with your body language, or your appearance, as much as you possibly can with the timing of a particular throw.'

During Warner's era, Charles Woodson and Ed Reed, regarded as two of the league's smartest defensive players, 'would look at you and they would read what you were doing'. Warner tried to turn these gifts against them.

'You used your eyes to show them something. Show them the left, throw to the right. Look at a receiver that's underneath – because they're going to jump that – and then attack them over the top. So those were a couple of guys really great instinctually, and when a guy has great instincts they're really tough to play against, so you have to try to use those instincts against them.

'A big part of our game is trying to make a bunch of things look the same so the defence thinks they recognize something.'

Quarterbacks like Warner do not rise to the apex of their sport only because of where they can throw the ball. They also reach the summit because they can throw the ball where their opponents do not expect.

'What you're always working on in practice is the timing and details of your route, and where your guys are going to be, so you don't have to think about that,' Warner explained. 'You know where they're going to be, and so the rest of that – for a quarterback – is manipulating the timing, or manipulating players, to coincide with the timing of when you want to make a particular throw. You always know where your guys are going to be, and you're trying to manip-ulate the defence, and then get the ball to your guy in the right place at the right time.'

Warner's conniving attests to how, as athletes rely on cues and anticipation to ascertain what will happen next – the games proceed at such a pace that they don't have a choice – they leave themselves vulnerable to being conned. While athletes are masters at reading what will happen next, their opponents can take advantage by mak-ing them anticipate one action, and then perform a different one. The greater the level, the more players must anticipate, as there is less time to react. As there is less time, the higher the standard, the more susceptible athletes are to deceptive information – so they must be better at recognizing when they are being conned.

Trickster-players

Tricksters can disguise the crucial cue to flummox their opponents. Shane Williams, the former Wales rugby winger and World Player of the Year, used his sidestep to leave defenders wrong-footed and on the floor while he charged towards the try line. 'The whole point of a sidestep is I'm trying to manipulate you into moving in a direction and then changing last minute,' he later explained. 'You've got to use the defender's momentum to put him off-balance. The wider I can take a defender and then change his direction of angle, the better.'[19]

Similarly, Torry Holt, an NFL wide receiver who was a seven-time all-star and a teammate of Warner's when the St Louis Rams won the 1999 Super Bowl, was a master of conning opponents.

'Each play for me I would show my opposition something different,' Holt recalled. 'Whether it was my release, whether it was the change in my speed, whether it was a head fake here to go in the opposite direction, those were all things that I would use over the course of a game to get myself an advantage. So when the actual play was called I've already set up and know exactly where to go to make that play work.'

One of Holt's trademarks was the head fake: shaping to move in one direction and then actually moving in the other. 'A lot of the trickery starts with your head and shoulders. So if I know I'm cutting to the right then I might feint to the left with my head and shoulders and then plant my foot and go out to the right.

'For really good fakes the head and shoulders have to be in unison. And again a lot of trust between you and the quarterback. For those fakes to really work and have an impact, the offensive line has to give the quarterback as well as the receiver the time to execute those moves.'

While elite players are better at deception, they are also better at picking up an opponent's attempts at deception and disguise. A rugby study showed how adroit elite players are at recognizing when they are being conned. Around 80 per cent of the time, top-level rugby players can predict what the opponent will do in the 100 milliseconds ahead of the opponent's action, making them resilient to deception and disguise. Less expert players could predict their opponent's actions only 25 per cent of the time and they show no noticeable gains in their ability to improve accuracy in that same 100 milliseconds viewing window, making them more susceptible to deception and disguise.[20] The best rugby players are able to pick up an opponent's sidestep 70 milliseconds quicker than novice players.[21] Novices are much more likely to respond to a fake in rugby by making an initial movement of a few inches in the wrong direction and open up space for a decisive break.[22]

Magicians know that looking in a certain direction can confuse people and set them up to be conned.[23] The best athletes can exploit this fallibility, too. In basketball, opponents make faster judgements and fewer incorrect responses when head orientation is congruent or aligned with the direction of pass, even when participants are instructed to ignore head orientation.[24, 25]

'Gaze direction is a particularly powerful cue that sports performers use to read the intentions of an opponent,' said Robin Jackson, a scientist at Loughborough University. 'If used selectively, it can be a way of deceiving an opponent, particularly if gaze direction aligns with contextual cues that help "sell" the fake.'

For players controlling the basketball, making sure their head movement and the direction of pass don't align can buy a few milliseconds of extra time. So, con artists can both give themselves more time before having to make a decision – and then, when they do, have more chance of it fooling their opponents.

'I'm constantly trying to deceive the defence and throw them off track,' explained Elena Delle Donne, who has twice won the Most Valuable Player award in the Women's NBA. One way she does this is 'deceiving them where you look one way and you pass it the other way.

'The biggest thing is just being able to make decisions quickly – so quickly that I don't even know that I'm thinking it through. I've drilled it so many times that I know if I get that head fake my next step has got to get me right by you and I know which way you're going to go and which way I need to go. It all becomes instinct.'

This instinct is so hardwired that when Delle Donne does a head fake is determined not only by her position and that of other players on the court but also by which defender is guarding her. 'There are some defenders that are very good at not jumping, and staying down, and those are defenders where you need to find a different counter for them. But then there's other defenders that I know if I give them just one head fake they are going to jump over me and I'm going to be able to draw a foul.'

For athletes in elite-level matches, there is essentially a constant trade-off. The earlier they commit to a certain action, the greater the benefits will be if their anticipation is right. But the earlier they commit, the more they will suffer if their anticipation is wrong and they are deceived; tennis players who make it too apparent which way they think the next shot will be hit risk giving their opponents large swathes of an unguarded court to exploit.

The best athletes can spend the entire match laying traps for their opponents. Earlier in a match, and in games when he was 40–0 up, Pete Sampras would consciously serve more than normal out wide – his less preferred serve – on the advantage side of the court, to make his favoured options more advantageous later in the match, when he needed them most. This is known as contextual deception, as opposed to the physical deception deployed by Delle Donne.

'People knew that serve down the middle on the ad side was my favourite so to open up the spots I would go out wide early in the match,' Sampras explained. 'If you're up 40–0, I might go out wide a few times just because I'm trying to get it out there so he doesn't cheat the other way. But come a tiebreak or break point, you might go back to your old faithful. It just depends on the flow of the match, who you're playing and what you can get away with.

'I definitely tried to mix it up, especially against the better returners. So against an Andre Agassi, if I could get the one out wide on the ad side, he can't cheat the other way. It's just like a pitcher or maybe a bowler in cricket – you just try to set up certain serves so when the big moment comes you're a little more free.'

Sampras would also vary his strategy on his second serve depending upon his opponent. 'Sometimes if he didn't return that well I'll keep coming in, I'll keep hammering that backhand. You play someone like a Chang or an Agassi you maybe stay back a few times here – you don't want to let him have a target. It just varied from day to day. At certain times if they know you're coming in every time it's good to stay back … It's just a chess game trying to keep the other person off guard.'

Similarly, Martina Hingis – for a period number one in the women's game at the same time as Sampras was in the men's game – was more likely to serve and volley 40–0 up than on normal points. Doing so, which was not her preference on the most important points, was a way of introducing a new strategy and disorienting her opponent, according to the tennis strategy coach Craig O'Shannessy.[26] The best athletes can use less significant moments of matches to maximize their chances of triumphing when it matters most.

Why bad balls get wickets

How do you enfeeble one of the greatest cricket batsmen of all time, and make them resemble an incompetent club player on a park green?

AB de Villiers – who reached number one in the world rankings in both Test and one-day international cricket – had made

46 runs in a Test match against Bangladesh in 2008. Then, Moham-mad Ashraful – an occasional spin bowler who was far off the stand-ard of the other bowlers – came on.

Ashraful's very first ball pitched so short that it bounced twice before reaching de Villiers – the sort of delivery that gives copious time for even a novice player to hit. Only, de Villiers hung back in the crease, bewildered to be facing a delivery of such ineptitude. De Villi-ers tried to thrash the ball through the leg side, but – his characteristic timing completely awry – he got a top edge, which looped up to Ashraful, who gleefully took the catch. For several seconds de Villiers remained in his crease, apparently thinking that the delivery was a no-ball – as balls which bounce more than twice are, but those which bounced only twice, as Ashraful's did, were not at the time.

'I was hoping for someone to call it a no-ball,' de Villiers said.[27] 'It is the first time in my career that I have been dismissed in such a fashion.'

In cricket, deliveries that would be considered bad balls at any level of the game – those that are very short, like Ashraful's to de Villiers, misdirected and wide, or full tosses that do not bounce before reaching the batter – get a curiously high number of wickets at the top level of the sport. It isn't that elite batters cannot play such deliveries – these are exactly the sort of balls they have been thrash-ing away from their childhoods. Batters like de Villiers can struggle against such deliveries because they aren't expecting them, and the balls are totally incongruous given the high standard of the match.

Information like the placement of fielders, the previous deliver-ies from a particular bowler and the bowler's run-up prepares bat-ters for what delivery will come next. But in top-level international cricket, the cues derived from this information almost never point to batsmen receiving wide balls that bounce in an easy way, at what is known as 'half volley length'. Paradoxically, this is what can make such deliveries lethal.

Players are more likely to make mistakes when the delivery does not align with the cues available before, and as, it is delivered. This tendency can make them vulnerable to deliveries that deviate from their expectations – sometimes because they are brilliantly disguised and executed, and sometimes because they are simply egregious balls.

A study in 2019 showed that elite batsmen make more errors when the ball they face does not match the contextual information that precedes the delivery, including when the ball bowled is conventionally thought of as very bad. While elite batters are far better than lesser players at reacting to deliveries when the contextual information aligns with the ball, the errors made by elite batters increase markedly when the contextual information does not align with what happens. Elite batters seem to actually play such balls worse than sub-elite batters, presumably because they are less used to them at the standard they play.[28] So when the best bowlers are bowling to the best batters, just occasionally deliberately delivering a bad ball can be a smart ploy.

'Skilled cricket batters can start to anticipate the possible line and length of the next delivery based on the score, field setting, state of the game, and previous deliveries from that bowler – not as a "pre-meditation" but a narrowing of possible outcomes,' explained Oliver Runswick, a scientist at King's College London and one of the authors of a study on why bad balls get wickets. 'While this offers a significant advantage in playing most deliveries, it can have its downsides. When less probable deliveries come, the batter is more likely to be dismissed.'

These findings were confirmed by research into full tosses – balls that don't bounce before reaching the batter, widely considered very poor deliveries – by Liam Sanders from Loughborough University. Analysing 70,000 balls by spin bowlers in Test matches from 2006 to 2015, Sanders found that, remarkably, full tosses got wickets *more regularly* than any other length of delivery. All the balls that would have bounced under 1 metre before the stumps – and so reached the batter before they had bounced – got a wicket every 27 balls, compared with every 61.2 balls for deliveries that bounced 4–5 metres before the stumps. The conventional wisdom about the worth of these two types of deliveries is not wrong – on average, full tosses conceded almost eight runs per six-ball over, while balls that bounced 4–5 metres before the stumps conceded just 2.2 runs every six balls.

But it is the very rareness of full tosses in Test cricket that can make them potent. In their desperation to hit full tosses some batters can be over-eager and make seemingly inexplicable mistakes, Sanders said. 'It seems there is a significant negative impact on anticipation and shot execution in skilled batsman when pattern recognition was broken – a lack of agreement between contextual information, such as the previous deliveries received, and the outcome of the event that followed.'

This is why, paradoxically, the worst deliveries in cricket can be effective at taking wickets. Even when their opponents don't mean it, elite athletes can be conned.

IO

The quiet eye

How elite athletes use their eyes differently under pressure

'A former player sent a picture of me shooting my free throws the other day. He said, "Oh my God, just look at your eyes, and look how focused you are. Look at your concentration."'

Rick Barry, one of the best basketball free throw shooters of all time

In the 2015 Rugby World Cup final against Australia, Dan Carter scored 19 of New Zealand's 34 points. All came with his boot. He kicked one drop goal, four out of four penalties and two out of three conversions – the second famously with his right foot, as New Zealand's dominance allowed Carter to fleetingly move away from his trusted left boot. Naturally, Carter was named man of the match in his final international game.

Over his international career, Carter scored 1,598 points – over 300 more than anyone else in men's Test rugby union history – including 1,453 points from kicks. This phenomenal record was underpinned by a kicking method that held up under pressure.

Whenever Carter was kicking, and whatever the stakes, he would look into the grand stand behind the posts and try to find a spot to aim for: 'I just focus in on that … I take three steps to my right and then I just tell myself to relax, breathe and control my heart rate and then I find that spot again between the posts.' By doing so, Carter ensured that his focus always remained on kicking the ball to that spot.

Before taking a penalty or conversion (drop kicks were different as these were during open play), Carter followed the same routine with his eyes. 'Move around a bit, find a spot where I want to kick the ball in that direction. And then I focus on the sweet spot, the part of the ball that I want to be kicking. That really helps me keep my head still. And I have one more look up at the posts, I visualize the ball going through so it's gone through which is good. It's always good to have that confidence with visualization, and from there one more breath and into my run. And if I am doing the same routine every time, I know that I am not thinking about missing the kick or thinking about I don't know what 30 seconds before the kick. So it's a real strong routine that I do before every kick.'

From training to the World Cup final, Carter never diverted from this essential method. 'When you do find things that work for you, you know it's important to stick with those.'

When he stepped up to take his kicks during the 2015 final, Carter 'was just in the moment. I wasn't thinking if I miss this we are going to put ourselves under pressure. I was just focusing on my routine, and going through those steps … wasn't thinking of what ifs – if I got it or if I missed; just focused on my routine. Exactly like I was during that week on the training field.

'I have seen a lot of kickers out on the training field and they are amazing, then they get into the game and they are not striking the ball as well as they are all week. To me that's come down to one thing – to control your mind, to be able to overcome the thoughts going on inside your head.'

When elite players like Carter perform such kicks under pressure they develop a fierce visual focus on their target, impervious to distractions or intense pressure – what sports scientists call the 'quiet eye'. Across myriad sports, elite players literally use their eyes differently when performing static tasks under the fiercest pressure. While less elite players tend to flit their eyes from point to point, elite players are more adept at honing in on a specific point and maintaining laser-like focus.

'By searching for the same spot, Carter visually controls his attention to the relevant spot' and 'prevents irrelevant information from disrupting his attention,' explained Retief Broodryk, a scientist from North-West University in South Africa who has examined the quiet eye. 'Typically, a coach will see that the kicker does not keep his head still and will respond by telling the kicker to keep his head still. As a result, the kicker will then shift his focus internally, to keep his head still. Focusing externally – on the sweet spot that he described – enables Carter to maintain attentional control and keep his head still.'

Broodryk measured the quiet eye duration of 18 rugby players as they executed penalty kicks from various locations 30 to 50 metres from the goal posts.[1] The quiet eye was measured during both the preparation and execution of kicks. Across all kickers, the quiet eye duration on the ball did not change during the preparation phase, but during the execution phase the quiet eye was 200 milliseconds longer on successful than unsuccessful kicks. A comparison of the top three kickers, who had accuracy rates comparable to those in professional rugby, with the bottom three revealed similar findings. The quiet eye was half a second longer for the best kickers – 932 rather than 482 milliseconds. A longer quiet eye begets greater accuracy – and not just on the rugby pitch.

The sportsperson's GPS

Joan Vickers, a scientist at the University of Calgary, defined the quiet eye as the final fixation on a target prior to the initiation of an action.[2] 'It helps players think of their quiet eye as being like a GPS system,' Vickers explained. 'Their brain needs to be fed very precise spatial information that is gained through an extended fixation on a critical location before the shot is taken.'

The mechanisms underpinning the quiet eye remain unclear. Scientists believe that the brain uses the quiet eye period to organize or program the movement needed to execute the skill. The duration of the quiet eye increases with more difficult tasks, which supports this notion. The quiet eye is also thought to help the ongoing visual control of the action, helping the athlete use vision to refine the action, and is believed to be crucial to maintain attentional focus and emotional control. It is likely that all these mechanisms are employed at the same time.[3]

Ongoing research work using brain scanning techniques to examine the neural processes underpinning shooting in archery has shown differences in brain activation between non-archers and archers. Archers have less brain activity during the quiet eye period than non-archers, such is their fierce focus. 'Participants with archery experience showed fewer active areas and more localized neural activation, suggesting more efficient processing of information,' explained Claudia Gonzalez, the lead scientist on the project from Thompson Rivers University in Canada. 'It seems that as expertise develops, a network of high efficiency and contextual processing develops in the brain.'

The quiet eye has been found in aiming tasks across a range of different sports. In everything from shooting,[4] dart throwing,[5] archery[6] and returning serve in volleyball,[7] those who fixate their gaze on the target for longer before initiating an action tend to be more successful. Paradoxically, while elite athletes move their heads the most during open play in matches – notably in football and basketball, when these movements are essential to game intelligence – they completely change their visual strategies during static, aiming tasks to focus more on precise points than less effective players. So in both open play and static situations, the best players use their eyes differently to less successful ones.

Away from sport, the best at aiming tasks tend to maintain their quiet eye under pressure. In law enforcement, elite armed response officers employ longer quiet eye periods on the assailant prior to pulling the trigger; rookie officers move the eyes from the assailant to their gun barrel using a rapid shift in their gaze, which can suppress their ability to process information.[8] More skilled surgeons employ longer quiet eye periods prior to dissections. When dissecting the laryngeal nerve, which is part of the voice box in the throat, leading surgeons had average quiet eye periods of 2.4 seconds compared with only 844 milliseconds for inexperienced surgeons.[9, 10] In sport and beyond, maintaining a quiet eye can help separate elite performers from the rest.

On cue

Stephen Hendry is one of the greatest snooker players of all time. During crux moments – like in his world record seven World Snooker Championship titles – he took slightly longer before putting his cue to the snooker ball.

'If it was a difficult long pot you'd maybe spend an extra second looking, making sure you got the potting point on the object ball before you got it down. Obviously, on more difficult shots, you'd spend more time down on the shot – taking the cue back and forward, you'd maybe take it back an extra time for a more difficult shot.'

The best snooker players tend to fixate their eyes for longer on both the cue ball and the target ball than less proficient players. Players tend to focus their eyes for longer before making potting shots rather than missing them, suggesting that the quiet eye is part of what sets the best players apart. When scientists shortened the time available to complete a shot, by asking players to pot a ball in less time than usual, the quiet eye period reduced and performance declined. When elite players were observed then – just as was true of Hendry – they tended to focus their eyes for longer before the most challenging shots.[11] 'I'd just try and take another second or so just to make sure

I had the right line on the shot or whatever. I more or less treated every shot the same.'

Before each shot, Hendry looked at the cue ball, the target ball and the pocket. 'My eyes would flit between all three when I'm down on the shot,' he recalled. Just before impact, 'I'd be looking at the ball that I was trying to pot – that would be the last thing I'd be looking at.

'If you take too long over your shots it can put you off, but certainly if it was a pressure shot or a difficult shot you'd take a second or two longer.'

Occasionally, even a player as good as Hendry would miss a crunch shot. When he did so, Henry said there was a pattern: he often took the shot too quickly, rather than giving himself sufficient time to clarify exactly what he was trying to do.

Hendry remembered 'rushing shots and getting down on a shot and not having decided that this was a shot I was supposed to be playing. My mind was on "I should be playing a different shot". Then I'd go down and miss the one you're playing. So making sure you knew what shot you were going to play before you get down to the table was very important. Even if it just meant taking another intake of breath just to make sure you've got that focus and you knew the shot you were going to play – I think that's the most important thing.'

Under pressure, athletes are more prone to rush than take too long. A study measured the quiet eye of international level shotgun shooters while performing under low- and high-anxiety conditions – practice or pseudo-competition. The elite shooters showed a decline in shooting accuracy under high rather than low anxiety, hitting the target 63 rather than 75 per cent of the time. One explanation for the decline was they used their eyes less effectively. Under greater pressure, the shooters fixated on the target later and then maintained sharp focus on the target – the quiet eye – for less time, 362 milliseconds rather than 403. These changes in gaze behaviour when anxious were accompanied by larger, faster and more variable movements of the gun barrel.[12]

'The information extracted by the eyes from the target object enables the motor system to be effectively organized in order to make an accurate shot,' explained Joe Causer, a scientist at Liverpool John Moores University. Under pressure some athletes use their eyes less efficiently, which can 'lead to the information extracted being compromised or incomplete, leading to a more variable movement pattern and poorer shot accuracy'.

Slowing down under pressure

When Annika Sörenstam, one of the best female golfers of all time, was making a crucial putt, she would wrestle with her desire to try to speed up. Yet she knew that was where trouble lay: 'I had a tendency to rush.' Under extreme pressure, Sörenstam consciously tried to fight this instinct and take enough time to gain focus. Sörenstam did this by developing a pre-shot routine that took 24 seconds; like Carter with his penalty kicks, she would endeavour to stick to this at all times.

'For me it was all about rushing it to get out of the situation. So, I really had to stick to my routine and take a few extra breaths and really feel I was taking a long time,' Sörenstam recalled. 'I would have to force myself to stick to my 24 seconds, so that I would feel like I was in slow motion. I felt like I was breathing or talking in slow motion because I had a tendency to be faster when there was a lot on the line.'

Sörenstam did everything possible to treat a putt – even if it was putting for one of her 10 major championship titles – as just another shot, focusing on what was the same, rather than what was different. 'Having a routine is really important, whether it's putting or chipping or driving. Go through the process as far as analysing what I need to do, getting good positive thoughts, freeing the mind, getting good feel, then executing and trusting myself. I'd try and look at every putt the same.'

Such consistent pre-shot routines are part of what distinguishes elite golfers from accomplished amateur players. Expert players have far more consistency in the length of both their routines and quiet eye periods, while poorer golfers have more inconsistent routines and quiet eyes.[13] The quiet eye period is embedded within these pre-shot routines, but is a much shorter and more specific period of time when the athlete prepares to program the movement, to establish control over attention, and fine-tune the action through visual control. When anxious, athletes often reduce both their pre-shot routines and their quiet eyes.

A study measured university golfers putting under pressure. It showed that at the tensest moments, players reduced the amount of time spent preparing for the shot from an average of 2.4 to 2.0 seconds. This change was accompanied by an overall reduction in the quiet eye period from 2.2 to 1.6 seconds, showing how the time taken over shots and the length of the quiet eye are often correlated.[13] The greatest change in quiet eye occurred during the actual execution of the putt, with the quiet eye shortening by around 300 milliseconds. Before crucial shots, the duration of the final fixation on the ball after it was struck by the putter reduced from 400 to 100 milliseconds.[13] The golfers seemed to move their attention away from the ball earlier when anxious, disrupting the putter's contact with the ball – suggesting that pressure has a greater impact during the execution rather than the preparation phase of the putt.

What is true in putting – that athletes reduce the quiet eye period when they are more anxious – is true across numerous sports.[3] A longer quiet eye appears to aid emotional control; athletes perform better if they focus attention externally on their target, rather than internally on their tiredness or stress.[14] When athletes are adversely affected by stress, they reinvest attention in aspects of their movement – like their swing motion when taking a golf shot, say – which they had normally performed automatically, so-called paralysis by analysis.[15]

'Stress puts pressure on our ability to maintain attentional control and even elite athletes can be susceptible to these negative effects,' explained Mark Wilson, a scientist at the University of Exeter. Maintaining their quiet eye could help athletes 'effectively block potential negative thoughts' that could hinder performance. 'Attentional control is critical for success, and elite athletes manage to control their emotions and focus on the task by maintaining their quiet eye periods.'

'It's so easy to get caught up in the moment, the pressure or what's on the line or what other people are doing,' Sörenstam reflected. 'It's kind of like an on-off switch – you switch it on, it's boom, boom, boom, then you turn it off and relax. You start conserving energy that way.'

Of course, some players are prone to taking too long before crucial putts. 'They cannot pull the trigger – they just keep waiting, waiting. I don't know what they're waiting for.'

Yet more players are prone to rushing shots than taking too long. Golfers with lower handicaps have significantly longer quiet eye durations on the ball when putting than higher-handicap players, focusing on the ball for over 2 seconds – nearly a second longer.[16, 17] On successful putts, the duration of the quiet eye period increases as the length of the putt increases, and when the green becomes sloped, and so harder to read.[18]

In elite sport, the body and mind are intertwined. And so, when athletes are exhausted, it doesn't just affect how fast they can run or how high they can jump but also how much they focus with their eyes: the duration of their quiet eye becomes less. A study of Canadian Olympic biathlon shooters – a winter sport that combines cross-country skiing and rifle shooting – showed that their shooting accuracy declined from 74 to 50 per cent following strenuous exercise, rather than rest. Like golfers under pressure, tired shooters did not maintain their quiet eye for as long as normal. From using their quiet eye for 2 seconds before pulling the trigger when they were rested, they only used their quiet eye for nearer a second when exhausted.[19] Biathletes that maintained performance under these high-pressure situations used a longer quiet eye, shielding them from distractions and avoiding an internal focus on the fatigue and pressure.

Training the quiet eye

The performance benefits of a longer quiet eye – especially when the stakes are high – are so great that sports are beginning to explore whether a better quiet eye can be taught.

There are some encouraging signs. International-level skeet shooters underwent an eight-week intervention using video-based feedback and instruction, designed to improve the efficiency of their gaze behaviours. Participants subsequently maintained a quiet eye both earlier and for longer than before the training intervention.[20] This change translated into better performance: the elite shooters who underwent visual training increased their shooting accuracy from 63 to 77 per cent. They then subsequently displayed an improvement in performance in competition for the six months post-intervention compared with how they had performed before their training.

Such interventions have been effective across a range of sports.[21] In basketball, a team that received quiet eye training improved free-throw accuracy by 23 per cent over two seasons.[22] In golf, two groups of elite players, with an average handicap of three, either received quiet eye training coupled with physical practice or only physical practice. Players who received quiet eye training maintained a longer quiet eye under pressure and reduced the number of putts taken per 18-hole round by 1.9 shots more than the group who did not receive quiet eye training.[23] A group that received quiet eye training when taking football penalty kicks were significantly more accurate in their ball placement and had 50 per cent fewer penalties saved than a matched-ability group who received no such training.[24]

'Players improve their performance when they adopt the quiet eye location, onset, offset and duration of experts in the game,' Vickers explained. 'Quiet eye training is usually done by first showing the player a video, frame by frame, of the quiet eye of an expert proto-type, and then showing them their own quiet eye as they perform the same skill. They quickly see what needs to be changed in their quiet eye location, onset, offset or duration. I think quiet eye training is also unique in that players rarely argue about changing their existing focus. They can see clearly what needs to be done to improve.'

Focusing on the basket

Rick Barry was the most successful basketball free throw shooter of his era – and when he retired in 1980 the most successful of all time, making 89 per cent of shots.

Barry was best known for how he took free throws. Unlike virtually every other professional basketball player in history, Barry shot his free throws underarm.

When he was 15, his father told him that throwing underarm – and aiming to get the ball over the front of the rim – would get more shots in the basket. Initially, Barry didn't want to shoot underarm; it looked weird, even emasculating. The first time Barry took underarm free throws in a high-school game, 'I heard a guy yelling at me, making fun of me in the stands.' Then, Barry 'heard the person next to him say "Why are you making fun of him? He doesn't miss."' Barry had his free throw method.

'It's the most efficient way to do it, I don't know why more people don't do it,' he said. 'It's like a big macho thing or something. It's ridiculous.'

In 2017, a study published by the *Royal Society of Science* suggested that Barry was right. It found that the underarm throw was optimal for free throws if the shooter could control the release angle and speed. For such players, throwing underarm increased the likelihood of the ball going in; when the ball approaches the hoop from directly above, as in underarm throws, the cross-section of the target is larger for the ball than when the ball lands at more of an angle, as when balls are thrown overarm.[25]

Even aged 75, Barry said that he could still throw free throws more successfully than many current NBA players. 'I can still get warmed up and I can still make eight out of ten,' he said. 'You don't think about the situation when you're shooting free throws, you just think about your routine.'

Barry doesn't just attribute his success to daring to shoot underarm. He also credits it to how he used his eyes. 'It's having a routine to do it the same way every time, and part of it was making sure that I was looking where my target was.

'I'd watched the ball until I got done bouncing it and have it in my hand. And then when I'd get it ready to go I looked at the rim. When I'm ready to go then I just would do a little motion of my hands to get them into a neutral position and then I'd start the shot. I had a routine – I did it the same way every single time.'

Elite shooters fixate their gaze for around 900 milliseconds on the front rim of the hoop during the free throw, Vickers found.[26] Less proficient shooters fixate their gaze on the rim for much shorter – only around 350 milliseconds – moving their gaze between different spots. 'When the quiet eye location is focused on the front rim, when it begins early before the shot begins, and when the duration is about one second, then the free throw percentage will be higher,' Vickers said. With a shorter quiet eye, 'the brain does not have time to organize the shot and performance suffers'.

The effect was so strong that it even distinguished between successful and unsuccessful shots for the elite shooters; on the rare occasions they missed, the best free throw shooters tended to fix their gaze on the rim for less time. Barry seldom did.

'I totally focused,' he recalled. 'A former player sent me a picture of me shooting my free throws the other day. He said, "Oh my God", just look at your eyes, and how focused you are. Look at your concentration."'

11
Southpaw advantage

Why lefties do better in sport

'It's strange to play a lefty because everything is opposite and it takes a while to get used to the switch. By the time I feel comfortable, the match is usually over.'

Monica Seles, former world number-one tennis player

The traditional Boxing Day Test match in 1982 was among the most thrilling Tests of all time. It ended with Australia falling to an agonizing three-run defeat to England, rendering Allan Border's defiant 62 not out in vain. It had been a typical innings from the left-handed Border, patient and resolute.

Ultimately, Border's innings did not change the Test match in Melbourne. But it did help Australia to unearth a great batsman many years later: Mike Hussey, who would join Border in the elite list of eight Australians to score over 5,000 runs in Test cricket while averaging over 50.[1]

As a seven-year-old boy, the Melbourne Test captivated Hussey – so much that it changed how he batted for ever. 'I was a right-hander but I loved Allan Border,' he recalled. 'I went straight into the backyard with my brother and said, "Right, I want to be like AB" – and just turned around and started batting left-handed.

'I do remember thinking it's pretty tough but I must have just persevered with it and got better and better.' Although Hussey is right-handed in everything else he does, from writing to throwing a cricket ball, he remained a left-handed batter. The shift meant that, rather than his stronger right hand being the bottom hand when Hussey held a cricket bat, his stronger hand would be his top hand. What started as simple boyhood imitation of a hero proved the prelude to Hussey building a brilliant Test career of his own, which included 19 centuries.

Hussey's decision that day, to switch the top hand with which he batted, aligned perfectly with sports science research. Feted left-handed batters Brian Lara, Ben Stokes, Adam Gilchrist, Alastair Cook, David Warner, Kumar Sangakkara, Matthew Hayden, Clive Lloyd and Graeme Smith are all right-handers; left-handers Michael Clarke and Aaron Finch also bat right-handed.

'I did feel as though – not initially but thinking about it many years later – it probably made sense,' Hussey reflected. 'I did everything right-handed, right-hand dominant, wrote at school right-handed, threw right-handed, bowled, played tennis, I even play golf right-handed. My right hand was probably a lot stronger and more dominant than my left hand. That helps in cricket with picking the bat up with the top hand and controlling the bat with the top hand. I found it to be a bit of an advantage.'

That December day, Hussey's brother, who was also right-handed, didn't switch hands. David also enjoyed a fine career, playing extensively for Australia in the limited overs formats. But while Mike played 79 Test matches, David never played a Test.

A transformative change

Much of sports science is concerned with increasing the likelihood of an event by a few per cent. But the research on the benefits of being top-hand dominant in a batting stance – that is, batting left-handed if they are right-handed, and vice versa – is of an altogether higher order. Professional cricketers are 7.1 times more likely to be top-hand dominant than amateur players, according to research carried out in 2016: a remarkable advantage conferred by switching their 'normal' hand, and among the most notable of sports science findings.[2] The study's authors – David Mann, Oliver Runswick and Peter Allen – found that the advantage was identical for both right-handers who switched to bat left-handed and left-handers who switched to batting right-handed.

'The idea for this "reversed stance advantage" really came to me when working at the National Cricket Academy in Brisbane,' Mann recalled. He observed that 11 of the 16 players in the squad, comprising the best young players in the country, all batted left-handed. Nine of the 11 were right-hand dominant. 'We started to realize the extraordinary number of high-quality cricketers who batted left-handed but threw with their right hand.' As of June 2020, eight of the 16 batsmen to have scored over 5,500 Test runs for Australia were top-hand dominant, with seven of those natural right-handers who batted left-handed.[3]

Just as Hussey found when he initially switched, in a child's early years it is easier to bat bottom-hand dominant – as a right-hander does when using a right-handed stance, Mann explained. The conventional stance may be beneficial when first learning to bat because the dominant hand is lower on the bat, making it easier to develop control in the initial stages of learning. But this advantage is transient and soon reversed. As batters evolve, a reversed, top-hand dominant stance allows them to have their dominant hand perform most of the work swinging the bat, which appears to provide better control than when the weaker hand is at the top of the bat.[4] Top-hand dominant players may be better suited to 'playing straight' – hitting the ball down the ground, past the bowler – a trait that might impress talent scouts and lead to such players having more chance of selection for underage youth programmes.

Ironically, one threat to the astounding advantage of being top-hand dominant is growing awareness of the benefits. An ongoing survey by the German sports scientist Florian Loffing found that one-third of all Test cricketers with an average of over 30 – a marker of a player making useful batting contributions – over recent decades were top-hand dominant, including Hussey. This figure has gradually increased over time. In the 1880s, the first full decade of Test cricket, no players who averaged at least 30 were top-hand dominant.

So, as more players switch their normal hands in their formative years, often encouraged to do so by their parents, the seven-fold advantage in being top-hand dominant may well struggle to hold. Even so, encouraging their son or daughter to switch their dominant hand remains, statistically, one of the greatest sporting advantages that any parent can bequeath to their children. The remarkable thing is how slow the cricket community has been to recognize the scale of the advantage and encourage all children to be top-hand dominant unless there are compelling reasons not to. 'The magnitude of the effect is so large,' Mann reflected, 'that it seems amazing that we have missed it and continue to teach kids to bat what we think is "the wrong way".'

Something sinister

Cricket has no simple name for those who throw with their right hand and bat with their left hand as the top hand. But baseball does – they are called 'sinister right-handers', the breed who switch their normal hands when batting. Just like in cricket, doing so brings a profound advantage.

Among the general population, only 2 per cent of baseball players throw right-handed and bat left-handed. Yet 12 per cent of Major League players throw right- and bat left-handed, a six-fold overrepresentation, similar to that of those who switch dominant hands in cricket. This finding is even more profound among the very best hitters: 32 per cent of elite hitters – those with a batting average above 0.29, including Ted Williams, the last Major League hitter to average 0.40 in a season, in 1941 – throw right-handed and bat left-handed. Elite hitters are 16 times more likely to throw with their right hand but bat with their left hand than non-professional baseball players.[5]

There are many possible reasons for the advantages enjoyed by sinister hitters. Players who throw right-handed and bat-left handed – or vice versa – have the dominant hand further away from the hitting zone of the bat, which provides a longer lever to hit the ball and generate power and elevation – a very similar benefit to that enjoyed by top-hand dominant cricket batsmen.[5]

'I do think it makes a difference for sure,' said Joey Votto, a six-time All-Star Major League hitter who throws with his right hand and bats with his left. 'I'll hit with right-handed batters and I'll think sometimes wow you're better than me, just from a pure skill standpoint.'

In their hitting stance, left-handers naturally stand slightly closer to first base than right-handers. And the left-hander's swing naturally generates momentum towards first base – for right-handers, their swing does not push them to first base in the same way – making it a little easier to run to first base.[5]

In baseball – somewhat like cricket in recent years – the emphasis on generating the most favourable match-ups means teams favour having an ample number of both left- and right-handers if possible. This perceived need for balance encourages sides to promote left-handers at a rate completely out of proportion to their share of the population.

'There's a bias toward left-handed hitters, because teams want to stack their line-ups with an even amount of righties and lefties so that it's not as easy to game plan for the opposing team,' said Trevor Bauer, a baseball pitcher for the Cincinnati Reds. 'A right-handed pitcher is generally better at getting a right-handed hitter out. So, if you have a lot of lefties then you gain an advantage because they have a better chance of hitting that right-handed pitcher. Obviously, it's different on an individual basis, but just league-wide that's generally how it plays out. Lefty hitters are more desirable.'

In both baseball and cricket, there has been a small rise in switch-hitting – hitting the ball like someone who bats with the other hand – in recent years. Such an approach extends part of the logic of batting left-handed – that you are more likely to generate a favourable match-up – but is also fraught with risk. It is hard enough to reach a good enough standard batting with one hand, let alone two.

While researchers have pointed out the technical advantages to being right-handed and batting left-handed, in both cricket and baseball, anyone who bats left-handed in these sports also benefits from an asymmetrical advantage in their practice. 'I get to face right-handed pitching 70 per cent of the time,' said Votto. 'That's a pretty clear advantage for a left-handed batter.'

Left-handers are used to facing right-handed bowlers or pitchers, but right-handed bowlers or pitchers are not nearly as used to bowling to left-handed batters. This lack of familiarity with left-handed batters results in more wayward bowling, with batters benefiting from this inaccuracy. Batters enjoy a clear advantage batting left-handed, regardless of their throwing hand dominance.[6] So, the familiarity advantage to batting left-handed is not specific to sinister right-handers or dominant left-handers, but rather benefits left-handed players no matter their throwing dominance.

A baseball pitch takes only 400 milliseconds to travel from the mound to the plate – scarcely more time than cricket players have to react to balls. And so anything that can make this process easier increases a hitter's prospects of making a clean connection with the ball. Conversely, anything that makes this process less familiar may render the task of hitting the ball even more disorienting. This explains why even though left-handers comprise just over 10 per cent of the population around the world, they account for 22 per cent of cricket bowlers and 30 per cent of pitchers.[7]

The proportion of left-handers across the globe has remained consistent for centuries, at around 10 per cent.[8] But left-handed bowlers account for 25 per cent of wickets in Test cricket since 2015, and six of the top 30 wicket-takers in Test history.[9] The leading wicket-takers in five of the last six Cricket World Cups have been left-arm bowlers. Unlike the case of left-handed batters, left-handed bowlers are almost uniformly left-handed in everyday life – they would simply not have enough strength to bowl with their weaker hand.

The 'southpaw effect'

In boxing, being left-handed – a 'southpaw', in the sport's parlance – also offers advantages. Loffing and Norbert Hagemann analysed over 3,000 elite boxers across eight weight categories between 1924 and 2012 to examine the win–loss ratios of left- and right-handed boxers.[10] Southpaws were generally overrepresented in boxing compared with the general population, and tended to have better win–loss ratios than right-handers. Perhaps surprisingly, left-handed boxers did not have a higher proportion of wins by knockout compared with right-oriented boxers. The authors believe that unfamiliarity with southpaws' fighting behaviour and their tendency to attack from directions or at angles different to those commonly experienced against right-oriented fighters could simply help them dominate a fight and win by points, not by knockout.

Left-handers on the tennis court may benefit from similar advantages. While they are used to playing against right-handers, right-handers are not used to playing against them. A study in 2009 divided right- and left-handed men's players into groups based on their tennis expertise.[11] Players then completed an anticipation test that required them to predict the direction and depth of an opponent's strokes on a computer screen. For all groups – national league players, local league players, and novices – right-handers' shots were easier to predict than left-handers' shots, even by left-handers themselves. Right-handed players were more adept at anticipating left-handers' shots at higher levels – but the deficit compared to how they could guess right-handers' shots remained, so the left-handers' advantage remained. Left-handers found it easier to anticipate right-handers than the other way around, suggesting that their greater practice against this type of player helped them gauge shots more accurately. Similarly, a study of volleyball players found that anticipating right-handed attacks was easier than left-handed ones.[12]

Athletes can anticipate the intentions and actions of right-handers more accurately than those from left-handers.[13] 'The righty has always got to change and adjust against the lefty but lefties don't – they play righties nine times out of 10 so they don't have to adjust,' said Craig O'Shannessy, a tennis strategy coach for Novak Djokovic and others.

The effect even exists in football, with goalkeepers able to anticipate right-footed penalties more accurately than left-footed penalties. A study asked goalkeepers to predict where the ball would cross the goal line. The difference in error score for left- versus right-footed penalty takers was 6.7 centimetres – the typical length of a goalkeeper's fingertips.[14]

Left-handers' natural advantage

The science of this advantage for left-handers in tennis, volleyball and other sports is rooted in what are known as perceptual frequency effects.[7] The more time that a player gets to identify certain types of patterns, like shots from players with a particular hand-dominance, the easier these become to detect. The more experience players gather, the greater the gap in their total hours facing right- and left-handers – in any given year, players will spend far more hours playing against right-handers, so the extra difficulty of combatting left-handers remains.

'The most convincing explanation as to why left-handers might have an advantage in interactive sports relates to their rarity and their opponents' low familiarity with left-handers' style of play,' Loffing explained. 'In exceptionally fast sports like baseball and cricket, incorrect anticipation and swing initiation can't be corrected in time, making it harder to read left-handed pitchers or bowlers.'

In tennis, left-handers also have a specific advantage. On the advantage side of the court – when the score is 30–40 – a left-hander's serve wide would be into a right-hander's backhand side. On break point, 'You've got your biggest weapon against their biggest weakness most of the time,' O'Shannessy observed. Around 75 per cent of all break points are on the advantage side – and left-handers are better equipped to cope with these because of the wide serve to the backhand side, which is the hardest return shot in tennis. When left-handers are returning serve at 30–40, wide serves are to their forehand side.

'It's strange to play a lefty,' Monica Seles, the former world number-one women's tennis player, once said. 'Everything is opposite and it takes a while to get used to the switch. By the time I feel comfortable, the match is usually over.'

The less time a player has to react to an opponent, the greater the advantage of being a left-hander. The greatest southpaw advantage lies in sports in which players are under the greatest time pressure to react, Loffing has found.[7] Essentially, the shorter the response time, the higher the overrepresentation of those who played left-handed. In sports like baseball, cricket and table tennis, being left-handed was overrepresented by about three times compared with the population at large. Yet, in squash, a sport in which the time to react to each action is greater, only 9 per cent of players were left-handers, fractionally under the global average.[7]

The stark discrepancy, Loffing said, is because when time pressure is not as great, there is still time for players to correct their inaccurate anticipation, rooted in them being less familiar with facing a left-hander. But when time to respond is more limited, such corrections are harder to make. And so the benefits of being left-handed are particularly pronounced in sports performed under severe time pressure.[7]

It has been suggested that being left-handed may offer innate neurological and biological advantages based on structural differences in how different sides of the brain are used to control action, but the paucity of left-handers in sports where the speed of play is slower challenges this notion.[15] So does the lack of left-handers in individual sports in which athletes do not directly interact with each other, like darts, snooker or bowling. These findings all point to the overrepresentation of left-handers deriving from how, because they are rare, they shape up better in head-to-head contests than right-handers. This advantage is not confined to sport. In the most violent societies, left-handers are nine times more common than in the most pacifistic societies, suggesting a Darwinian advantage to being different-handed to the norm.[16]

Southpaw serendipity

Unusually, Phil Mickelson's dad played golf left-handed. His son wanted to be like his father, and so – although he was right-handed – took to playing golf left-handed, too. 'We didn't realize it at the time, and when we did, we tried to teach him to swing right-handed but it was too late,' Mickelson's mother, Mary, later said.[17] 'He had such a natural swing, even at that age.'

Renowned for his smooth long swing,[18] Mickelson forged a brilliant golf career, winning five major championships. Inadvertently, mimicking his father gave Mickelson a significant advantage on the golf course. A study, which divided 150 golfers into groups based on their golf handicap, showed that the lowest-handicap golfers were *21.5* times more likely to play in a reversed stance compared with players with higher handicaps.[19] Playing with a reversed stance is thought to confer such an astounding benefit – three times more than for cricket batters who play with a reversed stance – because it means that the dominant hand is at the top of a player's grip. This provides extra control over the club, creating a smoother swing and more accurate shots.

Yet after New Zealand's Bob Charles won the British Open in 1963 it took another 40 years for another player to win one of the four major championships while playing left-handed. Of the four left-handers to win majors in golf, only Bubba Watson actually writes with his left hand; like Phil Mickelson, Mike Weir and Bob Charles write right-handed. Several left-handers, notably Curtis Strange, Greg Norman, Ben Hogan and Arnold Palmer, actually enjoyed glittering careers in this time – but they did so playing right-handed, benefiting from a reversed stance. The paucity of golf equipment and clubs historically made for left-handers encouraged many lefties to switch to being right-handed, and playing with your right hand was regarded as the 'correct' way to play golf.[20] Today, there is no such taboo to playing left-handed, and equipment is easier to access. The number of elite golfers hitting left-handed – even though their right hand is their dominant hand – has mushroomed in recent years.

While the science of hitting a cricket ball, baseball or golf ball with your dominant hand at the top of the bat or club is compelling, the stories of why the best athletes end up doing so are often rooted in chance. From Mickelson mimicking his dad to Hussey imitating Border, tales of athletes who have flourished after switching hands are another reminder of the role of serendipity in forging the best athletes.

12

The psychology of greatness

Why sport is played in the mind

'It's not always fun to go to training every day. Sometimes your motivation is s★★t to be honest. But there's something deep inside you that needs to sparkle.'

Ada Hegerberg, 2018 Ballon d'Or Féminin winner

As a young girl in Sunndalsøra, a village nestled between the mountains in central Norway, even extreme weather was not enough to stop Ada Hegerberg from playing football in her local park. 'I have thousands of memories when it was pouring down, it was snowing. It was all about getting to practice,' she recalled. 'Football basically meant everything.' Whatever the weather, 'you had to go there on your own and get the work done. That's how it was.'

As a young boy growing up in the township of Zwide on the outskirts of Port Elizabeth, in South Africa, Siya Kolisi was often unsure where his next meal was coming from. 'I used to go to school with no shoes on sometimes, and not eat for days,' he recalled. 'Every time I trained or played rugby I gave everything, because I thought maybe one day I would reach the top.'

The backgrounds of Hegerberg and Kolisi – a girl from a middle-class family in Norway, and a boy from one of the most deprived parts of South Africa – could scarcely have been more different. But both shared the psychological characteristics necessary to reach the apex of sport. Before the age of 25, Hegerberg won the Champions League four times and the inaugural Ballon d'Or Féminin award. In 2018, Kolisi became captain of South Africa when the side was in crisis. Within 18 months he led them to World Cup glory.

On 17 June 1991, the South African parliament voted to repeal the legal framework of apartheid. A day earlier, Kolisi was born to teenage parents in Zwide. Kolisi was raised predominantly by his grandmother. In his childhood, his family could not afford to buy him any toys. Kolisi had a brick, and 'would drive as if it was a car'.

Kolisi's mother died when he was 15, and his grandmother soon afterwards.[1] 'My grandma and my aunt were everything to me – they raised me when I was younger, but dad was rarely around.' One of Kolisi's outlets was rugby. There is a rich history of rugby played in the Port Elizabeth townships, with Kolisi's father and grandfather both accomplished players.[1] The young Siya was exposed to the game in a local school, Emsengeni Primary, and played outside school on local dirt fields.

His family taught him about 'using everything around me to get to where I need to be. And try not to complain and just use whatever you are given'. But his impoverished childhood gave Kolisi greater motivation. 'I always wanted more than we had, I always wanted what the other kids had.'

A defining day in Kolisi's early life was his first trial for the under-age provincial team, when he was 12. Kolisi did not have any rugby shorts, so he played in boxers instead. 'I couldn't afford shorts – and I didn't care how it looked, all I cared about was what I was going to deliver on the field … It's something I'll never forget.' Kolisi made the B-team.

Soon afterwards, he was spotted playing in an U-12 Eastern Province tournament by Andrew Hayidakis, a coach at Grey, a prestigious private school. Kolisi was promptly offered a full scholarship to the school.

The passion for sport generally comes from within athletes, rather than their practice being imposed upon them. It is harder to sustain intense training in a sport without fierce internal motivation like Kolisi's. In Norway, Hegerberg had a similar internal drive. 'My mum and dad never dragged me to the football pitch. I was the one waking up first in the house with my sister and dragging our parents out to play. It needs to come from yourself – the will … It shouldn't be the parents pushing your child to play football. It should come from within you.'

Hegerberg lived a 15-minute cycle from her local football pitches. 'Our parents wanted to develop responsibility in us from a young age. They never drove us to practice – we always had to take the bike … It kind of made us take responsibility, and I think that taught me a lot.' Playing against her elder sister, Andrine – who was born two years earlier and would become a fine professional footballer herself – provided Ada with extra motivation. The two would 'push each other' and 'drag each other out to go training'.

The young Ada became addicted to the thrill of scoring goals. 'That drove me to work hard and to push myself, because I want to feel that rush as often as possible.'

Her story highlights the importance of having an initial passion for the sport: athletes who engage independently with a sport as children are more likely to become elite.[2] Hegerberg's parents and sister – and, less significantly, her coaches – harnessed her initial interest, and encouraged her to commit to the sport with increasingly more time and energy.

Motivation: extrinsic and intrinsic

Psychologists differentiate between extrinsic motivation – external rewards like money or praise from parents – and intrinsic motivation – a drive that comes from inside the individual. High intrinsic motivation is associated with increased practice hours and higher self-motivation away from parental gaze, leading to better performance: a study of elite cricketers found that strong intrinsic motivation was associated with higher performance levels.[3] While both types of motivation can be useful for athletes, intrinsic motivation can be particularly important during childhood, according to Dave Collins, a leading sports psychologist.

Kolisi appears to have had both high intrinsic and extrinsic motivation. 'The hunger? Oh man it's because of the situation I was in, you know?

'I have no doubt I had more desire. I have no doubt I had more hunger and can't even lie about that or be modest about it – I really wanted it and still do,' he reflected. 'I'm one of those who wasn't supposed to make it.'

When he had the means to do so, Kolisi adopted his half-brother and half-sister. 'Hopefully my brother and sister will make something out of their lives, whatever they want to be they can achieve to keep our mother happy, wherever she is right now.

'When I get big-headed sometimes or when I think I've arrived or made it, I remind myself where I came from and who I'm playing for.

'I want to be amazing, because I'm not just playing for me – I'm playing for my family back at home, I'm playing for the people of my community, without me performing I can't help them. You know the more I do work, the more people want to work with me so that I can start building rugby fields or making jerseys for the kids in the township. So a whole lot of them rely on me because I relied on them, you know, and they helped me sometimes and they still do and they are my motivation.

'I want to break all these barriers for the kids to start believing that they can achieve whatever they want to achieve, whether it is in the ghetto or the suburbs.'

Kolisi's journey is sometimes romanticized. He has a very different view: 'A lot of people say it's a beautiful story what I had to go through ... I think we shouldn't have these stories.

'I think a kid waking up in the suburb and the kid waking up in the township or the ghetto should be waking up and having the same dream because they have the same equipment, the same facilities and opportunities. And that's why I'm working as hard as I can to try and equal the playing field by building sports fields, putting computers in classes and trying to get the kids to eat every day.'

Grit is the dedication and perseverance towards long-term goals.[4] It has been shown to differentiate athletes across varying levels of competition.[5, 6] Athletes who scored higher on a grit scale, a measure of an individual's perseverance to overcome obstacles or challenges developed by psychologists Angela Duckworth and Patrick Quinn,[7] accumulate more hours in practice and competition in football.[8] The extra practice time was associated with better anticipation and decision-making; such additional practice tends to be informal play – like Hegerberg playing with her sister – which is most associated with game intelligence.[9] Grit is associated with other psychological traits like conscientiousness, but the most important impact lies in perseverance and consistency of effort.[10]

'It's not always fun to go to training every day,' Hegerberg said. 'Sometimes your motivation is s**t to be honest. But there's something deep inside you that needs to sparkle, and if you lose that sparkle it's harder. I know where I am and I know where I want to go. It makes it very easy then to stand up every morning and to go work.'

Kolisi's description of his own drive echoes her words. 'Sometimes you don't want to get up, get out of bed in the morning, when it's cold in winter. But I have no choice – I have to go.'

Perfectionism of the best

In 2019, academics working in conjunction with UK Sport attempted to find out what differentiated the highest achieving athletes from those who did not reach the pinnacle. The study compared 16 super-elite British athletes who had won multiple medals at major championships with a matched sample of 16 elite athletes who had not won any major medals.[11]

Perfectionism – an intense commitment to a high standard – was shown to be one important differentiator of super-elite from merely elite athletes. Fourteen of the 16 super-elites reported perfectionist tendencies, compared with only five of the 16 elite standard athletes. The best athletes had higher levels of perfectionism and were more likely to be ruthless and selfish in the pursuit of their goals.

Athletes showing more perfectionistic traits tend to accumulate more time in sport-specific activities – everything from individual to coach-led practice – compared to those with lower perfectionistic tendencies.[8] Perfectionistic strivings are, in turn, linked to achieving higher performances. Endorsing the study of British athletes, a study of alpine skiers in the USA found that those with high levels of perfectionism had higher national rankings.[12]

Hegerberg's perfectionism meant that she could not celebrate her achievements properly. Whenever she won a Champions League, 'I would be enjoying it, but I would be moving too fast. The thing that has motivated me for years is to recreate success, and I maybe hurried a bit in that process. I think you need to enjoy the process and the big moments before you're ready to move on. But I think this perfectionism has had a positive effect as well – obviously I've managed to stay on top for some years, because of that philosophy.

'How do you recreate success? I think the mental aspect has everything to do with success. Everyone can work hard, but not everyone can be as strong as possible mentally to get to the top and stay there … Those who stay at the top have an incredible mentality.

'When things go well you can be even harder with yourself and work even more on fine details. If you don't do this, you're going to get a slap in the face one day.'

Hegerberg, like many of the best athletes, appears to be high in what psychologists call task and ego motivation.[13] Athletes high in task motivation use self-referenced criteria to judge success, and feel successful when they have mastered a task, learned something new, or improved their skills. Athletes with high levels of ego motivation use other-referenced criteria and tend to feel competent only when they have outperformed others. The optimal balance between goal and task motivation is athlete specific, though having both a high-ego and low-task motivation may lead to increased risk of burnout.[14]

Kolisi's constant yearning to improve and taste greater success suggests that he is similar. 'You never finish fighting because you know you can always improve. So that's what makes some sportsmen crazy – because they're always looking to improve each and every single time.'

After big victories, 'I am very happy – but then I look where I can be better the next time. Because at the end of the day you want to be a complete athlete, you want to have a complete game – you don't want to have just one or two moments in a game that are good, you want to have a whole game. And even if you do, you're still going to look for more or how you can do a couple of things better. So when you get to a place where you're just happy with your performance, I don't know – I don't want to get there yet. That will have to be my final game.'

What makes a 'super-champion'?

In 2016, a group of scientists compared three groups of athletes across a wide variety of sports. Those classed as super-champions had over 50 international caps or five or more World Championship or Olympic medals. Those termed champions had played in the top division but had fewer than five international caps, or been ranked in the top 40 and won no more than one medal in the World Championship or Olympics. The 'almosts' excelled at youth level but didn't make it beyond the second-tier league in team sports, or win any senior medals in individual sports.[15]

The study found that a positive reaction to failure was critical in explaining the athletes' differing trajectories. Super-champions were adept at using failure and disappointment – like being dropped, being moved away from their favourite position or losing big matches – to learn and drive themselves forward, as two super-champions interviewed anonymously by the study outlined:

I started a lot further back than other girls. So I was always really proud of that, how I'd manage to drag myself up to be a good enough person to be selected. I knew I wasn't as good as everyone else.

Not making that selection, especially after all that work. Several others just said f**k it, but I was never ever going to let them beat me. I just did double everything!

These stories reveal a fundamental psychological trait. 'High achievers seem to have a positive proactive coping and 'learn from it' approach to challenge even before they get started on the rocky road,' Dave Collins, Aine Macnamara and Neil McCarthy write in the paper.

Meanwhile, 'almosts' had a tendency to lament the unfairness of a situation or blame others. They did not seem as committed or as well equipped to deal with failure, as indicated by some comments they gave to the authors.

I loved fighting, but the training was just a chore. I would miss it if I could and always avoided the bits I was s**t at.

The previous year had gone so well … national squad selection, lots of support, then the winter of 2006 everything just blew up. I was suddenly lost … I didn't know where to turn and the support just seemed to evaporate.

It has been suggested that the best athletes are more likely to have experienced traumas early in their life.[11] Yet the study by Collins and colleagues did not find any evidence to support this notion, with super-champions no more likely to have had childhood trauma – like a parental death – than the other two groups.

But one aspect of their childhoods seemed to distinguish super-champions from the other two groups. Those who ultimately became champions more often had slower and bumpier progress. They were still outstanding young athletes, but they were more accustomed to failure, which made them better able to cope when they inevitably experienced a serious setback. The super-champions' experience of failure at an early age appeared to make them better able to adapt to later adversity. Some of the 'almosts' had no such experience – and then floundered when confronting failure for the first time. 'Things came so easily to me,' one recounted. 'I felt no pressure and really agreed when everyone told me "you're a natural".' Such an attitude is seldom conducive to adult success.

'There's a lot of literature to suggest attitude is the thing that makes or breaks champions,' said Collins. 'It's not having the traumas that is the distinguishing factor – the derailments, getting injured or not being selected. It's learning from these incidents that's key.

'Less than 1 per cent of people who achieve at the top level would have just been outstanding all the way through,' he said. 'Ninety-nine per cent of people who have an easier path early have it because they're bigger than the average player or they're more gifted or maybe Mum and Dad paid for extra coaching. What happens is because the ones that fall by the wayside don't experience challenges and more importantly, learn to overcome challenges, all of a sudden they hit a ceiling aged about 18, 19, 20 where everyone's as good as them, as big as them, as driven as them – or maybe even more driven. And now all of a sudden they just can't hack it.'

These observations point to the importance of providing constant challenges for developing athletes – sufficient opportunity to learn from failure. Collins has termed these 'speed bumps'. Moving out of Sunndalsøra to Oslo, the capital, when she was 11 was a particularly formative experience for Hegerberg. 'To challenge yourself as an individual – not only on the football side, but in life in general – you always need to try new things, and maybe stay outside the comfort zone.'

Playing with elder siblings is one way of providing bumps and teaching athletes how to cope with adversity; so is playing with those who are older and more physically developed, and regular exposure to new teams and situations. For girls, playing with boys – as Hegerberg did regularly – can provide a similar benefit. Aged 14, she was picked for a regional boys' team. 'That was a great experience for me, because obviously they were much bigger than me, but I was still capable of playing with them.'

Resilience

In October 2006, 20 seconds into a game away at Reading, Chelsea goalkeeper Petr Čech charged out to intercept a long ball on the left wing. As he attempted to do so, Čech's head thudded into the boot of Stephen Hunt, a Reading attacker. Čech was knocked out. Chillingly, he had to be removed from the field on a stretcher.

Čech was rushed to the Royal Berkshire Hospital. There, the extent of his injury was discovered, and he underwent emergency brain surgery later that night to insert two metal plates in his skull.[16] Čech was left with no memory of the blow. Doctors later said that the blow could have cost him his life.[17]

'For the first time in my life, after the operation, the first few weeks, I was not in control of my body,' Čech recalled. 'My body did what it wanted, and my brain did what it wanted.'

At the time he suffered the blow, Čech was widely regarded as the finest goalkeeper in the Premier League. The previous year, he had set a new record of 1,025 minutes without conceding a Premier League goal.

As Čech undertook gruelling rehabilitation in the weeks ahead, he had a huge scar on his head. When he began training again, he wore a head guard for the first time in his career.

'I had plenty of different issues and challenges ahead of me, but the most important part was listening to the body and to really be precise with everything I was doing – not to overdo things, not to be too cautious – and to find the right balance.

'It was a big challenge. At the same time, in my head, I was ready to do everything to give myself the chance to come back – I wanted to know exactly what I could do at the time to make things improve and to go forward, and with a positive attitude. I knew that if it takes a whole year it would have taken a whole year. Everybody told me it will take me a year to come back. I said OK, I don't care about the timeline.'

Only three months and one week after the blow that could have cost him his life, Čech returned, now in a head guard, to professional football. Immediately, he returned to being one of the world's best goalkeepers, recording eight consecutive clean sheets later that season. Čech would play for another 12 years in the Premier League.

Just as part of what separates the best athletes from the rest is their response to adversity, so elite athletes also tend to respond best to injury. Those who don't reach elite status can bemoan their misfortune when they get injured, as illustrated by the comments of one 'almost' in the study of super-champions, champions and almosts:

> I sort of lost enthusiasm for it because I did not feel like it was – I almost felt let down that I had, especially before the second operation … why was my injury different from anyone else's, how come mine had to be 14 months for the same surgery that someone else had done for three months.

The best athletes are more adept at channelling their disappointment at being injured to create the impetus for personal and sporting growth and develop greater resilience. 'That injury was pretty crucial,' recounted one super-champion. 'It just kicked me where it hurt and I was determined to get back.'

Another study examined psychological resilience in 12 former Olympic champions.[18] Elite athletes were shown to view injuries as obstacles to be overcome rather than irrevocable problems.

Čech's recovery embodies 'sport injury-related growth', said Les Podlog, a scientist at the University of Utah specializing in the psychology of injury. Sport injury-related growth is a state of mind characterized by higher levels of post-injury functioning and performance. Some athletes experience benefits from injury – greater tactical or technical awareness, improved technique, and improved strength and conditioning or flexibility.[19]

'The best athletes can increase their odds of experiencing growth by viewing injury as their new "competitive challenge", using injury as an opportunity to develop their athletic strengths and skills, and by mobilizing their social support network,' Podlog explained. 'By reframing the injury experience as a challenge to be overcome and by applying the same sport-specific skills honed over years of competitive play to one's injury recovery – a strong goal orientation, an ability to effectively manage pain, and a focus on controllable factors – athletes can emerge more robust following injury.'

Čech's return from injury was extraordinary, but it encapsulated elite athletes' resilience in coping with adversity, and the importance of a positive psychological response to setbacks – focusing on the opportunities ahead rather than what has been lost. Positive psychological responses to injury are associated with a higher and faster return to pre-injury level of performance.[20]

While the psychological qualities that the best athletes need are partly genetic, and partly shaped by a child's family and environment in their formative years, they can also be developed later in life.

'I spend every day on mental skills,' Hegerberg explained. 'All the people who manage to stay on the top level are very prepared mentally.' Hegerberg works regularly with a sports psychologist. Working with psychologists on goal setting, emotional control and relaxation can enhance athletes' performances.[21]

Hegerberg uses visualization particularly extensively. Sports psychologists often assist athletes in creating visualization practice sessions, in which they imagine competing in a particular event and what it will feel like. Visualization can enhance performance because it recruits different senses – sight, sound, smell and touch – to build a mental movie of the competitive setting.[22] Visualization can also facilitate skill learning, potentially by engaging the same neural pathways used in the real situation, as well as helping with motivation and relaxation. A study that interviewed seven leading athletes found that all had used psychological strategies like visualization, and tools to control their emotions to deal with the pressure associated with competition.[23]

'The mental aspect is everything to me,' Hegerberg said. 'Being able to perform at the highest level long-term is all about mental preparation.'

How struggling athletes turn it around

Two months into the 2016 Major League Baseball season, Joey Votto, ordinarily one of the very best hitters in the league – he was a former National League Most Valuable Player and had been an All-Star in four consecutive years – was in a rut. He normally had a batting average of over 0.3 runs. But after two months and 52 games of the season, Votto was averaging 0.213 – among the very worst in the league, and 50 per cent down on his normal record.[24] 'You're in the middle of a disaster, and you're like, "holy cow".'

Despite such an abject first third of the season, Votto ended 2016 with the second best average of his career, 0.326. After the All-Star break, Votto averaged 0.408, making him the only man since 2004 to hit 0.400 after the break. By far the worst season of his career became a record-breaking one.

'I was trying to flip the switch all year. I wouldn't say there was one moment. Sport is not really a movie – it's all just do it every day and there's no poignant moment, there's no special moment when a song kicks in and all of a sudden you go. You just keep chipping away at it and at some point you look up and you're like, "Whoa, I'm doing better than I was doing before," but then you have to remind yourself oh that doesn't matter because every single day that stain stays on you, so you've got to keep pushing.'

The metamorphosis of Votto's season illustrated his mental toughness. Mental toughness is the psychological capacity to drive towards a goal, particularly in response to challenging circumstances, explained Daniel Gucciardi, a psychologist from Curtin University in Western Australia. Players with the most mental toughness develop enhanced physiological endurance – their toughness allows them to tolerate more pain without it adversely affecting their performance.[25] Those with such traits adapt better to negative feedback and adversity.[26]

Mental toughness differentiates the best players from the rest. Studies of international and domestic rugby league players,[27, 28] high- and low-skilled bowlers,[29] cricket batters,[3] and high- and low-performing cross-country athletes[30] have all pointed to the same conclusion: the very best athletes tend to be mentally tougher than the rest. 'High levels of mental toughness enable individuals to achieve and sustain high levels of performance because they can optimally direct energy towards their personal goals, maximize congruency between their behaviour and valued goals, and efficiently adapt their thoughts and actions when confronted with stressors,' Gucciardi said.

'It's an odd game sometimes,' Votto reflected. 'You have to be resilient, and you always have to take a step forward. I think about baseball, especially being a hitter, I think about being a zombie – they shoot you in the gut and they take off your leg and then you just keep plodding forward.'

Like Votto, elite athletes tend to be those best at coping with adversity. In doing so, they draw on three main strategies. Problem-oriented coping strategies attempt to alter or manage the situation causing the stress. Emotion-oriented coping methods try to regulate the emotional impact of stressful events. Finally, avoidance coping tries to disengage the athlete mentally or behaviourally from the situation.[31] All three strategies can be effective.

In 2016, Votto appears to have used a combination of problem-oriented strategies – to help his bat swing – and emotion-oriented strategies – to keep himself calm and prevent himself getting too down and making turning his season around even harder. 'There was some technique issues that I was having, some luck issues that I was having – I was hitting the ball reasonably well, I just wasn't finding some holes. And then mentally I was kind of fed up, so I had to dig down deeper and be more competitive with every pitch, and with every at-bat. The game got tougher and I stayed kind of soft – and then it hardened me again.'

Coping strategies can vary by sport. Scientists have reported that professional rugby players use a more problem-oriented strategy,[31] similar to elite youth footballers.[32] In a sample of elite youth golfers, all three strategies were employed.[33]

His dismal start to 2016 galvanized Votto. 'I just remember always feeling like I had to catch up,' he recalled. 'I was so dissatisfied at the end of the year in some ways, because I wanted more, and I should have started off better. But with some distance from it, no doubt about it – it's one of the best achievements of my career, coming back from that.'

Votto showed the mental toughness needed of the best athletes. 'There are times where you just want to quit, but you can't, because if you quit now then you build the habit of quitting, and that's the worst kind of habit in my opinion. I'd rather get a D-minus and give it my all than get a D or an F and try again next test, if that makes sense.

'I just concentrate on what I need to do, what I'm looking for, how I need to feel. That's it. You get nervous sometimes, you feel what you feel, but typically that's the sort of thing that rides itself out or dissipates.'

Asked whether he has endured other similar barren runs, Votto laughed. 'O lord, have mercy. Too many. I most definitely have. I've had quite a few, and that's all part of being a Major League hitter.'

Votto believes that the frustrations of the start of 2016 made him 'stronger'. The next two years, he was selected in the midseason All-Star team. 'I think of myself as being more resilient and mentally tougher. But that was a tough stretch for me. I love those stretches because I do feel like either you wilt or you stand up to the challenge. And on that occasion I stood up.'

Feeling in control

Before each of his seven Wimbledon finals – all of which he won – Pete Sampras was consumed by a simple belief. Whether or not he won on Centre Court would be determined by how well he played, not by his opponent. 'If I took care of my game and my business, I should be OK.

'This is what I need to do – if I do this then I'm going to win. That was my approach to my matches. It wasn't anything else other than that. I had the weapons. If I served better, and moved well, and played my tennis then there wasn't anything that anyone could do. Not to be cocky – that was how I felt.'

The only player who sometimes felt like he 'took the racket out my hands' was Goran Ivanišević, a left-hander with one of the biggest serves in history; even so, Sampras beat Ivanišević in the Wimbledon final in both 1994 and 1998. 'Everyone else that I played throughout my career it was if I served well then the match would be determined by how I played; that's how I looked at it. It was very much a black-and-white approach to my game and my tennis. It wasn't a lot of wriggle room – I knew what I had to do. And if I did it I was going to win.'

Sampras's recollections are revealing. Elite athletes are more likely to perceive that they have greater control over the outcome of any sporting competition – and that the outcome rests more in their hands than that of opponents. This is known as an internal, rather than external, locus of control. An internal locus of control, coupled with high levels of self-confidence, reduces the anxiety athletes experience and how they control the anxiety they do feel.[34, 35] A study in 2015 showed that perceptions of self-control were significantly higher among professional than non-professional soccer players in Norway, suggesting that this belief in control is part of what separates the psychology of elite athletes from less successful ones.[36]

Like Sampras, Jamie Carragher – a footballer who said that his raw physical gifts were 'only average' – felt that the fate of the game was in his hands. 'I always believed if I played well, someone wasn't going to stop me.

'I was never really worried who I was playing against. Yes, I would think about it, and think about who I was coming up against, but I would never go into a game and be really thinking about who I was playing against; it was more about what job I had to do for the team.'

The costs to mental health

The great American sports writer Wright Thompson called his recent anthology *The Cost of These Dreams*. The title is apt: for athletes, reaching the pinnacle of sport often brings with it a profound cost. For all the glory of winning prestigious matches and trophies, there is no evidence of any link between achieving sporting greatness and being happy.

Being an elite baseball player is 'f***ing not even close to fun', Votto said. 'Being a Major League hitter, especially when you're struggling, is an odd experience. It's very lonely and confusing.'

Such is the burden of reaching the top of sport. Many of the traits that push athletes to achieve extraordinary feats can expose them to the risk of mental health problems.

The perfectionism that makes an athlete more likely to become elite can bring unwanted effects. Perfectionists' harsh self-appraisal increases the risk of burnout, overuse injuries, and mental health issues like low self-confidence, anxiety and depression. In one recent study, over 25 per cent of English football academy players reported mild to moderate depressive symptoms; 15 per cent exhibited symptoms suggesting the possibility of major depression.[37] The World

Health Organization found that 7–15 per cent of 18- to 24-year-olds in the UK suffer from depression.[38] So the best child athletes appear to be more likely to suffer from mental health issues, raising concerns about the pressure placed on athletes who are already prone to harsh self-appraisals.

Mental health challenges can be no less arduous at professional level. Many athletes have the technical and physical skills to cope with elite sport, but not the psychology. 'There's hundreds of them,' said Carragher of players with the sporting talent but not the mental attributes to enjoy a long Premier League career. 'The criticism of playing for a top club, the scrutiny – or that thing about as a player, you know, two games a week every week and being questioned, a mark out of 10 in the press. Yeah, there's plenty of players who couldn't handle that.'

Even for those athletes able to endure such scrutiny, the unremitting demands the career places on the player and their family can be a huge burden on their mental health. 'I was very competitive – like to almost a pathological degree,' recalled Marion Bartoli, who won Wimbledon in 2013. 'I couldn't accept losing anything.'

In team sports, training obsessively could be 'alleviation of guilt', said Kumar Sangakkara, who scored 38 Test match centuries. 'You don't want to have any doubt about the work you've done – how hard you've worked, and how ready you are to go perform. Because it does matter to other people. It does matter to me hugely – it does – but it also matters almost equally to another person, because if I score runs it matters in the final equation. So it's almost that kind of mindset – keep pushing, keep pushing, keep pushing … I don't know whether it was all healthy.'

A spate of athletes have spoken vividly about their struggles with mental health in recent years, and studies attest to how prevalent the problems are. In 2015, over one-third of professional men's footballers from Finland, France, Norway, Spain and Sweden suffered from anxiety or depression and a similar number suffered from disturbed sleep.[38] In some environments, the findings are even worse: around 45 per cent of Australian athletes reported experiencing symptoms of at least one of anxiety, depression or distress in 2015.[39]

In a survey in 2018, 61 per cent of US athletes agreed with the statement: 'When I am failing people are less interested.' Travis Tygart, the chief executive of the US Anti-Doping Agency, has said that a 'win-at-all-costs' culture contributed to athletes who 'chose to dope'.[40]

Athletes' desperation to win can lead them to explore using performance-enhancing drugs. As prize money and sponsorship deals get bigger, so do the incentives for coaches and athletes to find ingenious ways to cheat. At the Athletics World Championships in 2011, 0.5 per cent of competitors failed tests. But in an anonymous survey by WADA, only recently published, 30 per cent admitted to using illegal drugs in the year before the competition.[41]

Yet for all their challenges during their playing days, for the best athletes, the time after sport is often the hardest of all. Retirement is routinely described as feeling like a bereavement. Over half of former athletes in the UK have concerns about their mental wellbeing after retirement, the Professional Players' Federation found in 2018.[42] One in two ex-players do not feel in control of their lives within two years of finishing their careers.[43]

Worldwide the findings are no better. In football, 35 per cent of former players have depression and anxiety. Vast swathes of players seem ill-equipped for what follows their playing careers: 40 per cent of former footballers declare bankruptcy within five years of retirement, and a remarkable 33 per cent get divorced within a year of their careers ending.[43] The courage of athletes speaking about mental health in recent years has led to greater awareness of their challenges and improved support systems for players both during and after their careers. But in many sports there remains a pressing need both for more investment to help players and for broader cultural change in addressing mental health issues.[44]

The tragic irony for many athletes is that the very qualities that drive them to extraordinary feats stop them from fully appreciating them. For all that we idolize and envy athletes, in some ways they are the unlucky ones.

A few minutes earlier, Jean Van de Velde had been cruising to a remarkable victory in the British Open – one of the four major championships in golf, and widely considered the most prestigious. Now, he had his feet immersed in water. He had just removed his socks and shoes, seemingly to consider playing the ball from the Barry Burn, the river that runs through the Carnoustie golf course on Scotland's North Sea coast.

'What on earth are you doing? Would somebody kindly go and stop him, give him a large brandy and mop him down,' said the BBC's commentator Peter Alliss.[1] 'This really is beyond a joke now. He's gone gaga.'

For several minutes, Van de Velde considered his options while a bemused crowd watched.

'When I got into the burn three-quarters of the ball was outside of the water,' Van de Velde later recalled.[2] 'I didn't expect the tide to go up. Within 5–10 minutes, the ball was completely submerged. I couldn't hit it out of there.'

Van de Velde took a penalty drop – meaning that he forewent a shot, playing the next shot from near where it had gone into the water.

The 1999 British Open, the 128th ever staged, had developed into one of the most extraordinary in the tournament's rich history. Van de Velde arrived at Carnoustie ranked 152 in the world; he had never even got close to winning a major.[3] Yet he played four days of brilliant golf to set up an imperious position going into the 18th hole on Sunday evening. Van de Velde held a three-shot lead, so could afford to drop two shots on the last hole of the round, a par four, and still lift the Claret Jug. He would become the first Frenchman since 1907 to win the Open. All this history beckoned. Then came 20 minutes that would thrust Van de Velde into sporting infamy.

'Of course you probably get a little tighter at the end, but I was playing well, all at 16 and 17 holes – my nerves were holding,' he later said.[4]

Taking a driver – an aggressive option, given the lead he had, and one that surprised commentators – Van de Velde mis-hit his first shot, striking the ball further to the right than envisaged. Luckily for him, the ball landed safely between a bend in the burn, perilously close to the water. But there, Van de Velde's luck ran out.

His second shot – once again aggressive – was mis-hit and drifted right of where he had intended; freakishly, it bounced back off the railings of the grandstands, and then off the top of a stone wall, before landing 50 yards back in the rough. 'If anyone needs an advisor, he does,' Alliss said on commentary.

Then came the fatal third shot. Trying to hit the ball past the Barry Burn, Van de Velde miscued his shot. It landed in the water.

On the brink of defeat, Van de Velde regained his composure; on his seventh shot, he converted a seven-foot putt to tie the score. Alas, he was merely lengthening his ordeal.

The 45 minutes between the end of the 18th hole and the start of the playoff was 'not enough time to process what happened', Van de Velde recalled.[5] 'And way too much time to put it on the side and move on – straight on, and carry on with the same frame of mind and spirit.'

Van de Velde's very first shot in the playoff was disastrous – he had to take an unplayable, meaning that he lost a shot. Once his defeat was complete, he cried with disappointment.[4]

'I'm gonna have to live with it, not you guys,' Van de Velde said at the end of the Open. He would never win a golf major, and instead would always be the man who lost the sport's biggest prize. 'I was mad, sad, everything combined,' he later said.[5] 'The pressure, I was like … What the hell just happened here?'

'The worst over ever?'

Scott Boswell stood at the start of his bowling run-up, immersed in his own very public hell. It was the final of the Cheltenham and Gloucester Trophy in 2001, which should have been the highlight of Boswell's entire cricket career. Instead, he found himself unable to do what he had been doing his entire life.

'I became so anxious I froze. I couldn't let go. It was a nightmare,' he recalled. 'How can I not be able to run up and bowl, something that I've done for so many years without even thinking about it? How can that happen? What's going on in my brain to stop me doing that, and to make me feel physically sick and anxious and that I can't do something that I've just done so naturally?'

Boswell was an unremarkable fast bowler for Leicestershire. After a man of the match performance in the semi-final, he earned the right to play in the final at a sold-out Lord's Cricket Ground, regarded as the iconic home of cricket. It was the dream of every workaday county cricketer.

Before the final, Boswell had been unsure of his place, after losing form in the three weeks since the semi-final. At 10 o'clock the night before the final, Leicestershire's coach asked to see Boswell. He asked 'whether I was up for it and whether I could manage. So there was a seed put in my head before I actually played'. He was finally told he was playing 45 minutes before the game. Somerset, Leicestershire's opponents, won the toss and chose to bat on a sunny day. Boswell, as one of the opening bowlers, bowled the second over.

'The first couple of balls I felt OK,' he recalled. But from his last ball of the over, Boswell bowled an easy-to-hit short ball – a long hop, in cricket parlance – that was hit for four runs. 'It just didn't come out of the hands right … It just became a little bit stuck.' It signalled trouble ahead.

The next over began with a huge wide. 'I thought oh, Je★★s C★★ist, I've never bowled it that wide before – what's happened there? And that was it. I then bowled another wide, the crowd started to make a bit of noise, I'm thinking crikey. It went down the leg side so I've got one on the off side, one on the leg side, I've overcompensated and I'm thinking wow.'

An over in cricket comprises six balls – that is, six balls which are not considered a no-ball or wide. There are normally only a handful of such deliveries per innings. Boswell's second over in the final lasted 14 balls, as he repeatedly sprayed the ball too wide of the crease on either side. A YouTube video of the over – entitled 'The worst over ever?' – has been watched over 1.5 million times.[6]

Boswell felt like the over would 'absolutely never end'. This was, he admits, a 'choke'.

The science of the choke

Choking is widely described but poorly understood. A choke is a failure to manage anxiety and cope with the demands at a particular moment, leading to a catastrophic drop in performance.[7] As the pressure in a match rises, so can an athlete's anxiety.

Anxiety is a neurophysiological reaction to pressure or stress. It tends to arise during performances that trigger the fear of losing, or the perceived damage to one's standing. The symptoms of anxiety are both psychological – worry and fear – and physiological – like sweaty palms, which Boswell remembers having at Lord's, and increased heart rate. Anxiety uses up attention and working memory, hindering performance.[8]

Athletes find themselves thinking about processes that normally come automatically. This was Boswell's experience in the final. The simple act of bowling a cricket ball, on which his career had been built, seemed alien. 'When your conscious mind doesn't trust your subconscious mind you've got an issue,' he explained. 'When you're in the flow and you're not thinking about it, you just bowl and you're sort of using your subconscious mind – you just trust your skills.'

At Lord's, Boswell 'just didn't trust myself. I didn't trust my action and I didn't trust my skillset, and then when it was put under high pressure it failed.'

When athletes are anxious, they reinvest attention on the technical execution of the skill, those aspects of the movement that have generally become automated – 'paralysis-by-analysis'.[9, 10] Under normal conditions, the prefrontal cortex – an area of the brain located just above the eyes – powers brain activity, so people do not focus attention on the minutiae of how they perform a task. Under pressure, the prefrontal cortex goes into overdrive and effort is reinvested in the step-by-step details of how to perform the task.[11] In these situations, athletes can overthink and explicitly monitor movements that with practice have become automated. The athlete is essentially transported back to an earlier stage of learning when the action was cognitively controlled, inhibiting performance. This concept explains why Boswell, a 26-year-old in his seventh season as a professional cricketer, suddenly found himself unable to bowl straight.

As his second over became more farcical – six of his first eight balls were wides – Boswell recalled the crowd getting 'louder and louder'. To try to make the ordeal stop, Boswell increasingly rushed, taking less and less time before each ball. 'I just remember trying to race through my over to get it completed as quickly as I could, and it just kept going and going.

'Unfortunately I sped things up when pressure got to me, rather than trying to slow it down and take a step back, do the breathing, have a little smile – "It's only a game of cricket, off you go."' Boswell blames no one but himself but he was not helped by his teammates' peculiar reticence to go up to him and chat during his over.

At Lord's, the real problem was Boswell's method was not durable enough under pressure. 'I probably didn't have a bowling process if something ever happened. It was just absolute panic.' Boswell only ever played one more game in professional cricket, bowling one terrible over – including two wides – before being taken out of the attack.

Managing anxiety

Elite athletes are like the rest of us: they feel anxious and it impacts their performance. In the last 30 seconds of tight basketball games, WNBA and NBA players are 5.8 per cent and 3.1 per cent respectively less likely to make a free throw than at other points in the game.[12] When players take free throws in home matches, they are more likely to miss when the crowd is bigger. An extra 6,000 supporters at a game results in an average 10 per cent decrease in successful free throws, though away players are unaffected by the crowd size.[13]

Yet, compared to less proficient opponents, the very best athletes tend to feel less anxious in any given situation. They also channel the anxiety they feel positively. Higher self-confidence better equips athletes to deal with anxiety.[14] Athletes with low confidence view anxiety as detrimental to performance. But those with high confidence tend to perceive anxiety as a sign of being ready for the challenge ahead.[7] As such, they are less likely to choke under pressure.[14]

The best athletes are also more adept at brushing off disappointments during competition. Annika Sörenstam jokes that she never hit a bad shot in her life – 'I don't remember them.' This selective memory helped Sörenstam become one of the best golfers ever. Lesser players could be consumed by their mistakes, but Sörenstam clinically dissected what had happened, then got on to the business of trying to recover her position.

'You've just got to learn how to dissociate – make a quick analysis, boom. Forget about it, move on, don't carry it with you, learn from your mistakes. We all hit bad shots, it's just how do you regain composure?' Those with the greatest mental strength, like Sörenstam, have been shown to be the best at adapting to negative feedback – such as a golf ball hit poorly – and using it to improve their performance.[15]

When the time came to hit another shot, Sörenstam had dispensed with all thoughts of her previous mistake. 'It's about having a positive attitude when you're about to hit a shot and visualize a beautiful seven-iron rather than maybe a shot you hit with a seven-iron that didn't turn out so well.

'You've got to learn how to throw bad shots out and stand over the shot and say, "OK this is the most important shot." I always call it the now shot. The shot you're hitting now is the most important. Ten minutes ago is irrelevant and who knows what's going to happen in another 10 minutes.

'You have to learn how to throw out bad shots. I think that's the key to golf. We all know that the longest distance in the game is between the ears so you have to have a positive mind, you have to stand there and have tension-free golf swings. If you stand there and are worried about everything, it's hard to swing when you're restricted. When I play my best it's free-flowing and relaxed, no tension – just focus and have a target, but you're relaxed and your muscles can perform. There's nothing worse than when you try to do something and it's all tension and pressure and you can't breathe properly.'

Such mental strength enabled Sörenstam to perform even when struggling for fluency. 'It's amazing how strong the mind can be. Let's say you're not hitting the ball well, you can still scramble a score and get it done. Coming down the stretch, the importance of just sticking to your plan and being smart – you can play against people who are playing beautifully, all of a sudden they get a little rattled.'

Sörenstam was renowned for her ability to convert promising positions into victories. Remarkably, she came first in a major 10 times – more than she finished elsewhere in the top ten. 'My mind was probably my 15th club – I valued it a lot and I needed it.'

The best golfers make greater use of positive self-talk, goal setting, and relaxation skills, reporting less worry and less negative thinking.[16] Personality characteristics like hardiness and narcissism can further insulate the best athletes from the ravages of anxiety.[7]

'Of course I felt pressure,' Sörenstam recalled. 'But it was a fun pressure – I wanted to see if I could handle it, so just staying true to myself and believing in myself coming down the stretch. I always felt – who do you want to hit this shot or this putt? I wanted it to be me because I could trust myself.' The stark contrast with Boswell's experience at Lord's – 'I just didn't trust myself' – is instructive.

Sörenstam derived her strength from 'the perseverance I had, the determination, and knowing how many hours I put in. We all know that if it was 16 holes we would have different names on every trophy – it's 18 holes, it's a long way. You've just got to plug along and be there at the end.'

For Sörenstam, this meant sticking to her normal routine – the 24 seconds she liked to take for each shot – as far as possible, fighting her impulse to speed up. Under pressure, golfers approach shots differently, reducing the range of movement for the head of the golf club and applying greater force to the ball, suggesting that they rush.[17] In baseball, pitchers who flounder under pressure seem to rush their foot movements and the way they flex their elbows during pitching.[18]

Athletes weighed down by anxiety also use their eyes less efficiently, in both dynamic and static tasks. When table tennis players are anxious, they spend longer fixating on the ball and less time on their opponent, which may reduce their ability to pick up cues and anticipate what will happen next, forcing them to react to the ball.[19] When tennis players are anxious, they become less effective at picking up contextual information like the sequencing of shots in the rally and the probabilities associated with their opponent playing certain types of shots, which can have a negative effect on anticipation.[20] Other anxiety-induced perceptual deficits include hypervigilance – the 'deer in headlights' phenomenon – a narrowed field of view or tunnel vision, and drawing attention to irrelevant sights. In each of these cases, anxious athletes are likely to miss critical information.

When they rush, athletes tend to make worse decisions. Anxious athletes can act like rash gunslingers, overly risk averse poker players or chickens unable to make a decision.[21] One of Van de Velde's misjudgements on the 18th hole at Carnoustie involved being overly aggressive in his choice of clubs and approach – which commentators remarked on before the event, not merely with the benefit of hindsight.

Maintaining routines under pressure can help prevent such errors. 'Athletes should work with a sports psychologist to design a routine so that every aspect and element has a purpose,' said Chris Janelle, a sports psychologist at the University of Florida. 'The routine should be multifocal – stress resistant, attention focusing, and confidence building. It should also be flexible enough to be implemented as a framework for an entire season, as a pre-game preparatory tool, and as a moment-by-moment, play-by-play pre-shot routine.'

'That's the key – whether it's the first green or the 18th green on a Sunday at the US Open or a Pro Am, I just stick to the same routine,' Sörenstam said. 'By doing that you can deal with the pressure. People think, "People are watching, this putt means this." Or "This is a tough hole", or "It's an easy hole and I really should make it." All these things around you have an effect on how you feel and how you perform. But if you can get less of it into your bubble it makes it a lot easier.'

Frozen to the spot

It was the semi-final of the 1999 Cricket World Cup. One of the most extraordinary games of all time was reaching an excruciatingly tense conclusion.

South Africa needed 214 to beat Australia and reach their first final. If the two teams got exactly the same number of runs – which was unprecedented in World Cup history – Australia would qualify, by virtue of having finished higher in the pool stage.

The last over began with South Africa, down to their final batting pair, needing nine runs to win. On strike was Lance Klusener, in the midst of a stunning run of form that would lead to him winning player of the tournament.

The first two balls of the final over, delivered by Damien Fleming –
one of the shrewdest bowlers at the end of an innings – show-
cased Klusener's belligerence. Klusener crunched both deliveries
for four.

South Africa needed one run from four balls – with Klusener still
on strike. So Allan Donald, South Africa's number 11 – a brilliant fast
bowler but the team's worst batsman – would not need to face a ball.
He just needed to run to the other end to get the run South Africa
needed. In South Africa's changing room, one player had a bottle of
champagne at hand, ready to pop.[22]

This was 'nearly job done', Klusener recalled. 'I said to Al that the
first thing we would like to do is hit the ball for six, shake hands and
walk off, but at the same time if we can scramble a single run somewhere that also needs to be an option for us.

'One good ball and the game is over, or if you didn't take advantage of a single somewhere and then messed it up – there were so
many ifs and buts about it, but that was the plan. If we can get one
somewhere we're going to do that.'

After a protracted wait, Fleming delivered his third ball. Klusener
hit the ball towards a fielder, who had a chance to run out Donald,
who had advanced down the wicket to run before being sent back by
Klusener. South Africa would have been knocked out of the World
Cup had the ball hit the stumps.

'I'd have been out by a couple of feet if it had hit,' Donald later
said.[23] 'Sprawled on the floor, heart pounding, I thought "Thank
God, we've got away with it. We'll be OK now."' Before the next ball,
Donald told Klusener: 'Pick your spot, and hit it out of the park.'[23]

Fleming's fourth ball is cricket's version of Van de Velde's collapse.

Klusener did not time the ball as well as the first two deliveries in
the over, but started to run as soon as he hit the ball. 'That was in my
mind the opportunity to get one.'

The ball before Donald had run when he shouldn't; this time, he
didn't run at all, remaining motionless as Klusener hurtled towards him.
By the time Klusener hared past him, all Donald had managed to do
was drop his bat and look around forlornly. His legs wouldn't move.

'I looked up at Lance, saw him rushing to my end, and so I started
to run,' Donald wrote.[23] 'My legs felt like jelly, as if I wasn't making

any headway at all down to the other end. I tried to get my legs moving properly. It was a dreamlike sequence, almost in slow motion.'

Donald seems to have suffered from paralysis by analysis – a classic symptom of choking. When he finally started to run, he was out by yards. Australia were through to the final.

Stereotype threat: Why teams that choke once are more likely to choke again

Since 1999, South Africa's World Cup eliminations have straddled the full spectrum of sporting farce. In 2003, when they hosted the World Cup, South Africa were eliminated after misreading the required score and, remarkably, being knocked out after a tie once again. In 2011, they were cruising to victory in the quarter-final before a self-inflicted collapse against New Zealand. Four years later, South Africa missed several catches or run-outs before losing an epic semi-final against New Zealand.

The South Africa men's team have played in 19 global tournaments – the World Cup, the Champions Trophy or the Twenty20 World Cup – since that fateful day in 1999. Although consistently one of the leading cricket nations in this time, South Africa haven't reached a final. They have reached eight semi-finals – and lost every single one.

This litany of failures invites the question: when Donald was run out, was he paving the way for a whole era of South African World Cup failure? Did the run out not merely scupper South Africa's golden chance in 1999 but burden future generations of players?

Stereotype threat is the idea that when a negative image becomes associated with a group it takes on a life of its own, and the outcome and behaviours are more likely to be repeated. In a classic study, scientists asked male and female students to take an arithmetic test. Some students were told that males and females performed equally well on the test; the others were told that males performed better. When the scientists told the females that women performed equally well as men, they subsequently performed as well as males on the test. When females were told that women tended to perform worse, they performed worse than males on the test.[24] Being made aware of the stereotype seemed to impact whether participants would adhere to it or not.

Stereotype threat can permeate sport, too. It can affect 'any situation where you have the possibility or worry that people might judge you based on your inclusion in a certain group – that could be race, that could be gender, that could be the team you play on,' said Sian Beilock, the author of *Choke*.[10] 'Anytime you have the possibility of being analysed or evaluated or judged based on your membership of a group, that can create these anxieties that can lead to choking.'

In both sport and life, past failure can make future failure more likely. Since 1999, South African cricketers have lugged stereotype threat around with them, like an unwanted piece of oversized baggage, from one major tournament to the next.

South Africa's players have grown more anxious whenever the 'c' word is mentioned – but that doesn't mean they can escape it. 'We did choke,' South Africa's head coach Gary Kirsten admitted after a terrible performance in the 2013 Champions Trophy semi-final. He called the legacy of previous failures 'a dark mist that hangs over South African cricket in knockout events'.[25]

How to beat stereotype threat

As a South African cricket fan or – until the 2018 World Cup – an England football fan scarred by penalty shoot-outs could attest, failure seems to beget more failure. Every choke, real or perceived, creates more baggage the next time the team is thrust into the same position, making the hurdle even more overwhelming.

Yet people said the same of the All Blacks who, for all their brilliance between tournaments, became masters of floundering in the Rugby Union World Cup. After New Zealand's shock defeat to France in the quarterfinals in 2007, the All Blacks had not won the World Cup since 1987. In their defeats, they had lamented everything from refereeing mistakes to food poisoning.

'No longer can they dismiss the "choker" taunts – time after time the All Blacks redefine the term at World Cups,' a journalist wrote in the *Daily Telegraph*.[26] 'When the lights go down and it comes to showtime, New Zealand suffer horribly from stage fright.'

New Zealand won the next two Rugby World Cups. So while choking can be self-perpetuating, athletes' abilities under pressure can be improved. The cycle can be broken.

A multitude of techniques can improve performance under pressure. While some athletes are imbued with better psychological characteristics from birth, these are not immutable.[27] Interventions designed to increase mental toughness can improve athletes' performances.[28]

The more players practise, the more automated aspects of their movement become, helping athletes to manage anxiety and heighten attentional focus.[29] Maintaining pre-performance routines, as Sörenstam did, makes players more robust under pressure. Coaching designed to help players think independently, rather than being told what to do, helps develop implicit rather than explicit knowledge and gives players the best chance of avoiding choking.[30]

'If you're more explicit in how you acquire skills, you're potentially more likely to break down under pressure,' observed Phil Kenyon, a leading putting coach who has worked with major championship winners including Rory McIlroy, Justin Rose and Henrik Stenson. 'I try and encourage implicit learning, giving them a better chance of being able to handle things under pressure.'

It is often said that nothing in training can exactly replicate the pressures of the biggest moments in matches. Yet even if that is true, more pressurized training can help athletes cope with pressure on the field.

Whether preparing for public speaking or a big sports match, 'one of the really important things is to practise under the kind of conditions that you're going to perform,' Beilock said. 'There's often a lack of attention given to practising in high-pressure situations to get used to what you're going to perform. We know if you can do that you have the likelihood of being inoculated from choking.

'We know that students get better at taking tests when they take real-time practice tests – it's all about closing that gap between how you practise and how you perform.' There is, she said, no reason why the same principle would not apply to elite athletes.

A study of British national team badminton players put Beilock's ideas to the test. Players were divided into three groups: high-anxiety training – players were filmed when practising and told that national coaches would evaluate their performance; low-anxiety training, with no filming or coach evaluation; and a control group, who trained as normal. Before and after training, players had to anticipate serves from video and on the court. After training, players who had undergone high-anxiety training showed the greatest accuracy of judgement using a film-based test. Most importantly, these gains translated into better results in games – so the high-anxiety training made players better.[31]

Boswell now works as a well-regarded cricket coach for a club and school. His methods lean upon his own experiences of choking – and how to give players the capacity to hold up in the most pressurized moments.

His coaching sessions are divided into green – low pressure, with lots of coaching; yellow – with a bit more pressure; and red 'where they're under pressure, and there's a consequence at the end'. The sessions aim to put players 'under the same sort of scenarios that they're going to have when it comes to a match'.

He does not believe there is anything inevitable about choking – and that everyone can practise in a way that makes them less likely to choke. 'Could I have dealt with that differently if I was ever in that situation? Could I have had methods to slow myself down? I think I could.'

Boswell wants to stop others going through what he did. 'My mental and physical side just basically crumbled in front of God knows how many people watching live on television … I've only watched it once – and then not all the way through. But I watched about five or six balls and just thought "That's a car crash."'

'In the clutch': The Miracle of Medinah

Near the end of the middle Saturday of the 2012 Ryder Cup in Medinah, Europe trailed the USA 10–4. The USA needed just 4.5 of the 14 points still up for grabs to regain the Ryder Cup; Europe needed 10.5 of the 14 to win.

When Europe went 10–4 down, Ian Poulter was playing in one of the two afternoon four-balls still going on. 'When you look at the board and the first two matches of that afternoon session were red [the US team's colour], it was quite easy to see what the outcome was,' he recalled.

Poulter and his partner, Rory McIlroy, were behind in their four-ball. So were the other European pair, Sergio Garcia and Luke Donald. That meant Europe was on course to go 12–4 down at the end of the second day.

'As bad as it felt you knew that there's still a glimmer of chance – there's still two matches on the course,' Poulter remembered. 'Potentially it was looking like we were going to go 12–4 – which would have been catastrophic, and it would have been all done. But you have to still think in the back of your mind that you've got an opportunity if you can turn those two matches around, if you can get in at 10–6. It's been done before from 10–6.

'If we win the first four matches, all of a sudden we're all square. So that is all a process of telling yourself that that's a chance, there's a process of pride that kicks in that doesn't allow you to be beaten in that match, and you take yourself to a place where you haven't been taken before.'

Poulter was not used to Ryder Cup failure. In 2010, he earned the nickname 'The Postman' – because he always delivered points. Since making his debut in 2004, Poulter had won 10 points from 13 games, including six victories in a row by the time of his four-ball in Medinah.

After 12 holes, Poulter and McIlroy were two shots down in their four-ball: 'It was looking miserable.' Yet the very desperation of the situation – in the match and the Ryder Cup alike – drove Poulter on.

With even a draw of little use to Europe, Poulter and McIlroy had to attack relentlessly. After McIlroy birdied the 13th hole to cut the deficit to one hole, Poulter – with his eyes bulging – reeled off five consecutive birdies, in one of the most extraordinary individual passages of play in Ryder Cup history.[32]

'Finding yourself in that frame of mind is something which doesn't happen very often. And when you take yourself to that place you're able to deliver and turn matches around and execute shots one after another.

'I don't know if we'd have been three up in the match whether we'd have played any different. So it's one of those questions, how do you know how you would have played if you were three up? Would we have birdied the last six holes? I'm not sure. The fact of the matter was we had to be aggressive. We had to win that match. They birdied the par five, we had to birdie the par five. We had to control the match, we had to birdie the par four 16th – which they didn't do. So again, it was extremely simple in what it was we had to do – extremely simple. We had to win the match, we had to birdie every hole.'

As dusk fell over Medinah, Poulter secured a one-shot victory with a remarkable 15-foot putt on the 18th hole, celebrated by a roar of delight and a scream of 'Come on'. From being on the brink, Europe were revived.[33]

'When Poults gets that look in his eyes, especially the week of the Ryder Cup, it's really impressive,' his partner McIlroy said after the four-ball victory.[32] 'He just gets that look in his eye, especially when he makes one of those big putts, and he's fist pumping, and he'll just look right through you.'

Instead of trailing 12–4, Europe trailed only 10–6. It remained a grim position – only one team in Ryder Cup history had recovered such a deficit on the final day – but there was a different complexion to the tie. Poulter felt 'full of adrenaline, feeling we've got the opportunity now, we've got the chance', as he celebrated his putt.

'Great things happen in those moments. There were a lot of good shots executed all within a period of six holes, and it stemmed a level of motivation for the team. There was a big wave of momentum.'

A few hours earlier, Europe feared they had lost the Ryder Cup. Now, Europe were 'able to go to sleep on a high with winning the last two matches, having a team that now feel energized to go out to have an opportunity to win'.

The team also sensed a change in the US mood. 'They were extremely jovial and joyous on Saturday when they were 10–4 up. And momentum started to change, all of a sudden the pressure gets loaded off us and gets put back on them.'

Poulter, and Europe, took their form at the end of Saturday into Sunday. 'We have to win our matches, otherwise we lose the Ryder Cup. So we start to load the pressure on, we start to front-load the singles.'

Early in his match, Poulter struggled, going two shots down after four holes. Yet he still 'knew I'd win my point', Poulter later said.[34] 'It's a weird feeling when you're in the zone and all that mayhem is going on around you and you find that you are entirely focused on the shot, or the putt. All this adrenaline was flowing and I was thinking to myself: "There's no way I'm losing this."'

What Poulter described is called a 'clutch state'. Clutch states occur when athletes under pressure or 'in the clutch' are able to summon up whatever is necessary to succeed, to perform well, and perhaps change the outcome of the game. Flow states – which are similar but not identical – are when a harmonious state exists between intense focus and absorption in the event, to the exclusion of irrelevant emotions and thoughts, creating a sense that everything is coming together or clicking into place. Athletes with high mental toughness are more likely to experience flow and clutch states than those classed as less mentally tough.[35, 36]

'You don't think about it,' Poulter said. 'You don't have to think about it. You just go out and do your job. And you know that the more blue [the European team's colour] you put on the board, the more pressure you're loading on the team that technically won the Ryder Cup on Saturday, at some stage, to a team that's potentially going to lose one, so we're not under pressure and they become under immense pressure.'

Their fantastic record means that the European team in the Ryder Cup may benefit from stereotype lift[37] – the opposite of stereotype threat. 'You can get a boost of confidence from knowing that your team always wins,' Beilock explained. 'Anything that helps you focus on why you should succeed rather than why you should fail can be powerful.'

This has been Poulter's experience in the Ryder Cup: previous victories in the competition have galvanized him to perform better.

'My record in the Ryder Cup has been pretty good, so it certainly gives me a lift, it gives me a boost, focuses my mind to the task in front. And it's extremely simple, but it's win my match. So if I win my match I put a point on the board.

'It's always useful to know you've got what it takes to win … We know we've been able to turn matches around, we know we're strong in certain formats, and obviously that's definitely a confidence boost.

'We really need to do our job to the best of our abilities to be able to have a chance to win. And it's something as a European you're proud of that, we've been able to do that very well in the last 20 years.'

At 5.16 p.m. local time, Martin Kaymer calmly putted to win Europe's 14th point – retaining the Ryder Cup and sparking champagne-fuelled delirium. A few minutes later, Tiger Woods missed a straightforward putt that would have squared the tie 14–14; instead, Europe won 14.5–13.5, not just retaining the Cup but winning the tie outright. Blue had triumphed over red. The 'Miracle of Medinah' was complete.

14
How to lead

How players can inspire their teams to greatness

'There are hundreds, maybe thousands of ways to impact a game and your teammates. As long as you're doing positive actions to create just a little bit of a surplus somewhere, you are pushing your team – albeit in a small way – towards victory.'

Shane Battier, two-time NBA title winner, winner of the
NBA teammate of the year in 2014

Thirty-two minutes into the 2019 Rugby World Cup final, England were camped on the South African try line, needing just one final push to score the first try of the final. After a fiercely contested maul, the ball was passed to Billy Vunipola, England's most powerful player, who had only to make a metre of ground to score.

Before Vunipola received the ball, Siya Kolisi, South Africa's captain, crouched down low so that he was in the ideal position to make a tackle. As soon as Vunipola got the ball, Kolisi advanced on him, bringing him to ground with a pinpoint tackle that left Kolisi at the bottom of a group of players.

To Kolisi, this is a microcosm of what good leadership entails: being completely selfless in doing what the team needs. 'That's where you gain respect, when they see you finished but you keep on pushing because you're not only playing for yourself. There's a greater cause, there's so many other people relying on you.'

Kolisi's tackle came during a spell of extraordinary South African defence. England had 25 phases of attack, but were still unable to get over the try line. 'You start to believe more. Each set play that you win, each small victory.'

Eventually, England accepted a penalty – just three points, rather than the seven for a converted try. Kolisi's tackle was the closest that England came to scoring a try all day. In the final, Kolisi attempted 13 tackles, the third most of any player from either side. He was successful every time.[1]

Not quite 18 months earlier, Kolisi had been appointed captain of the South African national rugby team. He inherited a team in a mess. South Africa had suffered a humiliating 57–0 loss to New Zealand the previous September, and had recently slipped to seventh in the World Rugby rankings, an all-time low.

In a country in which sport and race have always been intertwined, Kolisi became the first black captain in the 126-year history of South African international rugby. He knew the enormity of his appointment, but also knew that it could not detract from his performances. 'It was just an honour to be captain. All the pressure was making sure that I perform – that was all I was focusing on.'

Kolisi is an undemonstrative leader. He leads by taking care of his own performance, and in doing so setting an example for the selfless rugby that he wants to play. 'The hardest pressure I feel is from myself,' he explained.

'I just have to play and show my teammates by the way I play, not by my words. Everybody can talk and say stuff, but if you don't show it on the field it means nothing.'

Kolisi's approach aims to make playing easier for his teammates. 'If someone makes a mistake, I always tell him try and forget and move on.'

Leadership by example

Anyone who observed South Africa's transformation could attest to the value of leadership in sport. Simply put, 'leadership is knowing what needs to be done, what needs to happen to achieve it, and how to influence others to cooperate in the process,'[2] said Stewart Cotterill, a leading expert on leadership in sport. Captains are essential because of how they share team-related knowledge – like tactics – and more specific task-related knowledge, like coordinating defensive roles during matches. But the best leaders go further. By behaving like a role model and demonstrating a good work ethic, they set an example for their teammates.

Captains who control their emotions and remain positive during the game display crucial motivational leadership behaviours; leaders can significantly impact teammates' confidence and their identification with the team. Successful leaders positively impact on team cohesion, athlete satisfaction, team identification, team confidence and the motivational climate.[3] How closely teammates feel connected to their leaders has been shown to be the most important factor in a player's leadership quality.[4]

In the most successful teams, leadership is not confined to the notional captain. Four main leadership roles have been identified: the task leader, who provides tactical instructions to teammates; the motivational leader, the greatest motivator on the field; the social leader, who cultivates a good team atmosphere off the field; and the external leader, who handles communication with club management, media and sponsors.[4] One athlete rarely fulfils all four roles, and nor should they: the number of different leaders in the team is positively correlated with team confidence, team identification and team ranking. Leadership should not just be centred on who wears the armband.

This is Kolisi's view, too. 'I don't talk about everything – each guy has a role in each department,' Kolisi explained. 'Every leader has to be able to follow and to serve.

'My leadership skills were making sure I helped the other leaders around me. I believe that I don't know everything, and some people are better than me at some stuff, and I make use of that – I believe in shared leadership.' This meant listening to other players, and giving them a platform to show their own leadership.

Like South Africa in the Rugby World Cup, successful teams tend to have several players beyond the captain who perform informal leadership roles. A study across nine different team sports found that only 1 per cent of players said that their team captain was the best leader on all four leadership roles – task, motivational, social and external. In 44 per cent of teams, the captain was not perceived as the best leader on any of the four leadership roles on or off the field.[4] Leadership is shared within the team: the coach, the team, the captain and the informal leaders together take the lead on different leadership roles.[2]

Captains must also be strong-willed and willing to take hard decisions when necessary. Five months before the World Cup final, Kolisi was captaining the South African domestic team the Stormers against the Crusaders, the New Zealand side who have long dominated the Super Rugby competition. At the very end of the game, the Stormers won a penalty. If they scored from a kick, they would draw 19–19; if they opted to run and managed to score a try, they would win. The romantic option would have been to go for the try – but 'nobody scored a mauling try against them I think in three years'.

With the crowd urging the team to boot the ball out for a lineout, and then go for a try and the chance to win, Kolisi took it upon himself to decide that the Stormers should actually kick for three points. 'My coach didn't want us to do that, but I took the ball and I said stuff them this is what we're doing – because I knew it was the best option.

'I just said OK, I've made a decision. We went for the posts and we drew the game. After the game the coach realized that was the best decision at the time.'

The decision to kick was lambasted. 'If ever you wanted to gauge whether the Stormers are an ambitious team or not, you just had to evaluate their decision-making with seconds to go against the Crusaders,' wrote the South African website IOL.[5]

Kolisi did not take heed: his actions were governed by what he thought was right for the team, not what was expedient. 'That was one of my favourite moments as a captain.'

In the days before the World Cup final, Kolisi remained true to himself. 'I never gave talks. I didn't need to. I mean, on this level, if you need motivation it's already too late − you should be motivated enough. I mean, who needs to be motivated for a World Cup final?

'Our coach spoke to us, and he reminded us once again why we were doing what we were doing.' The national team was 'the only people that could get South Africans to smile'. Before the game, Kolisi recalled hoping that a victory 'can maybe make people agree a bit and see eye-to-eye'.

When he got onto the pitch, Kolisi had a simple thought. 'These are the days we dream about, and when you get that opportunity you've got to reach up. I love that. That's when I want to test myself − when I'm uncomfortable. It's really tough, you know, you've got 20 million people behind you looking at you and just can't wait to do what you do best.'

After a player kicked the ball out to seal South Africa's victory, Kolisi ran to embrace a teammate and fell to his knees in celebration. Even in his live interview in the immediate aftermath, he used his platform to try to do wider good, pleading for national unity:

> The people of South Africa have gotten behind us and we are so grateful.
>
> We have so many problems in our country, but to have a team like this … We know we come from different backgrounds, different races, and we came together with one goal to achieve.
>
> I really hope that we've done that for South Africa, to show that we can pull together if we want to work together and achieve something.[6]

When Kolisi lifted the Webb Ellis Cup aloft in Yokohama, the moment rivalled Nelson Mandela handing Francois Pienaar the World Cup trophy when South Africa won as hosts in 1995. 'It was one of the best feelings ever to have those people around me, my teammates who know exactly what we all had to go through. From losing 57–0 against New Zealand, losing against Italy, losing against teams that we would never lose to in the past, and people not coming to our games in the stadiums – to 18 months with the new coach and going to win the World Cup.'

Best for the individual, or best for the team?

In team sports, the incentives of the player and their team do not always align. What seems best for an individual player might not be what is best for the team, if a teammate is in a better position.

This paradox is perhaps starkest in basketball. Historically, stardom – and the biggest pay packets – have flowed to those who score the most points, as one double NBA champion explained:

> If I wanted to maximize my earning potential as a basketball player, I would shoot the ball every single time I touched it, because there's a correlation between people who score points and the amount of money they get paid. Right? But we all know that if I took every shot every time I touched the ball, that is not a winning formula, and in fact we probably would fail to win very many games. In sports like basketball there's a delicate balance between doing what's best for you and doing what's best for the team.

That player is Shane Battier. When the NBA created a teammate of the year award in 2013, Battier came second in the first year and then won the award the following year, his final season. Uniquely, Battier has been involved in two of the four longest winning streaks in NBA history – 22 games with the Houston Rockets in 2008, and 27 with Miami Heat in 2013.[7] A team was better with Battier on it. The writer Michael Lewis christened him 'The No-Stats All-Star'.[8]

'He's probably the No. 1 smartest basketball player and person I've been around,' gushed LeBron James, one of the all-time greatest NBA players and a teammate when Miami Heat won consecutive titles. 'He knows everything.' Another teammate, Joel Anthony, described Battier's basketball IQ as 'off the charts'.[9]

While Battier was captain at times during his career, he did not need the armband to think of the team. Most successful teams have players that fill different roles – as energizers, team players and mentors – and whose actions lift their teammates. 'Informal roles provide an important shadow structure to those roles that are explicitly assigned to players,' explained Mark Eys, a researcher at Wilfrid Laurier University in Canada who studies group dynamics in sport. 'Players can fill in important gaps or supplement the formal structure without being told to do so. They just naturally arise within the team but are critical to team functioning and cohesion.'

This was true of Battier, ever since he was six or seven. 'I learned the best way for me to be effective was to be the best teammate I could be,' he recalled. 'When my friends on the playground – in soccer or basketball or baseball – won the games and I was a part of their success, people wanted me around.'

Battier learned the essential kernel of wisdom that sustained a fantastic 14-year career. 'Being a great teammate is paramount, and it was that attitude that kept with me throughout my entire basketball career, to the day I retired from the NBA. It was about what can I do to make this team successful? I knew that if my team had success I would be recognized. I knew it didn't work the other way around.

'I certainly wasn't the most athletic player on the court – there are people probably more skilled and more athletic. But I was really adept at executing game plans and limiting mistakes. And that's a really important part of winning.'

Most of a sports team, like an iceberg, lies unseen to the outside world: in training sessions and meetings far away from the games. It is here, Battier believes, that the cohesion great teams need is harnessed.

'The secret to cohesion is sacrifice, and you have to have a few catalysts – a few catalysts that light the pathway for cohesion and success. If you look at any great team, any great dynastic team, any great championship team, you usually have one or two guys, or ladies, who set the tone. These players are early to practice, care about the team, care about their teammates, put the work in, aren't afraid to be criticized – and that has a trickle-down effect on everybody else. If you look at the poor teams, the top players, the most influential players, may not take coaching well, or criticism well – they're lazy, they don't put in the extra work, they don't care about the team's success, and guess what? That trickles down to everybody else.'

This view is supported by research that examined the link between team cohesion and performance across 46 different studies.[10] The authors noted that groups with more task and social cohesion tended to perform better. The skill level of the team does not impact on the importance of cohesion: more cohesive teams are more successful at all levels of sport, not just elite level.

Task cohesion 'refers to a group's tendency to stick together and remain united in pursuit of instrumental objectives, like winning a championship,' explained David Eccles, a sports psychologist from Florida State University. 'Social cohesion relates to the satisfaction of a team's members with the social dynamics of the group. The relationship between cohesion and performance works both ways; teams that are more successful become more cohesive.' This finding suggests there is truth in former Tottenham and Barcelona forward Steve Archibald's aphorism – 'Team spirit is an illusion glimpsed in the aftermath of victory.'

Getting on personally with teammates is not a precondition for success; less socially cohesive teams can have high task cohesion. Andy Cole and Teddy Sheringham barely spoke throughout their four years playing together for Manchester United, yet averaged more than a goal every 90 minutes between them when playing together. Both were instrumental in the club's treble in 1999.[11] 'People wonder how on earth we could function like that,' Cole later remarked. 'Gary Pallister [a former teammate] once said to me, "I know you don't speak to Teddy and he doesn't speak to you, but at least you play well together." We did.'[11] Cole and Sheringham may have lacked any social cohesion, but they were such smart and skilled players they could still work together on the field.

A seminal study on team cohesion in sport examined the relationship between cohesion and team success in elite university basketball and club-level soccer teams in the USA.[13] A strong correlation was found between cohesion and success. but the authors reported that the strongest predictor of a team's winning percentage across the season was the average score for cohesion when aggregated across the entire team, rather than each individual's score per se; a low score between two or more players may not reduce the overall group's sense of cohesion to any noticeable degree. Overall, a team's level of cohesion links to the group's self-confidence and its perceptions of the chance of winning matches.

So not all members of a team have to get on; some clashes between individuals can increase cohesion in the long term if it releases tension.[13] But general agreement within a team on behaviours expected on and off the field leads to the development of shared group norms – what Battier identified as being early to practice, caring about their teammates, putting extensive work in, and not shirking criticism.

Team mental models relate to the shared knowledge that each member brings to the team. These models provide rules and guidelines for decision-making, coordination, communication and teamwork – they include shared knowledge of tactics and contingency plans for what to do in different situations. These models may function across a team, across units – like defence or attack – or across collections of players in specific situations; for example, central defenders need to share knowledge with their fellow centre-backs and with the whole defence.[14]

Battier's commitment to his teammates even extended to giving new players financial advice. Yet, for all his impact away from the court, Battier's greatest contribution was during games. He was renowned for his positional awareness, his penchant for getting back and supporting a player in need or diverting opponents to create space for a teammate. While his individual statistics were unremarkable, he empowered his team to perform better.

'You cannot allow your teammates to feel like they cannot succeed in any given situation because of you. If everyone has that mentality and everyone does what they're supposed to do, it's amazing how players will rise up to perform,' Battier reflected. 'The dirty secret of sport is no one wants to be an outcast. If everyone is rowing the boat in one direction, you don't want to be the weak link.

'Just being in the right spot, doing my job to the best of my ability, and offering support when I could and still being able to do my job, and doing all the little plays that are often the difference in executing a play and a play not being executed. They're very, very small things, but they all add up, and if you do them consistently and over time you see a difference in the scoreboard, but if you isolated it on one single play you're probably not going to notice anything. It's a lot of small additions to your team, to your team play, over a long period of time that makes the difference.'

Athletes across a wide variety of team sports have been shown to be able to identify structure in the opposition's offensive patterns and then use this to help anticipate what will happen next.[15] 'Being able to understand spatially what the correct spacing is, and where your place in the spacing is, is a very subtle but really important factor in basketball,' Battier explained. 'I really have worked hard to understand who my opponents were in every single game, and memorize their play, so I had a pretty good idea of where everybody was – or at least where they were supposed to be – at all times; it made my job easier. It's like having the answers to the test before you take it.'

No scientists have examined whether the same skills apply when recognizing familiarity in your own team's patterns and predicting the next action – but this seems logical. Over time, players develop extensive knowledge about their teammates' tactics, preferences and tendencies to make certain passes or runs and defend in a certain way.[16]

The team brain

One of Battier's qualities on court was 'to communicate very succinctly – most of the time non-verbally' with teammates. 'It makes a huge difference in how effective you can be.'

The best teams rely less on verbal communication than inferior teams, such is their implicit understanding.[17] Sides with more coherent team mental models have been shown to display greater empathy and understanding during matches – as if, like Battier, they have a team's collective mind, not merely an individual one.[14] Teammates who understand their shared and complementary mental models have less need to communicate verbally in high-pressure situations. A study of the NBA found that the most successful sides 'create a stock of valuable tacit knowledge', which was attributed to playing together longer, becoming more adept at anticipating each other's movements and having greater role clarity. Teams with a collective mind are more likely to thrive.[18]

This is one explanation for Europe's continued dominance over the USA in the Ryder Cup: after the 2018 competition, Europe had won seven of the last nine Ryder Cups. Ian Poulter has been at the heart of those successes, with Europe victorious in five of his six appearances; in 2012, Poulter won all four of his matches during Europe's come-back at Medinah. He offered one simple explanation for why Europe has often seemed more cohesive than the US team: the difference in how players travel to events on the European and US tours.

'In America everyone gets a car, so within that two-year span you never travel from a hotel to a golf course generally with a potential teammate. But in Europe you're sharing courtesy cars with one, two, three other players, or even a bus to get from a hotel to a golf course. Well, when you do that generally you're chatting, you're bonding with potentially another teammate, so even a silly little thing like that all helps in the big picture when two years down the line you're paired up with one of the guys that you generally socialize with ... It comes extremely naturally to us to be able to get along as a team, and because of that we have a huge comfort level – and a team for us is very much a team.'

When teammates use these shared mental models, similar neural activity occurs in each team member's brain. These are called 'hyper-brain networks'.[19] A study of duets playing guitar chords showed that the neural activity pattern in each musician's brain resembled the other more closely when the musical patterns were closely cou-pled.[20, 21] During flight simulations, pilots and co-pilots activate sim-ilar neural structures in their brains, particularly during take-off and landing.[22] For the best team players, their brains are coordinated in a way that allows them to pre-empt each other's actions; it is as if they can read each other's minds.[23]

'It's amazing – when you put the time in, and the repetition in, how instinctive all these things become,' Battier reflected. 'I never had a conscious thought of, "I need to give LeBron the ball on his right hand because he's right-handed", or "I need to stand here because I know that Dwayne Wade may need my help on this play." It's through repetition and the familiarity that you build with your teammates – you just know when they need the ball.'

When non-verbal communication was not adequate, Battier spoke to teammates with simplicity and directness. 'There's not a lot of time for niceties in basketball. Everything has to be short, everything has to be explicit. There's not a lot of time to worry about someone's feelings or whether they get the message in a way that's not offensive. So there's a lot of swearing sometimes, a lot of terse talk. But if both parties understand that we need to talk this way, directly and frankly, to complete the mission and to win the game, it's easy to get beyond the tone and the tenor and maybe the directness of the message.'

The best team players embrace the most mundane jobs. Perhaps the best distillation of Battier's game was one of the least glamorous tasks in basketball: running back on defence. Each time, this act was statistically overwhelmingly likely to have no impact at all. But over the course of a game or a season, it did.

'Running back on defence is never going to be in the highlights reel. It's never going to garner a post-game interview. No one's going to buy my jersey because they say, "You know what? Shane Battier is great running back in transition defence." I knew every time I ran back on defence there was a chance that I would stop the transition break and make a team play out of the half court. Now, once the team is forced to play out of the half court they are significantly less effective than they are in transition – probably by 200 base points. If I do that a few times a game, no one will know the difference, but I may have saved my team a point or two, which is huge, because every point differential on the scoreboard is worth three wins at the end of the year. That's something no one would ever be able to understand, but if you do that enough, and over the course of an 82-game season, that's significant points that you save your team.'

This was Battier's philosophy playing basketball, and the qualities so beloved by his teammates. 'There are hundreds, maybe thousands, of ways to impact a game and impact your teammates. As long as you're doing positive actions to create just a little bit of a surplus somewhere, you are pushing your team – albeit in a small way – towards victory … It's amazing what you can accomplish when no one cares about who gets the credit.'

Communication: the secret of doubles

By the end of 2019, Jamie Murray had won seven Grand Slam doubles titles and been ranked as the men's number-one doubles tennis player. Over this fantastic career, Murray has played with over 50 partners, giving him an insight into what separated victorious doubles teams from those who lost.

'Team energy is so important,' he explained. 'Energy and togetherness will get you through a lot of matches. If you're really together and believe in each other and trust each other, that's going to get you through. Whereas if you're playing with someone who you don't know what they're doing or thinking in that moment and maybe you don't have good vibes with and the trust is not there, then you're probably going to lose more of those matches than you'd win.

'You can see when a team kind of falls apart – they maybe stop talking, or they're not bouncing around the court. You just feel it if they sort of tap out or one of them's tapped out, and they lose their way. And it can get away from you quick.'

Being a great doubles player, Murray said, is about 'being able to move well with your partner, be in sync with your partner, and stay in the moment'. An analysis of communication between players in NCAA Division One doubles – the top level of US college doubles – video-taped five female doubles pairs, analysing how communication differed between winning and losing teams.[24] Winning teams spoke twice as much as losing teams and used significantly different communication sequences. Victorious sides not only communicated more, they also communicated differently, speaking more about task-relevant action statements – what they should do in the match, like getting to the net sooner – and being more consistent in their interactions from point to point. More speaking in losing teams was about matters irrelevant to their tasks – including complaining about conditions in the game or their shoes.

'Teammates share knowledge that allows them to coordinate their moves smoothly,' observed Gerson Tenenbaum, a sports psychologist from Florida State University and a co-author of the tennis study. 'When required, they decide upon new manoeuvres that give them an advantage over their opponents. They also encourage each other by using verbal and non-verbal communication. When losing a point or being behind, they plan strategies and motivate each other. By doing so they always remain "in the game".'

The origins of this rapport generally start well away from the court, Murray reflected. 'It's an intense relationship. You're on the same schedule with that person every day – you're waking up the same time, you're going for breakfast, you get in the car to the courts together, you're practising together, you're having lunch together, then you're waiting together for the match, and then obviously you've already spent like eight hours with that person or so. And you've got to put yourself in a stressful environment with them, to try to win the match. It's a lot easier to go through those tough situations with someone that you actually enjoy spending time with.

'The chemistry is important, obviously. I guess the more openness you have in your relationship the better – it's easier to sit down and discuss things when things are not maybe going as well.'

The smaller the number of players in a team, the more important team cohesion has been shown to be to success, perhaps because any set of players have to spend more time together.[10]

'The more battles you go through, I guess the more you learn about each other, and the team gets stronger,' Murray reflected. Several researchers have shown that cohesion is developed through mutual sharing of ideas and open discussions.[25, 26]

'The more you play with that person, you obviously start to understand how they like to do things in certain situations – what shots they like to play, what serves they like to hit, at break point down or something, for example. And you just build up that trust over time, whereas obviously if you're just pitching up and playing with a random person for that one week it's a totally different mindset.'

In doubles tennis and beyond, team cohesion can imbue players with greater self-belief. A study in 2015 found that cohesive teams gave themselves a higher chance of winning than less cohesive sides, lowering the pre-match anxiety of the more cohesive teams.[27]

Many teams are not really defeated by their opponents but by themselves. 'That happens every week, you know? People lose their energy, they lose their togetherness, and that's the main reason that they win or lose.'

Playing as one

In 2019, the Golden State Warriors became the first NBA team in 52 seasons to make five consecutive Championship finals. While Golden State had a side brimming with talent, talent alone is not enough – especially in US sports leagues, which are set up to ensure a level of competitive balance. Building a culture that prioritized the group, not the individuals, was at the core of Golden State's achievement, reflected head coach Steve Kerr.[28]

'We've had great talent, but it's talent that fits together well,' Kerr said. 'Basketball is a game of five players having to play as one, and our star players all complement one another – they all do different things, they make each other better, a rare occurrence when you put all-star players together. Sometimes they overlap and they get in each other's way, but not our team.

'It's just the culture that we've built as a group. We have players who take great joy in each other's success, which sets a tone. And we talk all the time about the importance of passing the ball, moving the ball on to the next player. We have so many playmakers that there's no reason for us to try heroic shots. We can just make the simple play over and over again and we're going to get great shots, and our guys enjoy that, and they believe in each other.'

Coaches can drive team cohesion. A study asked male and female athletes across numerous sports to identify coach behaviours that either negatively or positively affected motivation. Inspirational direction, personal relationships and support all increased motivation. Abusive language, inequality, poor communication, player ridicule and hierarchical structure that differentiated players were demotivating and deleterious to team cohesion.[29]

Those coaches found to be adept at promoting team cohesion had several common traits. They teased players. They set team goals. They used motivational speeches to foster unity. They were realistic in describing the challenges they faced against opponents. Crucially, they did not single out players for specific criticism after matches. The coaches tried to instil a culture of winning – or occasionally losing – as a team, not as a collection of individuals. The athletes reported that having an open dialogue with the coach was important, and that social get-togethers helped cohesion.[30]

The final secret ingredient

'What's my legacy?' legendary basketball coach Gregg Popovich once joked. 'Food and wine.' Danny Green, who played under Popovich for eight seasons at the San Antonio Spurs, explained to ESPN the merits of Popovich's famed dinners. 'Dinners help us have a better understanding of each individual person, which brings us closer to each other – and, on the court, understand each other better.'[31]

Famously, after the Spurs suffered an agonizing overtime loss to Miami Heat in game six of the NBA finals in 2013 – when they would have sealed the title with a win – Popovich still organized for the team to go out for dinner together immediately after the game. They came agonizingly close to winning game seven two nights later, and then thrashed Miami 4–1 in the NBA finals the following year.

'I was friends with every single teammate I ever had in my [time] with the Spurs,' one former Popovich player told ESPN.[31] 'That might sound far-fetched, but it's true. Those team meals were one of the biggest reasons why. To take the time to slow down and truly dine with someone in this day and age – I'm talking a two- or three-hour dinner – you naturally connect on a different level than just on the court or in the locker room. It seems like a pretty obvious way to build team chemistry, but the tricky part is getting everyone to buy in and actually want to go.'

The lessons of building team cohesion through culinary outings has been observed by Kerr, who has made a point of taking Golden State out for regular dinners. The idea, he has said, is from his time playing for Popovich.[32]

Such an approach does not always work. Eccles showed that some players find attempts to build team cohesion by requiring them to attend social events reduced opportunities for downtime away from the sport and negatively impact feelings of autonomy and self-control. In his paper, 'one athlete referred to these weekly "bonding" nights with his teammates as "f★★★ing pasta bonding night"'.[33]

'Cohesion depends upon the way the players see each other, the way the players interact with each other, the players developing respect for each other and believing that they're all on the same page,' explained Roy Hodgson, the former England manager. Sometimes, a manager must 'encourage certain players to be less selfish' during games – and, occasionally, even do the opposite.

'You won't find many players at the level that I'm working at who will say to you, "I do not believe in teamwork", or "I do not believe that teamwork is important, I think I am more important than the team." You won't find many that say it, but of course there will always be some who unfortunately have that in them somewhere, and don't buy as fully into the team concept as others, and that's because we're inevitably dealing with very different individuals.

'To be successful footballers, they need individual success. They need newspaper people to write that they're good players, they need clubs wanting to sign them, get them to sign new contracts, and give them more money because they are so valuable to them. So, the problem with teamwork, in a way it's much more important to the coach and the leader in some ways than it is to the individual player, because the individual player can actually survive bad team-work, whereas the coach and leader can never survive bad teamwork because he is defined by the results.

'That is where the real crux in leadership and coaching lies – making certain that you produce a team that is cohesive, that does understand not only the importance of teamwork but what that actually means on match day. And what it requires of you is sacrifices to make certain that the whole is greater than the sum of the parts.'

It a lesson that, in their different ways, Kolisi, Battier and Murray have long absorbed.

The England men's football team and penalty shoot-outs: they go together like teenagers and acne.

From 1990 to 2012, England were eliminated from the World Cup or European Championship on penalties six times out of ten. They lost six of their first seven shoot-outs in major tournaments – the worst record of any men's national team in the world. With each failure, the dread of shoot-outs increased and, it seemed, the certainty that England would flounder next time a game was decided by whether players could beat a goalkeeper from 12 yards.

And so before the 2018 World Cup, there was an unspoken fear among England fans: the spectre of penalties. Gareth Southgate, England's manager, had missed perhaps the country's most famous penalty of the lot, against Germany at Wembley in the semi-finals of the European Championship in 1996. England's fear of penalties had only intensified since.

'Practising didn't help us too much on this occasion,' England manager Roy Hodgson said after England lost their sixth penalty shoot-out, in 2012. 'You can't reproduce the tired legs. You can't reproduce the pressure. You can't reproduce the nervous tension.'

Before the 2018 World Cup, Southgate and his backroom team took a very different view. Rather than cling to the comfort blanket of penalties being a 'lottery', a familiar refrain of previous England managers,[1] Southgate and his team researched penalties extensively. They scoured football, other sports and science for any clues about how to improve.

England analysed all the research on penalties, interviewing academics about their findings and how they could be used to gain an advantage; they also commissioned their own research. Every member of the squad did psychometric tests to help Southgate compile his list of penalty takers.[2] From March – three months before the World Cup began – players practised taking penalties when they were tired, just as they would after playing extra time.[3] To put extra pressure on themselves, players often told the goalkeeper where they were aiming before shooting, effectively reducing the margin for error. And they practised the walk from the centre circle to the penalty spot, so this would not be a novel feeling during a shoot-out. Everything was done to prepare players for the cauldron of a shoot-out.

Rather than tiptoe around the topic, players were encouraged to discuss penalties, and how they would approach their shots from 12 yards in front of the nation's gaze. 'We speak about pressure, pressure moments, key moments in the game,' said Marcus Rashford, a crucial player for England in the World Cup and since. The team did not try to deny England's traumatic history in penalty shoot-outs, but instead tried to channel it to their advantage.

'For us it was to get rid of people thinking – it's England in a penalty shoot-out, and we're probably not the most confident. So I think as a team we were just determined to put whatever England had done in the past behind us. We believed that we could do something special with that England squad, so we were just focused.'

England's preparations created a novel feeling for the players involved. Before the shoot-out with Colombia in the second round of the World Cup, 'it felt like we were going to win a penalty shoot-out, which probably England teams haven't had for a while', Rashford recalled.

Over the preceding months, England had developed a routine that players could stick to in shoot-outs, to keep the focus on the task at hand, not the consequences if they missed. Before each penalty, Jordan Pickford, England's goalkeeper, handed players the ball. This method aimed to give players as much control as possible over what happened in the seconds before they took their kick.

When Rashford stepped up to take England's second penalty, with England 2–1 down in the shoot-out, 'Picks just gave me the ball – we used that little routine as something to settle us down, so it felt just like how it was when we practised'. Although more than 20 million in the UK and millions more throughout the world were watching, for Rashford 'it was a normal situation'. The routine with Pickford helped normalize a moment that legions of former England players found an ordeal.

And so as Rashford embarked upon his penalty, he was not consumed by fear of failure, just by the task – ordinarily simple enough for such a skilful player – of beating a goalkeeper from 12 yards. He managed to 'just put everything to one side. And at the end of the day it was just a penalty, and if you do what you've been practising then nine times out of 10 you'll score. You just want to be clear on what you're doing.

'Mentally, you need to relax and think about how many times you've scored penalties, and just getting that confident feeling when you're stepping up. So I just try and concentrate on that.

'Doing the actual penalty wasn't as bad as people think – when you're as focused as we were at the time it was almost normal.'

Rashford did his trademark shuffle run-up, and then dispatched the ball emphatically to the bottom right-hand corner. David Ospina, Colombia's goalkeeper, never had a chance. After celebrating, Rashford completed the last bit of his routine – going up to Pickford, wishing him good luck for the next penalty he would face.

A few minutes later, England won their first ever World Cup penalty shoot-out. Pickford – following advice given by England's backroom staff about which way to dive – parried a penalty from Colombia's Carlos Bacca with his left hand after diving to his right. Eric Dier calmly scored the decisive penalty, triggering pandemonium and, for England fans reared on penalty failure, disbelief.

'We did our research, with [Martyn] Margetson [the goalkeeping coach] and the analysis staff,' Pickford explained after the game. 'I had a fair feeling. Falcao was really the only one who didn't go "his" way. But it's about: set; react; and go with power.'[4]

No longer is an agonizing penalty shoot-out defeat the first image that people have when England are mentioned. 'I think right now everyone has a different picture, a different painting in their heads of the England national team,' Rashford said.

For now, at least, the curse had been lifted.

Generations of England teams have clung to the notion that penalty shoot-outs hinge on the luck of the Gods. This is a domain in which there is no rhyme or reason to what happens – except, it seems, that England will lose.

Yet there is more research on how to win penalty shoot-outs than almost any aspect of sport. Scientists have scoured the wreckage of England campaigns past and found that the notion of shoot-outs as unknowable and impervious to analysis is a myth. There are, instead, distinct patterns that help predict who is most likely to win or lose a shoot-out – and make teams more likely to win in the future.

In a curious way, repeating the cliché of penalties as a 'lottery' increased the chances that England would lose. 'You can never recreate on the training ground the circumstances of the shoot-out,'[3] England manager Glenn Hoddle said after losing to Argentina on penalties in the 1998 World Cup, foreshadowing similar comments by his successors. Such a belief amounted to 'self-handicapping', as if England were 'preparing to fail' and getting their excuses in early for doing so, said Sian Beilock from Barnard College in New York. If shoot-outs are a lottery, what is the point in practising? By not practising penalties with the intensity of other skills, England stymied their penalty-taking skills, making a shoot-out seem even more daunting when it did come. A study interviewing those who took penalties in a shoot-out between Netherlands and Sweden in 2004 found that those who thought that the result was more down to luck were more likely to have destructive interpretations of anxiety than those who believed that it was down to skill.[5]

'In history – and this is not just England – teams and coaches avoided penalties to begin with by not talking about them, by not practising them, by trying to pretend that they didn't exist,' said Geir Jordet, an academic considered a leading expert on penalty shoot-outs. 'Then you're in the quarter-final of the World Cup and you have penalties – and you've never talked about it because you were afraid that speaking about it would get into people's heads. And now you're there and they're on their own and they're scared and they haven't received any help. Then you have disaster.'

With penalties, just as in other pressurized moments of sport, those who want it to be over as quickly as possible are more likely to get the wrong result. Southgate himself learned as much in 1996. Before he took his sudden death penalty against Germany, 'All I wanted was the ball: put it on the spot, get it over and done with,' Southgate wrote.[3]

The perils of rushing penalties were demonstrated in a study by Jordet and a team of academics. They analysed 366 penalties to explore the relationship between the time players took and their success in shoot-outs. When players started their run-up less than 1 second after the referee blew the whistle, the success rate was a paltry 58 per cent. Players who took longer than a second scored 80 per cent of the time.[6] Extreme pressure can lead players to 'get it over and done with', like Southgate. When they do so, their performance suffers because their focus is weakened.

In 2018, scientists measured footballers' gaze behaviours before taking penalties. Those who maintained focus on the ball for longer were significantly more likely to score. Successful penalty takers fixated on the ball earlier in the run-up and maintained fixation on the ball for longer after making initial contact with their foot. Longer fixations on the ball – the quiet eye – led to more accurate penalties, with the ball being placed nearer a corner of the goal. Those who missed more often moved their eyes off the ball earlier, towards where they expected the ball to go, before they had even made contact with the ball.[7] This finding replicates those in basketball, golf and rugby union that a longer quiet eye helps athletes perform better.

Taking time

These findings help explain England's appalling history of penalties. Analysis of shoot-outs in major tournaments has shown that players who look like they want to escape miss more often.[8] In 2009, Jordet analysed how long players from different countries took between the referee's whistle and taking their shots. English players took the least time after the whistle – just 0.28 seconds – of any country analysed. Players from Germany, who have the best record of any nation in shoot-outs – in World Cup shoot-outs, they have scored 17 out of 18 penalties, winning four out of four shoot-outs – took 0.64 seconds, over twice as long as English players.[9]

'There's definitely a tendency that players miss more when they take less time,' said Jordet. 'If all they think about is getting out of the situation as soon as possible, their focus is already not on producing the right mechanics to strike the ball – it's on something else. Maybe they only have 60 per cent of their capacity left to execute the technique properly because they're already thinking about the consequences, about how they don't want to be there.'

Before the 2018 World Cup, England were aware of the need to take longer over their penalties. 'There's research to show that English players are quick to the ball when the whistle goes,' the FA's technical director at the time, Dan Ashworth, said before the game against

Colombia.[10] 'You look at the other nations, they take a bit more time. [Cristiano] Ronaldo's self-control [before a penalty] is incredible.'

Historically, England have erred in how they have used their eyes before taking penalties, again suggesting that they want to avoid the situation. When penalty takers are under intense pressure, they tend to maintain a fixed gaze for less time. They move the ball around more, and fixate for shorter periods on the goalkeeper. Jordet's analysis in 2009 found that English penalty takers in shoot-outs avoided the keeper's gaze 56.7 per cent of the time; German penalty takers avoided the keeper's gaze only 29.6 per cent of the time.[9] England players have used 'an avoidance strategy', Jordet said. They try to deal with the stress by either looking away from what's stressful – the goalkeeper or the goal – or rush towards the ball, which would effectively end the penalty as soon as possible, so they could get out of there.' The more players want to get out of there, the worse their results are likely to be.

In 2006, Jamie Carragher scored his penalty against Portugal – but he had taken it before the referee's whistle. He then missed his retake. 'I had to wait until after he blew his whistle. I didn't realize,' Carragher later said. 'I obviously don't take that many.'[11]

The urge to rush can be particularly great when the ball is not placed exactly on the penalty spot, so players must return to the spot to move the ball around, drawing out the whole process. In a shoot-out in the 2002 World Cup second round, Gaizka Mendieta had the chance to send Spain through against the Republic of Ireland.

Mendieta had a long run-up before each penalty. He had placed the ball on the spot and walked to the start of his run-up when he noticed that the ball was not placed cleanly. When the referee blew his whistle, Mendieta smiled and nonchalantly walked back to the penalty spot to reposition the ball before then returning to the start of his run-up and restarting the whole process.

'I put the ball on the spot and the ball moved,' he recalled. 'I walked back to put the ball in the right place. People afterwards in the dressing room told me how could I have been that calm in that moment. You have to follow the routine that you have, that process, before you take it because it all takes care of the actual action.' Mendieta scored the decisive penalty, putting Spain into the quarter-finals.

Routines that hold up under pressure

Often, England have failed to ensure that, even in practice, one penalty replicates another. 'England's penalty practice sessions at the 2006 World Cup seemed to be based on a group of players standing with balls at their feet on the edge of the area, taking a kick whenever there was an opportunity,' Ben Lyttleton recounted in his insightful book *Twelve Yards*.[12] Such haphazard training meant that England did not develop the consistent routines that were a hallmark of the 2018 team. In 2006, players went up alone and picked up the ball from the referee or the opposing keeper, rather than from their own keeper. This all explains how Carragher was not fully aware of the need to wait for the referee's whistle.

The strongest penalty takers have the most durable routines. Mendieta scored 31 out of the 34 kicks in his career, one of the finest records of any penalty taker.[13] All the while, he stuck to exactly the same method – waiting for the goalkeeper to move before slotting the ball into the other corner.

'I had a routine,' Mendieta explained. 'From the moment the penalty is given, if there's any trouble in the box or around the penalty spot stay away from it and focus on taking the penalty and how I'm taking the penalty. Then, from the moment you put the ball on the spot, you take the steps back.

'I always waited for the goalkeeper to move and tried to go the other way. So it was a whole process that helped me to focus … I would run up and look at the goalkeeper rather than the ball and when he moved I would kick the other way – or try to kick the other way. If he didn't move, then I would go one side with pace and quite a heavy touch so he wouldn't reach the ball.'

This is known as a goalkeeper-dependent strategy. Scientists have suggested that a goalkeeper-independent strategy – choosing a side and sticking to it, regardless of the goalkeeper's action – may be better for the majority of players.[14] Whichever method a player adopts, they are best-served sticking to it, especially during the biggest moments – just as Mendieta did when scoring in a penalty shoot-out in the Champions League final in 2001, after earlier scoring a penalty in normal time.

'The process, the penalty, the technique was exactly the same – that wouldn't change from a training session to a Champions League final,' Mendieta explained. This ensured 'you're just focusing on what you had to do rather than thinking I've got millions of people watching'.

When diverging from the norm, players have more scope to think, increasing the risks of it going wrong. Indeed, the greater the pressure in a shoot-out, the worse kickers perform. A study of over 1,000 shoot-outs from 1970 to 2013 by Ignacio Palacios-Huerta, a Spanish economist, showed that the side that takes the first penalty wins 60.6 per cent of the time.[15] Since about 80 per cent of all penalties are scored, the team who go first normally go into the lead, so the side going second must score to keep up – or, from the fifth round of penalties onwards, score just to remain in the tie.

'The psychological pressure of "lagging behind" clearly affects the performance of the team that kicks second,' said Palacios-Huerta; similarly, in chess, he pointed out, the player going first wins 57 per cent of matches that aren't drawn. As the pressure ratchets up in shoot-outs, so the quality of kicks plummets. When scores are level going into the fifth penalties, the team shooting first score 76.2 per cent of kicks – but, should that be scored, the scoring rate for the other team, who now need to score to avoid defeat, falls to 62.5 per cent. Goalkeepers are about as likely to save the penalties; the discrepancy in outcomes is driven by teams who take the second kick being much more likely to miss the target altogether.[15, 16]

For players from teams with a history of losing – like England or the Netherlands – past failure makes future failure more likely. Players from countries that had previously lost penalty shoot-outs are more likely to miss in future shoot-outs for their national teams, even when they had played no part in the previous failures. Those representing countries that have won their past two shoot-outs score 89 per cent of penalties; those from countries that have lost their last two shoot-outs score a paltry 57 per cent of their kicks – and just 46 per cent if they were personally involved in both those shoot-out defeats.[17]

This is stereotype threat at work. 'Of course, you can't help but think about Southgate, Batty, Pearce, Beckham, and Waddle, and all those penalty nightmare misses of old,' Ashley Cole later wrote of England's penalty shoot-out defeat to Portugal in the 2006 World Cup.[9] 'It lurks in your mind somewhere, adding more pressure and a little bit of fear.' Cole didn't take a penalty for England in 2006, but did take one against Italy in Euro 2012. He missed, and England lost. Again.

But just as bad penalty-taking habits can take hold in teams, so can good ones. While penalties are a mano-a-mano contest, there is a strong team dimension to who performs best. Good habits – taking enough time before kicks, maintaining a stronger visual focus on the ball and having a general routine before the penalties, like Pickford handing takers the ball – can spread in teams, making the kickers themselves more likely to score.

So for all that penalties are an individual pursuit, the sides that are most likely to triumph are those that 'have prepared, have a routine as a team', said Jordet, using England in the 2018 World Cup as an emblem of how teams can develop methods more conducive to success. 'The overall aim of the preparation was that they would go into a penalty shoot-out and they would own it – instead of being passive victims.'

Even celebrating together can improve the team's chances of winning. When teams celebrate each penalty scored, it significantly increases their chances of success – infusing teammates with a positive attitude before their kicks. Such behaviours have a negative effect on the opposition – after more assertive celebrations opposing teams are more than twice as likely to miss their next shot.[17]

From observing how teams around the world prepare for penalties, and being interviewed as part of their own penalty kick research, Jordet even suggested that 'The country in the world who is now leading the preparation and the documented deliberate effective approach to penalties is England.'

How to save penalties

On his professional football debut in 1996, Mickael Landreau's team Nantes conceded a penalty. Landreau saved it, securing a draw. 'It was a great memory – it played throughout my career psychologically.'

This set the tone for a remarkable career in which, far more than his 11 caps for France, Landreau became renowned as one of the world's best penalty-savers. That debut save was the first of 39 penalty saves throughout his career. Historical statistics on penalties are patchy, but Landreau's record is among the very best.

'I think it's 50 per cent a lot of work, because there's a lot to analyse – the player, which side he goes, what he changes before striking the ball,' Landreau explained of his method. 'And the next 50 per cent is intuition.'

Landreau described his penalty-saving method as one of 'permanent adaptation'. Sometimes, he would play on the kicker's ego, as when confronting the great Brazilian Ronaldinho.

'His personality made me want to challenge him,' Landreau explained. Landreau deliberately stood near his right-hand post, seemingly leaving the whole of the left side unguarded. But as Ronaldinho stood up, Landreau rushed towards the centre of the goal. Ronaldinho kicked the ball to his right – near where he had originally been standing – and his penalty was saved.

Mostly, though, Landreau followed a more conventional method. 'Before each match I watched the potential penalty kick-takers to see if there were any changes depending on where they were shooting – the way they ran, the moment in the match.'

Unsurprisingly, goalkeepers' chances of saving a penalty have been shown to be much higher if they know the probability of the kick going left or right, based on the penalty taker's tendencies, and it aligns with what actually happens in the match. But there is a risk – the reverse effect is observed if the information relating to the penalty taker's tendencies does not align with what actually happens. So, while using penalty-taker tendencies can have significant advantages, it can come at a substantive price if the penalty taker does not execute the expected outcome.[18] Landreau hedged against this risk: he prepared meticulously but as penalty takers ran up to take their kick, he 'watched a lot of momentum and potential changes'.

There is less than half a second between a ball being kicked firmly from the penalty spot and it crossing the goal line. On average it takes a goalkeeper 200 milliseconds to react, and 350 milliseconds to dive left or right – more time, in other words, than it takes for the ball to reach the goal from 12 yards. If a goalkeeper merely reacts to the kick, and the ball is placed anywhere near either post, their chances of saving the ball are minute. So goalkeepers must anticipate where the kick will be taken, not merely react to it. But they have to do this while not allowing the takers to anticipate where they will move, getting their timing just right. 'It's very important to stay a long time on your feet and don't give the solution to the player – it's very important to dive at the last moment,' Landreau said.

Elite goalkeepers pick up early cues from the penalty taker's approach, the position of their non-kicking leg relative to the kicking leg, and the angle of their hips relative to the goal.[19] When goalkeepers save penalties, they tend to hold a steady fixation in the space between the ball and non-kicking leg for longer, allowing them to extract information from surrounding areas while using peripheral vision to follow the arc of the kicking leg.[20] Goalkeepers use all this information to anticipate where the shot will be kicked, increasing their chances of diving the right way. Unless the ball is kicked to the middle of the goal, there is simply no time to wait and see where the ball is being shot before starting to move.

The best penalty-savers are better at predicting the direction of shots before the ball is kicked – picking up cues from kickers before making contact, giving themselves more time to move to intercept the ball in flight. A study asked expert and novice goalkeepers to observe filmed sequences of penalty takers; the clips were stopped at different points during the penalty taker's approach, run-up and kick. The goalkeepers had to predict which of the four corners of the goal the ball would be placed to. Immediately before ball contact, expert goalkeepers could predict which corner the ball would be shot to on 51 per cent of occasions; novice goalkeepers could predict successfully only 39 per cent of the time.[21] The more of the penalty that is seen, the greater the chances of success.

This raises the question of how goalkeepers can optimize when they move, not just where they move. Goalkeepers who are more agile when diving have an advantage – they can watch more of the kicker's motion and delay their dive fractionally.[22] Because they moved later, more agile keepers have been shown to be less susceptible to being conned by penalty takers who use deception to lure keepers into thinking they are kicking the ball one way and then kick it another.[23]

Landreau used cues from the start of a penalty taker's run-up to help determine which way he dived. 'But you have to be very focused to leave as late as possible, so that the shooter cannot change course.'

The little black book

It was the biggest moment of Maddie Hinch's professional life: a penalty shoot-out to decide who would win the gold medal in women's hockey in the 2016 Olympic Games. And so she turned, again and again, to her little black book.

Scribbled in this black book were details of what the penalty takers from the Netherlands, Great Britain's opponents in the final, liked to do. Before each penalty, Hinch returned to look at the book for a few seconds.

'I had seven or eight people in my notebook that I thought would take penalties,' she recalled. 'It was one line for each player – so essentially it was quite a small amount of information on the day that had come from huge amounts of information gathered over a couple of years.'

Hinch had been preparing for the possibility of the tournament being decided on penalties for months. Before the Olympics, she had compiled a database on likely penalty takers from all 12 competing teams, recording what they liked to do during shoot-outs. While penalties in matches were with the ball in a static position, in penalty shoot-outs, uniquely, players have 8 seconds to run from the 25-yard line and try to score. 'It's like going into an exam – if you do your homework you just feel a little bit more ready and less nervous. You just feel prepared.'

Hinch had played in two previous shoot-outs against the Netherlands. 'I knew what worked and didn't work so well.' But on those occasions she didn't have her little black book to turn to.

'That was part of my routine as well. I wanted them to see that I was ready and had some information. They were still a bit like what's in it? And it could have been blank for all they knew. It was part of my routine and my mind games.

'I knew what my routine was from the moment the whistle blew and we were going into the shoot-out. When I was walking to the bench I knew how much I wanted to drink, where I wanted to go and stand, I knew I wanted to look through my notebook. I also used it as a bit of a time delay so when I saw the players stepping up it just gave me a few seconds to reread the notes.'

Before each penalty, 'I remember just walking over, saying something to the umpires just to distract myself. Then it was like routine mode – I'd touch my toes, I'd look down the line and I'd just stare at the strikers. I wanted them to look at me.'

The Netherlands' first penalty was taken by Willemijn Bos. Hinch 'knew she wanted to shoot early, I knew what side of the goal she wanted to shoot'. To unnerve Bos, Hinch started running in line with her left post – where Bos wanted to shoot. 'I could see her looking at me thinking, "S★★t she's still on that side." I'd left her the other side of the goal wide open. But it wasn't in her routine so she hesitated and that's what caused her not to execute that well.' Bos ended up aiming towards the right post – opposite to her favoured side – but her shot was inaccurate. Hinch parried it away with her legs.

For the second penalty, from Ellen Hoog, Hinch needed a completely different strategy. Hoog liked to shoot early, so Hinch remained rooted in her goal, the exact opposite of her approach to the first penalty. Hoog's eventual shot was saved; Hinch's delaying tactics meant that the klaxon marking the end of the 8 seconds for the penalty sounded before Hoog scrambled the ball into the net. Another plan had played out exactly as Hinch envisaged.

The third penalty was the one time that Hinch had to depart from this fundamental method. It was taken by Laurien Leurink, a young Dutch player. Leurink had barely taken penalties before – she wasn't one of the seven Dutch penalty takers in their semi-final victory over Germany – so, when Hinch glanced at her little black book, 'I remember looking at my book and thinking, "S★★t there are no notes."' Hinch tried to make it look like she had normal notes, like those she read before saving the first two penalties in the shoot-out.

Against Leurink, Hinch relied on her ability to identify cues even against a player she was unfamiliar with. Leurink shaped to go to her left, but then shifted to her right and then tried to beat Hinch on her near post. Hinch read the shot and dived to her left to make a brilliant save.

Such qualities of anticipation distinguish elite goalkeepers, even when they have no prior knowledge about a player's tendencies. A study asked elite and non-elite hockey players to anticipate the direction of an oncoming shot from film while they lay supine in a brain scanner. Expert players were significantly better at predicting shot direction prior to ball-stick contact, with accuracy levels around 10 per cent higher than with non-experts. Strikingly, the study showed that elite players' brains were activated in different regions compared with non-experts, with far greater activation in areas associated with the action observation system, an area of the brain responsible for stimulating the action that follows. This finding highlights how experts' brains adapt and are moulded to the specific demands of saving penalty shots because of their extensive practice in the task.[24]

'Expert penalty-savers look in different places to the intermediates and novices, allowing themselves to pick up more task-relevant information,' said Zoe Wimshurst, the author of the study. 'In the hockey penalty stroke this information seems to come just from the stick, with any movements by the body being more likely to distract and confuse.'

Hinch knew that, just as she prepared for the penalty takers, so they would try to prepare against her. In warm-up matches just before the tournament, Hinch intentionally experimented with other strategies. These were suboptimal strategies to save penalties in these lesser games, but meant that Hinch was ideally placed to save penalties when they mattered most – in the Olympic Games. 'I varied it so much that I had so much in the locker that I could have pulled out that they couldn't prepare for all of it. There were certain things that I hadn't shown yet.'

There are, Hinch said, many similarities between their approach and England's men's football team before the 2018 World Cup. The most significant is how they tried to imitate the pressure of penalty shoot-outs. For a year before the Olympics, England ended almost every training session at Bisham Abbey, their training centre, by being divided up into two teams and facing off in a penalty shoot-out.

Coaches made this training competitive, driving players to improve. Players' scores over time were recorded and made public to the rest of the group. 'You didn't want to be the worst goalie or the worst penalty taker – that's what you were trying to score or save.'

Players' specific tendencies were also documented – like which side they shot to, or where they dived – so they could see which options were working. Players would then know what their best options were and which they should focus upon improving.

Over these months of training, Hinch set upon her method for what to do in between penalties. 'I'd let the players go to the 25-yard line first and I'd take a little bit longer to get to the goal. I'd really try and test the boundaries of that – almost get the umpire to tell me off. Because they're still waiting on the 25 and the longer they're there, the more they're thinking.'

Her extensive preparations not only improved Hinch's penalty-saving; they also brought her peace of mind. 'There's enough pressure and butterflies to deal with as it is – let alone an underlying guilt of I could have done more.'

No details were too small. 'The girls would even look at details like as I'm walking over with the ball what am I doing with the ball? Some of them would dribble it but they felt nervous – so they were like we should just carry the ball there, pick it up and put it down on the spot.'

To avoid anxiety about penalties affecting them during the game, players did not know who would take penalties until after; there was a group of potential penalty takers, whom the coach Danny Kerry shuffled depending on the opponents and their performance. In training, players practised reacting in exactly the same way – with quick high-fives down the line – to both penalties that had been scored and missed, to avoid being weighed down by despair if a teammate missed. 'In the shoot-out we just got back in the same position – we've done this a million times, we'll do it again,' Hinch recalled. 'All these tiny details, we looked into more than any other team.'

After Hinch saved all four of her penalties, Hollie Webb had the chance to seal the gold medal with England's fifth penalty of the final. Webb was not one of England's regular penalty takers. But as she walked up, 'I was very calm in the moment,' Webb recalled. 'I knew if I scored that would be it. I remember just thinking I'd rather run out of time than rush it.

'It was all about processes. You knew what you were doing – you didn't have to think about any of that because it's all been rehearsed prodigiously. All you had to think about when it was your turn was walking up there and executing your shuffle.

'Everything was very normal – we'd been in those places and we tried to replicate an Olympic final so many times before. Obviously you can only do that to some extent but it really did feel like it was normal. That helped the nerves.' For all that was at stake, 'it didn't feel any different to just practising at Bisham Abbey'.

Preparation could go a long way to making Webb's shot easier, but not to prepare her for the feeling when, after dribbling and turning, she slammed the ball into the net just before her eight seconds were up. 'It went from a moment of pure calmness to what it meant for the sport and just the wider craziness and the team all running towards me. The bit after it had gone in – that is a bit of a blur. That was all a bit mad.'

PART THREE

Training smarter and the science of success

16
Practising smarter

How athletes progress from good to great

'Putting yourself under pressure in training actually makes the games easier.'

Dan Carter, 2015 Rugby World Cup winner with New Zealand, three times the IRB World Player of the Year and the highest points scorer ever in men's Test rugby

When she has a free throw, Elena Delle Donne bounces the basketball three times. Then, she says a few words to herself and 'I let it fly'. And, 19 times out of 20, Delle Donne scores.

Delle Donne is the most successful free-throw shooter in basketball history. By the end of 2019, Delle Donne had landed almost 94 per cent of her free throws in the rim – remarkably, over 3 per cent more than nearest rival, Steph Curry.[1, 2] She once made 59 consecutive free throws; all told, she has made 944 out of 1,006 attempts.[3]

For Delle Donne, the road to perfection – or as near to it as possible – begins in practice. During breaks in training, while her teammates sit down and have a drink, Delle Donne shoots free throws instead. This work ethic is in keeping with the entire philosophy that governs her practice; it is best to train when she is physically and mentally tired to replicate match conditions.

'I practise free throws during all of my workouts and shoot them right after doing tough drills so I'm tired,' Delle Donne said. 'Generally, when people are tired their mind is the first thing to go. So, if I can lock in and knock down free throws while tired it helps me in game moments when it's on the line.'

Before she leaves a practice, Delle Donne must make 10 successful free throws in a row. Such discipline imbues her with the confidence to shoot free throws when they matter most. Her record in playoff matches is even better than overall.[4, 5]

'I find it super important to stick to my routine,' she explained. 'You should never rush on the line but there's also no reason to draw it out too long. I think routine is super key and sticking to the routine stops me from overthinking.'

The Delle Donne method is founded on simplicity, enabling her to repeat it under the fiercest pressure: bouncing the ball, setting herself up to shoot, and uttering a few words to herself. 'I always say something right before I shoot the free throw. It is personal to me. So, maybe when I retire, I'll let that piece of information go – but it is something that is super positive and gives me confidence.'

One of the hallmarks of Delle Donne in these crux moments is her unstinting focus on where she wants the ball to go. In the seconds when she is about to throw the basketball, 'I always stare right at the front of the rim right before the shot and as I shoot … It's important to fixate on the rim. This is the target so in order to hit your target you have to keep your eyes focused on it at least until you release the ball.'

Deliberate practice

'All animals are equal, but some animals are more equal than others,' George Orwell wrote in *Animal Farm*.[6] So it is with the hours of practice in sport; some hours are more equal than others. Higher-quality practice – known as deliberate practice, which tends to be more onerous – counts for more than lower-quality practice.

The concept of deliberate practice was proposed by Anders Ericsson and a group of scientists in the late 1980s.[7] The authors asserted that deliberate practice – practice which was explicitly undertaken to improve performance, effortful to carry out and brought no immediate rewards – was essential for refining skills. Deliberate practice could lead to skill development at an accelerated pace.

During deliberate practice, learners identify skills that need improving, rather than merely passively accumulating experience without pushing themselves to improve.[8] Deliberate practice is physically and mentally demanding and not always enjoyable. But this means that deliberate practice generates constant feedback, which can be used to refine performance.[9]

Another tenet of deliberate practice is the notion that high-level instruction and coaching are available when necessary. The absence of direct instruction from a coach differentiates deliberate practice from purposeful practice, which is also designed to challenge athletes, but is not grounded in empirical findings about what someone needs to improve in the same way.[10]

Not all agree with Ericsson. In 2016, a group of scientists examined the relationship between the number of practice hours accumulated during the sporting career and the level of attained performance in sport. The authors reported a moderate relationship between all types of practice and performance that accounted for 18 per cent of the variation in performance.[11] Ericsson argued that all forms of practice are not equally effective in improving performance.

When the analysis was restricted to the hours accumulated in deliberate practice, he said, a substantially stronger relationship was found, highlighting the importance of deliberate practice.[12, 13]

Delle Donne: deliberate practice in action

Eric Thibault is the assistant coach of the Washington Mystics. One of his responsibilities is effectively to be Delle Donne's personal coach, and help perhaps the best women's basketball player of all time explore the full outer reaches of her talent.

After each WNBA season, Thibault and Delle Donne sit down to discuss her previous campaign. Then, they hatch a plan for what she will do over the off-season. This process does not judge her by conventional WNBA standards, only by the player that they think Delle Donne can become. 'We're talking about somebody who is already one of the best players in the league, so we came at it from the angle of these are going to be incremental gains,' Thibault explained.

Before the 2018 season, Thibault and Delle Donne identified a relative weakness of her game: her lack of assists. 'Our biggest room for improvement – your ability to make teams pay for over-helping and giving you too much attention,' Thibault wrote in his write-up of Delle Donne's 'offseason outline' for 2017–18. In the outline, he wrote:

> You have a career average of 1.6 assist per game, with 1.2 turnovers per game. For the sheer amount of attention you receive, you could achieve three assists per game without breaking a sweat (and without reducing your shot attempts). In terms of impact on our offense, that is 'low hanging fruit'. For example, Tamika Catchings bounced between three and four assists for most of her career, and she drew less attention as a scorer than you do. Most of it is just developing the technique and timing (and, obviously, having other people make shots). For how much you have the ball, your turnover numbers are good. We would just like to turn the 'escape' passes against help and double teams into 'attack' passes.

In 2018, Delle Donne went from 41 assists in the season to 67, comfortably the highest yet in her career. In 2019, her career best increased again, to 68.[14]

Thibault has helped Delle Donne improve the efficiency of her shots – taking more shots from the most optimal places, either very close two-pointers or shots from just outside the three-point line, and fewer deep two-pointers. He breaks down the court into three sections: the left block (on the left of the basket as the player looks), the middle, and the right block.

Delle Donne's off-season notes for 2018–19 detailed the ways that she could improve her shooting even further:

- Shot distribution – more focus on getting shots at the rim, drawing contact, taking a % of mid-range jumpers and making them 3s/layups/fouls;
- Only 18% of shots at the rim … our team 22%, league average ~30%;
- Elena shoots ~70% at the rim;
- Above league average at every distance, but needs to redistribute;
- One midrange -> rim per game brings the % of shots up to 25%.

Thibault used video analysis and data analytics to break down Delle Donne's shooting percentages all over the court. Before they got the technology, he or another coach would write down all of Delle Donne's shots during practice. The analysis encouraged Delle Donne to take more shots in areas she is strongest, and to improve in comparatively weak areas.

'It wasn't so much an area where she didn't shoot well, it was more about balance,' Thibault explained. 'She would kind of revert to what was comfortable and not always maximize what she could do in terms of getting to certain areas of the court.

'We looked at statistical data from different areas on the court – did she have balance from the left block in the post? Was she unpredictable? Was she able to go to the middle of the floor and to the baseline equally well? We just found a couple of areas where she was under-utilizing her skillset. She only liked to go to her right hand one side of the court and so she was wasting an opportunity on the other side of the court to do the same thing.'

While Delle Donne was efficient all over the court, 'she barely ever turned to her right shoulder from the right block', doing so in just four out of 51 possessions in 2018. 'A team that did its homework could sit on her left shoulder and anticipate a shot ... We wanted to make her harder to predict. If we wanted to go from a 90–10 split to a 60–40 split we had to modify our workouts.'

In some drills, Thibault barred Delle Donne from turning on her left shoulder when receiving the ball in the right block, forcing her to turn on her right shoulder, which she favoured less. 'We might make her play one-on-one against one of our coaches or practice players where she couldn't start by going the way she would normally go. We'd make her try to score going the other way.'

Delle Donne seldom delves into the statistics herself, but trusts enough in Thibault to act on his findings. 'He'll be like, "Hey, when you're on this block you tend to go this way 50 per cent of the time – if we can get you to go this way more you're going to get more points." So a lot of it is percentage based, and trusting his information. And then we'll even watch film and I'll be able to see: "OK, I need to be better at going right here because everybody's starting to force me this way."

'When he creates my workouts he'll get me to these spots and we'll work on going different ways or upping my percentage in this spot. It's kind of like he works all that magic and I just show up and we work those spots.'

Thibault introduced drills to encourage Delle Donne to take more three-point shots. 'We spent more time making that a part of her routine, shooting them in different ways – moving without the ball, or shooting it off the dribble – and just trying to increase her attempts from that part of the floor because she was so efficient.'

Analysis identified times when Delle Donne's performance slipped. 'Sometimes it's like "Hey, you're getting weak at minute 42 of the workout and we've got to figure out a way to get your endurance a little better"' she explained. These findings pushed Delle Donne to train to improve her shooting when most tired, replicating the feeling at the end of an intense play off game. 'We'll do certain drills that are high conditioning, and then we add shots to them at the end. So that's a way to figure out how to push through the fatigue and mentally get past being exhausted but still be able to shoot.' A heart rate monitor is attached to Delle Donne during workouts, to ensure her intensity matches that needed in games.

In training, opponents are sometimes allowed to foul Delle Donne in a way that would be barred – officially, at least – during games. 'I'll always have a defender who's contesting each of my shots, and there's times when I'll have them push me at the waist, so I still find a way to finish and make the shot while being hit.' So if Delle Donne is fouled during a game, she has learned how to take a shot regardless. 'If you can finish while being exhausted and also getting hit here and there I think that's a great thing to practise.'

The ferocity of her training makes actually playing matches seem easier. 'I like to make practice way harder.'

Delle Donne believes that her rise to being the best player in the WNBA has been underpinned by the evolution of her practice. 'Now that I've gotten older you have to work smarter, and realize quantity is not the best recipe, especially for my body. So just trying to be efficient through the workouts, and know like hey, today we are going to work mid-range, and that is the focus, and we are going to get these shots in, we are going to do a little bit live, a little bit with no defence and then some with defence. Each day you just go in with an idea of what's the thing we're working on today, and then it helps you to get a way more efficient workout.'

While Delle Donne is fortunate in her physical gifts – most obviously her 6 feet 5 inches height – she has also risen to the acme of basketball because of her relentless focus on self-improvement. Delle Donne may not call it by this name, but her practice methods with Thibault bear all the hallmarks of deliberate practice.

ASPIRE

Unwittingly, Thibault's approach to helping Delle Donne fulfil her talent generally follows the ASPIRE model suggested by skill acquisition specialists Paul Ford and Ed Coughlan, from the University of

Brighton and Cork Institute of Technology respectively, for implementing deliberate practice in sport.[15]

Analyse – using empirical data where possible, the areas that the athlete needs to improve to reach the next level.

Select – aspects of performance for practice and the short- and long-term goals for the athlete to achieve.

Practice – sessions should ideally be individualized and designed by coaches to ensure that they are sufficiently challenging using principles of 'desirable difficulties' and 'challenge points'.

Include – relevant and appropriate feedback.

Repeat – but in a variable and random manner to ensure there is sufficient variability.

Evaluate – improvements in performance as objectively as possible – and repeat the cycle.

The approach provides a structure that helps ensure that athletes continue to engage in deliberate practice, evaluating their strengths and weaknesses and pushing themselves. 'The description of Delle Donne and her coach identifying, selecting, practising and evaluating aspects of shot efficiency generally follows the ASPIRE framework,' Ford said.

'I can't say we have consciously used the ASPIRE model, though as I read it I found myself nodding along,' Thibault said. 'That balance between repetition and unpredictability and variability is exactly what we try to figure out from day to day.'

The optimal challenge point

When seven-times world snooker champion Stephen Hendry practised, he had a favourite drill. Hendry would spread all 15 red balls out on the table, and put all the colours on their spots. Then, Hendry would have to clear the table – not once, but 10 times.

'I'd try and do that 10 times in a row – and if I did seven and missed I'd have to go back and do it again. So when you get to seven, eight clearances you're under pressure because you don't want to start again.

'The aim was to clear the table. And consequently, when you get to a match and a tournament, as soon as you get the chance, you just automatically clear the table.'

Training in any sport can become sterile. That is particularly true of snooker, given the lack of variables to manipulate. 'The practice side of snooker gets quite difficult because the table never changes so it's difficult to find new ways to practise,' Hendry explained. 'It's very hard to mix things up.'

Through his arduous training, Hendry ensured that his practice retained an essential edge. This edge meant that Hendry was constantly pushing himself. And it meant that, sometimes, the matches themselves could seem less pressurized than practice. After all, in match-play, Hendry only needed to clear the table once, rather than 10 times.

Hendry's drills were an example of overload training: the notion that practice should be harder than matches. Such a method achieves two aims. First, it develops an athlete's skills. Second, the match pressures are replicated in practice. Athletes may become better equipped, in terms of both their physical and mental skills, to deal with the challenge they face in matches.

While the practice undertaken by Hendry led to meaningful gains in his performance, it does not fully fit the criteria for deliberate practice outlined by Ericsson. The absence of direct instruction from a coach, as well as the apparent lack of availability of data to identify areas or shots to improve, differentiates deliberate practice from purposeful practice.

'When someone identifies a particular set of specific goals and designs a practice activity that provides immediate feedback and opportunities for repetition of the same or similar tasks, then we call this purposeful practice,' Ericsson explained. Purposeful practice will result in the potential for meaningful improvements, but, according to Ericsson, this type of practice is generally not as efficient as deliberate practice.[10, 16]

The optimal challenge point is the sweet spot for training. This is the point at which practice is difficult enough to push athletes to develop new skills, but not so challenging that it is completely beyond their existing capabilities. Mark Guadagnoli and Tim Lee, scientists at the University of Las Vegas, Nevada and McMaster University in Canada respectively, developed the concept.[17]

'If an appropriate level of challenge is created during practice, some degree of short-term failure should occur, allowing an opportunity for growth,' Guadagnoli explained. 'As a general rule, if you find that someone has more success than about 70–75 per cent of the time during practice, they're probably not being stressed appropriately.'

Practice is not about succeeding all the time but about playing on the edge between success and failure, pushing athletes to higher levels. While the optimal challenge point differs between athletes, depending on their character and motivation, the optimal challenge point for an elite athlete is likely to entail failing around one-third of the time. Such regular failure – desirable difficulty – yields effective long-term learning.[18]

This was the experience of Dan Carter, the highest scorer in the history of Test rugby, in his kicking training. He prepared for kicking during matches by aiming at a smaller target in practice.

Because of the natural curve that left-footers get, 'there is a bad habit of left-footers pulling the ball to the right of the posts', he explained. So Carter and his coaches devised a bespoke training routine. In practice drills against teammates, he would get 10 points if he kicked the ball exactly to the left post. He would get two points if he kicked the ball through the midline of the posts, but only one point if he got it between the middle line and the right post, encouraging him to aim to the middle of the posts and just to the left of the middle. This strategy allowed him to fight the left-footer's natural tendency to pull the ball to the right of the posts.

During practice Carter's coaches would often tell him where to take his kicks from, replicating the variability in kick location and distance during matches. 'It's randomized so it's not like I sit in one position. I do not actually know where the kick is going to be from one attempt to the next. I tell my coaches I am having 12 kicks today, you decide where they are from.'

As Carter improved, the kicks that his coaches made him perform became harder. As athletes develop, the difficulty of their training must rise as well to maintain optimal learning; keeping the challenge static will force the learner to a point of diminishing returns. When practice is too easy, or the coach provides all the answers, it bypasses the effort and engagement necessary to learn.

To be most effective, practice must be sufficiently difficult so that it actively engages learning.

Carter's dropkicking practice followed the same principle as the rest of his training. 'Putting yourself under pressure in training actually makes the games easier.' Carter liked players to run at him 'from different angles, yelling' while he practised dropkicks. 'It is something that you have trained up against before so you have answers.'

Competing against both opponents and himself in training drove Carter to constantly modify and improve his kicking. During matches and training alike, a coach or analyst would record each kick on video, allowing him to work with his kicking coach to understand what he did when he kicked at his best and what went wrong when he missed. 'I have a lot of footage now of when I am kicking well and when I am not kicking well. I can often see it on an iPad – looking at my good and bad habits. It's a good way to monitor your kicking and to find ways to improve.'

Avoiding arrested development

The feeling of reaching a plateau on the sports field is a familiar lament for athletes. Why, suddenly, do athletes cease improving, despite following exactly the same training routines that helped them to improve to a certain level in the first place?

In many professions – including on the sports field – there is not necessarily a relationship between someone's experience on the task and their actual performance.[6] People typically reach a plateau in their performance, seemingly incapable of improving to the next level. A plateau, Ericsson asserted, 'is not the maximal level that could have been attained if the individual kept working with a coach – thus we refer to this premature plateau as arrested development. In other cases, some individuals do keep working with a coach and continue to improve. But at some point they stop engaging in deliberate practice and thus similarly will not improve further.'

To Ericsson, the problem is that athletes continue to do what has taken them that far. Even at the pinnacle of their sport, athletes should continue to evolve their training methods to avoid arrested development. From learning to drive a car to learning to serve in tennis, as people develop more skill, the way that they perform it tends to change; the act of doing the task becomes more automatic. While this is true of the best athletes on the field, paradoxically during practice their brains are less automatic than those of less elite athletes – because they are still engaging new cognitive processes that will add to their skills and ultimately increase performance.[10]

'When someone merely engages in activities in the domain and thus is not designing practice activities to attain particular goals beyond the current level no improvements are expected,' Ericsson said. 'That is the reason why some golfers and tennis players remain at the same level even after a decade of regular weekly playing. Only when athletes sets goals that are beyond their current performance and thus outside their comfort zone and then engage in purposeful, and ideally, deliberate practice, does it elevate their performance.' The best ice skaters fall down more during their practice sessions than ice skaters who are not quite as good.[19] Elite athletes are always trying to introduce new challenge points to their practice.

Leading athletes are also more inclined to work on their weakest areas. In one study, scientists asked groups of expert and intermediate Gaelic footballers to practise two types of kick towards a target from the hand and off the ground using their stronger and weaker foot; the players were free to practise the skills however they wanted over a six-week period. The expert group practised the skill they were weakest at 65 per cent of the time; the intermediate group practised the skill they were weakest at only 35 per cent of the time. Expert players spent longer reflecting on their performance before, during, after and between practice sessions and rated practice as more effortful and less enjoyable – but, perhaps as a result, improved at a faster rate than the intermediate players.[20] At the end of the training period, the experts displayed a more marked improvement in performance.

Perhaps most revealing of all was another study involving two matched groups of youth and intermediate Gaelic footballers.[21] A training group – taught to self-reflect on their performances – improved performance at a significantly faster rate than the control group, who weren't given any guidance, even though their number of hours practising the skill was identical. Forensically analysing how to spend practice most efficiently can help athletes improve faster.

Steph Curry's constant evolution

Steph Curry is such an extraordinary basketball shooter that fans flock just to watch him train. It has become an iconic sight; about an hour before each Golden State Warriors match, Curry is on court, receiving basketballs to shoot into the basket.

He begins by taking shots from just a little past the mid-range line. Then he moves further away, past the three-point line, into the corner of the court. These shots require extraordinary precision to execute – and Curry makes them even harder, taking the shots off-balance, with one leg off the ground, or leaning back, replicating the pressure exerted by an opponent.

'You find some very unorthodox ways to challenge yourself,' he explained. 'It's mostly balance work in terms of challenging yourself and making it a little bit harder in your practice than in the game – things click. That's how all balance works – that is the foundation of your jumper shot.'

Curry's pre-game routine does not finish until he has taken shots from inside his own half, long past what is futile for virtually any other professional basketball player. 'In terms of trying to sustain it and shoot at a high level it's about practising the shots I'll take in games and repeating that motion over and over and over again.'

This is how Curry has become the best three-point shooter in the history of the NBA; as of the end of 2019, he had scored 20 per cent more three pointers per game than anyone else in history. Curry is at the apex of a revolution.

The attempt to refresh his practices is at the core of how Curry has changed the way the game is played. He even went through a phase of wearing goggles in training. 'It's just an extra stimulus that could test you and challenge you, take away some of your senses so that you could really lock in focus. As hard as I could make things in practice, that's the easier it gets in games.' Using such goggles can help athletes develop multisensory function. Wearing goggles that prevent athletes from seeing their limbs during practice encourages them to use non-visual information to move their limbs, freeing vision to focus on what is happening elsewhere on court.[22, 23, 24]

As Curry has improved, what he demands of himself in training has become ever more onerous. 'I've got to continue to push myself. I hesitate sometimes to open the veil on that because there is a process to building your game and I do not want children kind of jumping steps in terms of their development. Once you get to high school, college, you can start to add more and more.

'No matter how well I shoot, I feel like I can get better.'

Delle Donne's offseason outline for 2018–19 included one very specific goal. She wanted to join Curry in the hallowed 50–40–90 club – maintaining a 50 per cent field goal percentage, 40 per cent three-point field goal percentage and 90 per cent free throw percentage over the regular season. No WNBA player had ever achieved this feat before.

In 2019, Delle Donne became the first ever woman, and only the ninth ever player in the NBA or WNBA, to join the 50–40–90 club.[25] It was the latest mark of her greatness, but also of her ability to make good on the plans she hatched with Thibault. 'It's funny to look back on that,' Thibault recalled. 'Sometimes with Elena you can say something or make a suggestion or work on something, and she's so capable of quickly turning around and implementing it or reaching a goal.

'When you have somebody that's that elite and invested in their success and willing to work on what to other people may be pretty marginal things – a normal athlete might say oh that's good enough, I'm already shooting X percentage, that's already a great percentage. But when you have somebody that's that willing to be coached, that's already at that level, it just makes you want to help them any way you possibly can.'

In the 2008 Olympics, the women's Great Britain hockey side floundered. They won only two of their six games and finished sixth.

The team needed to change. So did Danny Kerry, their head coach.

'I was what most people would consider a performance coach, very process-driven,' Kerry recalled. 'The reality was that I had little or no knowledge of how to build relationships, little or no self-awareness about why I behaved the way I did.'

At a debrief meeting after the Games, Kerry received 'some pretty frank feedback' from players. They told him he was autocratic and unapproachable.

After the Beijing Olympics, Kerry's players began to notice a profound shift in his style. 'He changed an awful lot as a result of feedback from players,' recalled Hannah MacLeod, who played for Great Britain from 2003 to 2016. 'He went from a coach whose approach was "this is how you develop skill, off you go" to giving more ownership to the athletes and helping them understand how to learn themselves.'

One manifestation of Kerry's new style was his attitude to giving feedback: 'Feedback should be sought by athletes,' he said. When this is the case, 'they are more likely to be open to that feedback.'

Reducing the frequency of feedback and providing athletes with more control over how and when they receive feedback has been shown to encourage more trial and error learning. Giving feedback selectively aids skill retention, encouraging more independent and flexible learners.[1]

'Providing feedback after every practice attempt can create a dependency on coach-directed feedback and place too little emphasis on problem-solving,' said David Anderson, a scientist at San Francisco State University. If learners become overly dependent on feedback, 'performance will suffer when the feedback is no longer available during competition'.

As athletes become more skilled, their ability to detect and correct mistakes improves.[2] For coaches, the challenge is to accelerate the error detection and correction process by fading out feedback over time. To expedite the process, coaches can provide summary feedback after a number of practice attempts, rather than after each one, use a question-and-answer approach, and ask athletes to identify what went wrong before giving feedback.

After the 2008 Olympics, MacLeod noticed Kerry become more open to new ideas. 'People who saw the game of hockey in a completely different way – he listened to them because they challenged his thinking,' MacLeod recalled. 'He encouraged players to think and voice opinions. He definitely would not have done that back in 2008.'

'I made these changes so that athletes learned to take more ownership of their performance,' Kerry reflected. The process requires coaches 'to understand where the athlete group is as a whole at a point in time, and then try to progressively shift to a more athlete ownership model of coaching. You have to essentially grow these skills in athletes.'

Until 2008, Kerry's training sessions were very traditional, focused on relentlessly repeating drills. 'We would go from pass the ball along a line 50 times and then move onto a different passing technique and passing it 50 times,' MacLeod recalled.

After Beijing, Kerry became increasingly aware of research on skill acquisition. More random and less blocked, repetitive practice enhances how athletes retain skills, and how they transfer them to where it really matters – matches. Blocked, repetitive practice leads to the best performance during practice, but these improvements do not transfer as well to competition as dynamic practice involving small-sided and possession games.[3] Game-oriented practices also develop game intelligence, including anticipation and decision-making.[4, 5]

'All you're doing with traditional, prescriptive coaching is isolating technique and making people repeat the same actions. You are not developing their skills or ability to perceive,' Kerry said. In his more variable training, Kerry emphasized 'binding action with perception', so players could adjust to different situations. No longer would one practice session resemble the next. As much as possible, he made each training scenario meaningfully different.

'In every session now I'm thinking about the design of space, the number of opponents, the types of cues that you want the athletes to either consciously or unconsciously perceive and then take appropriate actions.' The emphasis in training moved from players being as successful as possible within the narrow confines of blocked practice to experiencing the widest and most random range of scenarios.

Manipulating constraints – like rules, the number of players involved or the pitch – reflects how constraints change during matches. Isolating skills under fixed practice conditions, using drills and grid-based practices, does not.[6, 7] 'There was a big shift towards a constraint-led approach' so players could 'make the right decision in the context of realistic match situations', MacLeod recalled.

Players need to learn to adjust during matches, make decisions in response to a continuously changing environment and withstand pressure. 'Coaches often have an ideal view of what an action should look like, rather than whether it's functional under pressure,' Kerry said. 'Our session designs created an ability for athletes to adapt under pressure in the moment.'

The squad was even involved in evaluating and designing training. Kerry asked players to provide feedback at the end of each week. He reminded the players what they had set out to achieve in training, and asked them whether they had done that, and how they could have done things better. 'We could say "How about this?" And the training the next week would look a little bit different,' MacLeod recalled. 'I've never ever seen a coach do that before.' The changes meant 'all of a sudden you're not going through the motions ... We are responsible for the quality of training and the training sessions, as well as the head coach.'

The common thread informing Kerry's entire approach was encouraging players to think for themselves. 'There was a massive shift in what training looked like from 2008/09 to Rio,' MacLeod observed. 'You were constantly thinking, "How can we do things better?" It gave us the ability to really impact our training environment and have a sense of control over where we were going which builds confidence, builds trust and makes the environment that we were then working in very rewarding.'

Kerry encouraged players to talk through possible scenarios in matches – including some unpalatable ones. 'We'd talk about "what if" scenarios,' MacLeod recalled. 'Those conversations were unbelievably important in terms of where we got to. So if we weren't experiencing it in training we were talking about what would happen and what it would look like and what was in our control and therefore what are our processes.'

The new approach essentially did two things for players. It exposed them to more scenarios – increasing the likelihood that players were prepared for what they then experienced on the pitch. And it made players familiar with confronting unexpected problems and then working through them – so that even when they encountered a completely novel situation, they could identify it and adapt.

These changes were made with one goal in mind. 'In my world essentially we are judged on two weeks every four years,' Kerry explained. 'Constantly in my head the decisions of what we do and when we do it, how we do it, that trade-off between a long-term development towards that two-week window and the short-term needs of a particular tournament.'

During the 2012 and 2016 Olympics, MacLeod recalled several instances of Britain conceding a goal just before half-time, or facing an unwanted obstacle – like losing their captain to injury, as they did in 2012. The team had practised and discussed coping with such problems. 'At half-time someone would say we're just in our training environment. We'd felt that pressure, we'd felt those situations – it was literally all we needed to do, remind ourselves that we are so prepared for big matches and high-pressure environments because of the conditions that we'd created in the training centre. There was that confidence – we'd been in that situation and we knew how to execute our skills in so many different environments.'

From coming sixth in 2008, Great Britain came third in the 2012 Olympics – their first medal in field hockey, in either the men's or women's competition, since 1992. This built a foundation to improve further in 2016.

Great Britain faced a brutal schedule – eight matches in 14 days, culminating in an excruciatingly tense final against the favourites, the Netherlands. After the final finished 3–3, Britain defied the national stereotypes to win on penalties. Kerry's transformation culminated in the nation's first Olympic gold in women's hockey.

'Coaches can have a huge bearing on how athletes own their performance, they can have a huge bearing on the culture within a squad, they can have a huge bearing on the mood and appetite for trying, a huge bearing on how they respond to bad results,' he reflected. 'Had I not had the journey I've had – through Beijing and then through London and into Rio – I don't feel I would have had the adaptability and the different skills to tap into at different times to help us achieve what we achieved.'

With the 'old Danny' in charge, MacLeod is adamant, 'We wouldn't have won gold in Rio.'

Training to play

Every coach has a different style and a unique journey. Yet Kerry's metamorphosis embodied many of the traits that have been found to give coaches the best chance of helping athletes to become elite.

The central paradox in coaching lies in the contrast between performance and learning. What is best for short-term performance is not always best for long-term learning – and, as such, long-term performance.[8] 'You may see improvements during practice, but these may not be sustained,' said Nicola Hodges, a scientist at the University of British Columbia. A training session may look structured and organized, leading to good performance during practice, but actually inhibit learning. Another training session may appear random and chaotic, but be more conducive to learning. Learning can't be observed directly during practice, but has to be inferred from changes in performance in competition over a prolonged period of time.[9, 10]

Coaching that improves players during practice may hinder them outside the training ground. The extensive use of demonstrations, instruction and verbal feedback will improve a player during practice, but it does not promote long-term skill retention, or skills that can transfer easily to match situations. Being more hands-off, and allowing players to think through problems themselves, will initially lead to slower learning in practice – but it will mean athletes learn in a deeper and more robust way.[11]

Judy Murray's experience coaching her sons, Andy and Jamie – both in their childhoods and during their careers, when she was not their official coach but still provided important advice – attests to how coaches can challenge players. Murray's style focused on asking the boys questions about how they'd played and why, designed to help them learn independently and take ownership for their games.

When coaching the boys, Judy often devised games to push them and force them to play in a different way. Sometimes, they wouldn't be allowed to hit the ball in the service box during rallies; sometimes, they could only win the point by hitting a volley, or by bringing up their opponent to the net, so they had to use drop shots. 'You're able to influence the practice to challenge the player to make them think,' Murray explained. 'You're always trying to create different challenges.'

The different games Murray played with her children were 'all helpful, if you're going to develop an all-court player,' she said. 'To give the kids all the variety, all the tools that they would need to cause trouble, avoid trouble, get out of trouble, whoever they were playing against. So they had a plan A, a plan B, and a plan C. That was what I always tried to do.'

There is a tendency to 'over-coach', Murray reflected. 'They coach that the most important thing is to be able to win with power. Well, of course if you're playing against someone who is more powerful than you or is better at the power game than you are, and you have no plan B or plan C, you're going to lose. Whereas I always tried to develop creative, thinking all-court players … I coach to enable them to play the game.'

The array of games meant that the Murrays constantly had to plan and execute different skills. Such random practice is more difficult than merely repeating drills, and involves greater cognitive effort than blocked practice, so athletes learn more; scientists refer to this as contextual interference effects.[3, 12] Blocked practice activates areas of the brain associated with daydreaming, showing it does not engage athletes. More random practice – like the Murrays used, or Great Britain's hockey team did after 2008 – better engages areas in the brain 'central to long-term retention of skills', explained David Wright, a scientist at Texas A&M University. And it can lead to players having more tools to call on when it really matters.

One study assigned 30 college baseball players to three groups.[13] In separate random and blocked groups, players received two additional batting practice sessions each week for six weeks; a control group received no additional practice. The random and blocked groups both received 45 pitches – 15 fastballs, 15 curveballs and 15 change-ups. The random group received these pitches in a random order; the blocked group received 15 of each type in turn. After six weeks, the random group showed far greater improvement; the random group were 56.7 per cent more likely to hit the ball compared with only 24.8 per cent for the blocked group. Similar results have been found in badminton,[14] golf putting[15] and tennis.[16, 17] When different groups spend an identical amount of time on blocked and random practice, those undergoing random practice show greater improvements.

'You could improve passing down the line and do it exceptionally well,' said MacLeod, now Great Britain women's U-23 hockey coach. 'But how you make the decision to do that and execute the skill in the environment of a match – it's very difficult to transfer that. So can I go from passing the ball down the line to actually making the correct decision as to when to pass? Can I get the right pass selection and execute my skill when I'm perhaps off-balance?' Random practice can give players the answers to these questions.

The errors players make in training teach them how to detect and correct mistakes. After players have had prolonged exposure to random practice, they subsequently learn other skills more quickly, Wright found. Other new skills are 'acquired at a much faster rate than preceding novel skills, which suggests that random practice may offer broader, or transferable, learning benefits – providing a how to learn advantage.'

How smarter practice helped Justin Rose reach number one

Putting coach Phil Kenyon has attempted to incorporate these techniques into his coaching. Kenyon started working with Justin Rose in 2017. The following year, Rose, with vastly improved putting, became world number one for the first time.

'His putting practice was very blocked – it didn't have a lot of variability in it, and it was really predominantly based around technique rather than skill,' Kenyon recalled. 'One of the things that we did was to give him some improved concepts – what he needed to work on technically. But then I spoke to him more about the need to develop other skills, and to incorporate a little bit more variability in his practice.

'If you stand and hit the same putt, once you've hit that putt you've learned from it – you've learned what the slope was, what the speed was, stuff like that. So, previously, he would spend a lot of time on a straight putt working on technique, and he wouldn't have enough variability. If you've got a lot of variability in your practice you have to read every putt. You're going to read more putts in a practice session if you hit a putt from a different location than if you hit five putts from the same location. So by adding variability it would challenge him more from a green-reading perspective, which ultimately showed up some weaknesses, then we looked to improve those.'

Kenyon introduced Rose to a putting training method called spiralling. This entails starting to putt from close to the hole, then gradually moving the putt further away, spiralling the putting point further away from the hole. 'Every putt is a different distance and a different angle as you circle around the hole at different distances,' Kenyon explained. 'He would have to go and do that every day at a different hole – to read every putt, predict the break, and then there's a scoring challenge so it adds a little bit of variability and pressure.' Most importantly, the method 'gives him feedback on his ability to read the green'.

This approach to teaching putting has been endorsed by research.[18, 19] Variable practice involves, for example, hitting a forehand drive in tennis to targets positioned at varying depths on the opponent's side of the court, whereas hitting the ball to the same target is specific practice. In golf, players were assigned to either variable, specific or no-practice groups when putting.[20] The variable and specific groups practised over six consecutive days, doing 10 blocks of 18 putts each day – 180 putts in total. Those doing variable practice, varying the distance on each putt as in spiralling, putted fewer shots successfully during practice than those in specific practice. But the variable practice group was more accurate during the subsequent putting trials, showing their skills developed faster.[21] As Kenyon does, coaches can increase practice variability by manipulating the slope, and speed, of the green, rather than merely changing the length of each putt.[22]

The science of skill acquisition even suggests Kenyon could have pushed Rose further by asking him to not only alternate the length and slope of the putt but also to play a different shot on each attempt, putting one shot and chipping the next or vice versa. In one study, scientists asked groups to practise putting and chipping under practice conditions ranging from blocked – the same shot played repetitively – to random, alternating between chip and putt shots on successive attempts.[23] Those who trained under more random conditions, flipping back and forth from a putt to a pitch, improved more than those who practised under blocked conditions.

Traditionally, it was thought that blocked and specific practice created less variability in practice, and that less variability created more stability and skill. But it is now widely thought that variability during practice is crucial to learning – the more the better – since it creates athletes that can adapt to the same variable conditions that exist in competition. This variability enables athletes to better adapt their skills to the different demands of competition.

The extra feedback Rose acquired on his putting helped identify, and correct, weaknesses. 'You could start to see some biases in his green reading where he sort of under-read certain putts,' Kenyon explained. 'We started to refine some aspects of his green-reading, and give him specific feedback within those processes at appropriate times so he started to develop that skill.' These methods mean 'you're continually stressing the player so that they're pushing themselves'.

Just as Kerry found with England hockey, Kenyon's experience attests to how athletes can achieve greater success if they incorporate more random and variable practice into their training.

Empowering players

A fundamental philosophy informs how Norway nurtures skiers. 'I want my athletes to think for themselves. We need athletes who are smart,' explained Eirik Myhr Nossum, the head coach of the Norwegian men's national team. This philosophy – and the ownership athletes take over their training – may help explain why Norway is the most successful nation in the history of the Winter Olympics.

Other nations 'have coaches who are asking every athlete on their team to do the same training', Nossum said. 'My goal is to create a framework or a philosophy of how we're going to do something and then discuss with the athletes how we train these parameters in the best way. So the athletes are very important in the development of the training programmes.' Nossum terms coaches 'partners' for the skiers.

'We are independent – that's something I have recognized compared to cross-country skiers in Germany or Russia,' said Ragnhild Haga, who won two gold medals in the 2018 Winter Olympics for Norway. 'We are very much our own bosses. We write our training plan, and our coach's job is mostly to support us and say, "Yeah, that's a little too much, or that's a little too little training," so we learn much from other athletes and support each other.

'We learn to feel our own body, and when we are tired we rest … Of course we have a good relationship with the coaches. But we own our projects very much, so people in my team know what to do in training and competing.'

Coaches are certainly not redundant at elite level. But too much overly prescriptive coaching can inhibit a player's development. Trent Woodhill, who worked with Virat Kohli, Steve Smith and many leading cricket batsmen, is fond of saying, 'A coach can help a bit, but he can mess you up a lot.'[24]

More hands-off coaching offers significant advantages for skill learning. When athletes are given more control over their learning, as in Norwegian skiing, they are empowered to decide when they would like feedback and instruction and how they would like to structure practice.[25] The approach may not be optimal for athletes not naturally inclined to stretch themselves as much as possible, but has strong advantages for those with the high levels of self-motivation typical at the top of professional sport. 'Allowing athletes control over instructions or feedback – even control over how many practice trials they need – is often better than coach-controlled schedules,' said Hodges. 'Learners have relatively good insight into how they are doing on a trial-to-trial basis and so can make decisions about when they need help.'

Implicit learning

Coaching methods that discourage athletes from over-analysing the skill learning process can lead to techniques that are more durable under pressure. The use of sayings like 'scratch your back' when serving in tennis can lead to more implicit, rather than explicit, skill learning – encouraging learning without conscious awareness of what specifically is being learned.[26]

Athletes are far better served if they can develop an external focus when performing actions – concentrating on the effect of the action, like the racket trajectory or ball flight, rather than the action itself.[27] Focusing on the minutiae of the action can push athletes 'to use conscious control processes that are relatively slow and interfere with automatic control mechanisms', explained Gaby Wulf, a scientist at the University of Nevada, Las Vegas. But, 'when instructions promote an external focus, performers use unconscious, fast, and reflexive control processes – which makes their movements more automatic.' Such an external focus leads to better balance, more efficient muscle movement and even reduced oxygen consumption, helping athletes withstand gruelling conditions better. It remains unclear whether interventions that encourage an external focus of attention work equally well with the very best athletes as they do with novices.[28, 29]

Implicit learning and an external focus both embrace the notion of reducing the importance of coach-directed, prescriptive instruction, though the optimal levels of instruction vary according to the skill being practised and the learner's characteristics. The challenge for coaches is to identify each athlete's sweet spot.

'This sweet spot differs between athletes,' Nossum observed. But to generalize, across sport the sweet spot of coaching intervention for players – those aspiring to be elite and those already at elite level – is for less prescriptive coaching than often used.

A video analysis of coaches working with players at three levels of excellence, including the Premier League, in England examined how coaches structure practice sessions when working with youth players ranging from nine to 16.[30] In over 80 practice sessions analysed, coaches required players to complete drill and grid-related activities 65 per cent of practice time; elite youth players were engaging in realistic game-based activities only 35 per cent of the time. No differences were noted either across age or skill level; coaches seemed to structure sessions the same irrespective of age and skill. Coaches rarely oversaw prolonged silence of over 6 seconds; instead, they constantly cajoled players, perhaps partly to justify their own jobs. In coaching, a theory versus practice divide may exist at the very highest echelons of sport.

Rather than filling every silence because they feel they ought to, the most effective coaches act less as owners of all knowledge and more like facilitators. They help discover the best way for them, even in sports like football, which are dependent on complex strategies and interplay between different players.

'Discovery learning' at La Masia

A more hands-off approach to instruction is embraced at La Masia, Barcelona Football Club's academy. In 2010, La Masia became the first youth academy to have trained all three finalists for the Ballon d'Or in a single year – Andrés Iniesta, Lionel Messi and Xavi – and has continued to produce a slew of elite players ever since.

'There are two main tenets of how we try to develop players,' explained Isaac Guerrero, head of coaching at FC Barcelona. 'First, we have to talk more to the player through the task itself – the context we are designing – rather than via verbal instructions. Our goal is to create a context for learning implicitly rather than through pre-established and conventional models. In this sense, we must change the focus away from explicit guidance in favour of discovery learning. We need an attentive coach, who can "talk" to the players by manipulating the constraints of the task and not via explicit, verbal instruction and feedback.'

Second, the idea is that what matters is 'effectiveness and individuality rather than right and wrong – so players should be taught to do what makes them most effective, and harnesses their individual strengths, rather than act in a prescribed way.

'Unpredictability is the defining characteristic of football,' Guerrero said. 'We must train our players to handle the variability inherent in our sport, and we can do so through less prescriptive methods of instruction, encouraging implicit learning.' Barcelona's practice sessions have a strong emphasis on recreating match-like conditions using rondos and small-sided games which mould players who can make decisions for themselves. A mark of successful coaching at La Masia is creating players who ultimately have only a very limited need for coaches.

The aim, Guerrero explained, is not to tell players what to do but to create an atmosphere of 'discovery learning'. Such a philosophy aims to cultivate creativity. 'As coaches, we want to avoid promoting rules that invite the player to do what they are told,' Guerrero said. 'Our role is to act as facilitators, creating environments where players can learn autonomously.

'We always ask key questions: are we constraining players too much, preventing them from being creative and adapting their behaviours to the situation? Are we limiting their actions to only those we deem valid based on our view of the game? As coaches, we must ensure that rigid rules don't lead players to play by the rules. Players need to learn to adapt to the context and sometimes to create their own rules – our role is to create a context where players can learn to problem solve and find solutions to the challenges created by the game.

'Coaches need to limit the explicit instructions they provide so that players are encouraged to perceive and make their own decisions. Our goal is to create a predominantly implicit, rather than explicit, process based on task variations rather than instructions from the coach. We are developing players that won't be dependent on our coaches; a player that will be autonomous.'

Such an approach has moulded the players Barcelona have produced, as Xavi, one of La Masia's finest ever graduates, explained in 2018:

> Some training centres believe that repeating the same things leads to perfection. It's heart-breaking. If the coach says: "Xavi, pass the ball to Matias, who passes it to Javier, Javier to Xavi, Xavi to Matias again, and so on for 10 minutes, what's the point? What does it improve? Maybe the passing technique, OK, but when do we activate the brain? We are stuck on elementary mechanical principles. During training, some players are even asked to run 10 metres for no useful reasons: "After the pass, you have to sprint!" But where? Why? Running is good, doing it smartly is better.[31]

The boot-throwing days are over

In the UK, and many other places, the seeds of change have taken longer to sow. But awareness is growing of the benefits of less prescriptive coaching.

'You need the environment for learning,' said former England manager Roy Hodgson. 'You need the environment where the serious athlete feels that – in this environment, and in this group – the way the group is being managed, I've got the chance to improve myself as an individual and as a team player.

'Learning or improvement comes about through positivity and encouragement, and not abuse and criticism. I've always believed in that.'

Hodgson believes in players taking ownership and shaping how they are coached, not merely doing as they are told. 'When we're coaching out there, and we're making our point, we would welcome a player saying "I'm not sure I understand this" or "I'm not sure that's something that I think I should be doing",' he said. 'Then it will be us making certain that we really spend the time with players convincing them of what we're saying, and that what we're saying is the right thing. Or for us to maybe switch and say "well, hold on, that's a very good point you've got there", so maybe we'll change our viewpoint on the subject.

'That's the way it should be. And if you get the right environment and you don't make players cower in your presence so they're unwilling to say "This is what I think and this is what I'm feeling", that's the way you will progress. In the old days, if you like, where there was less intention perhaps to involve players in the process, many players would be wary of making comments which went against what they were being told.'

Such enlightened methods are becoming more common. Hodgson has worked in football coaching for over 40 years – a journey that has encompassed managing England, Inter Milan and multiple successful stints in the Premier League. While Hodgson's style was never in keeping with the caricature of the boot-throwing football manager, he has observed a shift in how players learn over his career, with players increasingly empowered to shape their training, rather than merely taking orders like mute children.

'The major change would be it's become less coach-led,' he explained. 'It very much was a group of players who quite happily put themselves forward to say "what have we got to learn, and you stand in front of us and you tell us everything, and we won't say anything". And, maybe we'll do it and maybe we won't, and basically speaking we expect it all to come from you.' A combination of changing social norms and the rise of video analysis – encouraging players to watch and analyse their own performances – is leading a shift in the culture of how elite coaches and players interact.

'We've come around much more to being a bit less coach-led – us trying to get more from the players themselves, the players themselves to take responsibility, to take accountability, really, for their game,' said Hodgson. The shift is welcome: athletes who take more control of their own learning tend to adapt better to different challenges and ultimately morph into more successful athletes.

18

The next frontier

Technology and innovation in sport

'The scientists are embedded in the very infrastructure of the club.
The questions we address arise from day-to-day interactions with the
coaches and other support staff. We try and find solutions that are
driven by data and science.'

Javier Fernández, data scientist at the Barcelona Innovation Hub

The beautiful city of Barcelona in Spain is home to one of the world's most famous sports clubs. Futbol Club Barcelona is a symbol of Catalan culture, cherishing their famous motto 'Més que un club' (More than a club). Barcelona have long pushed the boundaries on the field. Increasingly, they are also doing so in their use of science and innovation off the pitch.

The Ciutat Esportiva Joan Gamper is the club's training complex, named in honour of Joan Gamper, the club's founder. The complex is nestled in Sant Joan Despí to the west of central Barcelona. The training complex, which also caters for basketball, handball and *futsal*, includes the club's legendary academy, La Masia. The original academy was located in an historic Catalan farmhouse, built in 1702; the current academy is located on a new site that opened in 2011.

While La Masia will continue to be at the heart of the club's future prospects, Barcelona believes that the team can be helped by what happens in an adjacent building which houses the Barcelona Innovation Hub, launched in 2017. With its drab grey outside and rows of desks by windows, the building could pass for an accountancy firm. But those inside the building aim to do nothing less than create a world-leading centre for generating sports knowledge and innovation – and help Barcelona win even more trophies in the process.

Barcelona's vision is to create a community that collaborates with brands, entrepreneurs, universities and research centres to bolster knowledge and innovation in sport. The club aims to create new products, technologies and services that can benefit its players, the club's partners and society in general – simultaneously improving the team's performance and generating extra revenue. The five areas Barcelona are focusing on are medical services and nutrition, sports performance, team sports, sports technology and social sciences.[1] Projects follow a consistent four-step process: innovation; knowledge acquisition; knowledge generation; and knowledge dissemination.[2]

The Barcelona Innovation Hub has links with major universities including the Michigan Institute of Technology – one of the world's foremost research institutions – but it is also a university in its own right. Barça Universitas is the Hub's digital platform for transmitting knowledge and allowing new ideas, concepts and products to spread beyond the club grounds. It organizes major conferences in sports science and medicine, offers Master's degrees and other online courses, and has a coaching academy on site.

'In Barcelona, we have one of the biggest laboratories in the world in terms of players and coaches,' said Carles Bargalló Segura, an engineer by training who currently works in technology and innovation at the Hub. The Hub services the needs of over 2,000 male and female athletes across five sports. The sports science department has 28 staff members on site, a number that dwarfs many academic departments at leading universities. Here – in theory at least – cutting-edge research and a leading sports club meet, propelling both fields forward.

Javier Fernández, a data scientist in Barcelona's sports science department, leads the process of making sense of the tactical performance data gathered at the Innovation Hub. Fernández has a background in high-scale software development and the application of artificial intelligence – typical of the skills that Barcelona look for when recruiting for the hub. Fernández maps football concepts and Barcelona's playing philosophy into actionable algorithms to gain better insights into the game. His main focus is providing data-oriented tools to help the club's football analysts answer complex questions on individual and team performance.

'The beauty of the Innovation Hub is that we are actively engaged with coaches on a daily basis in a way in which most universities are not,' Fernández explained. 'The scientists are embedded in the very infrastructure of the club. The questions we address arise from day-to-day interactions with the coaches and other support staff. We try and find solutions that are driven by data and science.'

The sports technology area focuses on three main areas: artificial intelligence, virtual reality and player tracking. Barca's data analytics team complements the coach's expert eye with quantitative and contextual analysis of player positions relative to the ball. By integrating positional data with other information – individual events during matches along with physical workload, medical and environmental data – the club can identify what impacts on performance and the chances of injury, helping it to stay at the top.

The best coaches make the best decisions but, increasingly, such decisions are underpinned by science. Who should they recruit, sell and select? How do they best prepare players, physically, technically, tactically and mentally? The challenge is to manage data in a way that translates into successful decisions. GPS player tracking systems monitor every player in training and matches – fans have been getting used to seeing GPS vests under players' shirts – so coaches know what distance each player covered, at what speed, including accelerations and decelerations. Barcelona's GPS technology – Wimu, co-developed with a Spanish technology company – can even track recovery times and the force of impact collisions with opponents.[3] Alongside GPS tracking, the club uses automated video editing systems to analyse tactical and technical skills across all teams at the training complex. Factors analysed include the number of passes and the distance and interactions between players; each player's heat map highlights the focus of activity around the field. Each youth team has at least one analyst.

Optical tracking systems monitor player movements and positions, with and without the ball, with a high-tech system built into Camp Nou, the club's iconic stadium. In both matches and training, sophisticated algorithms based on artificial intelligence analyse large datasets to identify important trends and their impact on match-day outcomes. The idea is that nothing is left to chance.

The market for state-of-the-art technologies to monitor player movements and actions is growing at a phenomenal rate: the industry is expected to grow from $280 million per year in 2018 to $2.05 billion in 2024.[4] The industry is moving towards smaller and less invasive sensors or wearable technology – for instance, smart fabrics could be inserted as a simple patch on the Barca shirt, camouflaged under the badge of the La Liga logo, enabling the club to monitor player function in a non-invasive manner. Barcelona plan to integrate new technology and data increasingly strongly to stay ahead of the competition.[5]

Such ambitions illustrate the work being done by the most innovative sports teams in the world to use technology to improve their athletes, and help them attain higher levels of performance. While Barca's Innovation Hub is not entirely unique in concept, it is likely that more and more sports teams will follow this path.

Though not all technological innovations will yield meaningful improvements for athletes, how teams use technology will play an increasingly important role in determining the best athletes in the years ahead. The growth in technology spans numerous areas and fields, not all of which can be covered in one chapter. This chapter focuses briefly on five categories: data analytics; technology on the field; sleep, neuroscience and diet; injury prevention and nutrition; and technology off the field, including virtual reality.

Data analytics

In September 2019, footage of a conversation between Rafa Nadal and Roger Federer, two of the best tennis players of all time, was disseminated on social media. Federer was playing a singles match against Nick Kyrgios in the Laver Cup – a competition that pits Europe against the rest of the world – with Nadal supporting his teammate.

During a change of ends, Nadal addressed Federer: 'Under five shots, when the point is going, you are winning more than him, like 8–5 for you, I checked.'[6] Nadal was imploring Federer, who was one set and 5–4 down at the time, to play shorter rallies. He did – and went on to win. The interaction was a snapshot of the growing importance of data analytics in sport, and how, as well as clubs using data to influence player recruitment, such data is being used to improve player performance.

While often reinforcing existing perceptions, data can also challenge them. So far, perhaps the most intriguing finding from data has been that, across myriad sports, athletes would be best served by playing in a more attacking way.

Fourth down in an American football game is the last phase of play before the offensive team must give the ball up to their opponents unless they can move it forward 10 yards. Traditionally, most sides punt the ball down the field, returning possession to the other side deep in the opposition half, rather than 'go for it' – choosing to run with the ball again, in the hope of carrying the ball 10 yards, whereby their team get another fourth down. Most teams are wrong. The average NFL team gives up 0.4 wins a season, from their 16 games, because they don't 'go for it' enough.[7]

'There are several plausible theories for why behaviour hasn't matched theory, but ultimately the decision to punt is a lower risk play,' explained Michael Lopez, the author of the paper and now the director of analytics for the NFL. 'In high-pressure settings, choosing low over higher risk is something lots of non-coaches would probably do, too.'

What is true in the NFL – that teams generally use a suboptimal strategy, which is simultaneously more defensive and less likely to lead to victories – has been found across a range of sports. In football, when teams are losing they make substitutions later than the data says is optimal – perhaps because managers want to avoid admitting their initial selection was a mistake, or to avoid the risk of bringing on attackers and then conceding more goals, leading to a humiliating defeat.[8,9]

In ice hockey, goalkeepers are pulled off too late in matches by teams that are losing – meaning they have less chance of suffering a heavy defeat, but also less chance of salvaging a draw.[10] In the NBA, analysts have found that attempting threes, rather than twos, yields higher expected returns – even though three attempts fail much more. This simple mathematics has transformed the sport, leading to the number of three-point attempts per game nearly doubling since 2010.[11]

As well as pushing players and teams to play in a more efficient – and, generally, a more offensive – manner, data analysis is leading teams to evaluate players differently. In invasion sports there has traditionally been limited information on what players do the vast majority of the time on the pitch – when they don't have the ball. One of the most significant developments in the years ahead will be in the quality of tracking and analysing data that teams use to measure what their players do without the ball, and how players could improve their actions when not in possession.

'Previously teams only really had data on events involving the ball,' said Bill Gerrard, who has worked with the Major League Baseball team Oakland Athletics and as a data analyst for AZ Alkmaar in the top division of Dutch football. 'Some of the most cutting-edge data analytics is in using tracking data to analyse offensive and defensive shape. Tracking technology now provides positioning data on all the players continuously, allowing teams to identify players who are not positioning themselves optimally.' Especially important is 'how quickly players reposition themselves during the transitional phase when possession has just been won or lost'.

As tracking data becomes more accurate, it should be possible to measure information about a player's body posture in invasion games like football, said Hector Ruiz from the data analysis company Stats

Perform.[12] 'That means that you know how a player is standing with respect to the ball, the direction they and the rest of the players are facing, whether the ball is near their strong foot. This opens the door to a whole new dimension of analysis.'

Not only is technology developing, but the ease of accessing data is improving for athletes. Artificial intelligence is now enabling available smartphone technology to automate and enhance the ability to quantify where basketball shots are taken during practice, explained David Martin, previously head of sports science at the Philadelphia 76ers.[13] Other companies are using artificial intelligence to automatically recognize a number of different basketball plays during a game and automatically tag these plays for team analysts – of whom the 76ers had 12 at the start of 2020.[14, 15, 16] 'The focus is typically on talent identification and development but also game strategy and evaluation of how well a player executes plays,' Martin said. 'The strengths and weaknesses of opponents gets plenty of attention leading into games as coaches explore viable tactics.'

Professional sport will always be far too unpredictable to be played by algorithm. But in the years ahead the best athletes, and their teams, will use data with greater shrewdness in pursuit of a competitive advantage – including using artificial intelligence to reduce large datasets to create simpler conclusions for coaches and athletes. This is crucial: data is valuable only if it can be used to improve performance on the field.[17] As the aphorism has it, 'Not everything that counts can be counted, and not everything that can be counted counts.'

Technology on the field

At the end of 2019, *The Irish Times* named its global sports star of the year. It didn't give the award to an athlete. 'No man or woman, team or country, had a year in history to rival the now properly global running shoe phenomenon known as the Nike Vaporfly,' the journalist Ian O'Riordan wrote while anointing the shoe as the sports star of the year.[18] 'Take a look over any of the times that counted in 2019 – from the big city marathon to the local park run – and chances are the Nike Vaporfly are right there on the ground beneath their feet.'

The selection was warranted. In 2017, the Vaporfly, a shoe with new carbon-fibre plated technology, launched. It promised to shave 4 per cent off running economy – translating to an increase of about 2.5–3 per cent in running times. In the world of shoe technology, such hype is not uncommon. But this time, it was justified.

In 2019, 31 of the 36 podium positions in the six world marathon majors were by those wearing Nike Vaporfly shoes.[19] An analysis by *The New York Times* found that athletes wearing the Zoom Vaporfly 4% or ZoomX Vaporfly Next% – the two most popular versions of the shoe, which have retailed for around $250 – ran 4–5 per cent faster than a runner wearing an average shoe, and 2–3 per cent faster than runners in the next-fastest popular shoe.[20] Both the men's and women's record marathon times were set by runners in the Vaporflys, which typically shave 90 seconds off a marathon time.

The shoes are much more impactful than other so-called one percenters. Indeed, so tight are the margins at the top echelons of marathon running that in most cases not wearing the Vaporflys can effectively rule you out of contention.

It is a snapshot of how technology can transform sport – opening up new frontiers, and, some fear, even distorting the essence of sport. In 2009, FINA – swimming's international governing body – permitted full-body non-textile polyurethane swimsuits to be used in races. So profound were the benefits for swimmers that in the first five days of the 2009 World Championships, 29 world records were set. The following year, FINA banned the full-body non-textile polyurethane swimsuits – trying to make who won more about swimming and less about who had the best swimsuit.[21] The same effects have been seen in cycling, with advances in bike technology credited as being crucial in British cycling's recent successes.[22, 23]

Nike is not content with the 4–5 per cent advantage in running economy the Vaporfly shoes have been shown to deliver. It is believed that the next iteration of Nike's shoe, the Nike Alphafly, could improve running economy by 8 per cent. A wave of other shoe companies is also attempting to develop shoes that deliver similarly spectacular performances.[19]

'Shoe selection has always been important for an athlete to max-imize his or her performance, but it was much more individualized,' explained Geoffrey Burns, a specialist in running biomechanics from the University of Michigan. 'Now it's discriminatory in com-petition. If you are on the line in traditional racing shoes, you have to be several minutes better than the competitor next to you if they are in a next-gen shoe like the Vaporfly.' As such, technology is 'absolutely' becoming more important in determining who wins marathons. 'Performances now have a greater and greater attribu-tion to engineering.'

This Vaporfly technology threatens to change who even becomes a professional runner. It is possible that 'young athletes who want to break through will never be seen unless they have this shoe,' said sports scientist Ross Tucker. For instance, the runners who get scholarships to US universities are those who are most successful in races – and if these come to be dominated by those with Vaporflys, those without them may be denied the opportunities.

Even for those who can afford them, the Vaporflys will still change who actually wins. Traditionally, running has been a sport in which equipment mattered little. But, among any two runners, there are discrepancies in their responsive to the Vaporflys: some may show an 8 per cent improvement in running economy, Tucker explained, but others only 2 per cent.

These differences could be multiplied further as the shoe design becomes more individualized and precisely tailored to each athlete's physiological needs. 'This is exciting scientifically, but scary socio-logically,' said Burns. 'It creates enormous issues of access, and brings in greater and greater perpetual uncertainty into performance attri-bution. That's troubling for a sport whose value proposition was its brutally and beautifully clear honesty.'

The Vaporfly is an extreme example of how, if they are both expensive and not regulated properly, technological advances will have a big impact on which athletes go on to be the best. If there are a series of different shoes all promising to transform athletes, it could be which technology is best that ultimately separates different athletes on the podium: a microcosm of how, across sport, technology could play a bigger part in deciding who wins.

Sleep and neuroscience

The hyper-professionalism of sport is leaving no area of an athlete's life untapped. Sports teams like Barcelona are showing ever-increasing interest in areas previously considered in the private domain – even sleep.

Stresses on the brain arising during practice, performance and recovery impact on the brain's anatomy and function.[24] These neural changes allow athletes to learn new skills and consolidate and refine existing ones. Learning is thought to arise as a result of changes in the amount and location of neurotransmitters within and between neurons, and across regions, in the brain. These neurons are connected by neural synapses. Rather than being consolidated in any specific region of the brain, skill learning is thought to be encased through large, distributed and dynamic neural networks. The quality and quantity of sleep can have a profound effect on the brain, so a player suffering from poor sleep can have weakened physical and mental capabilities – and their performance on the pitch can suffer.

Perhaps the most surprising finding is that learning is not limited to practice itself but continues away from training – particularly during sleep intervals – via a process termed 'consolidation'. When someone is awake, different parts of the brain interact dynamically. During sleep these interactions are dampened, allowing space for memory consolidation and learning – so athletes who sleep better accelerate their learning. Sleep also aids good health, performance, recovery, the prevention of injury and increased participation in training.[25] In the hunt to unlock greater performance, then, sleep is an essential frontier.

Many athletes still sleep in a way far from conducive to peak performance. A study in 2017 found that 78 per cent of leading athletes report issues with insomnia ahead of competition.[26] Changing sleep patterns can bring substantive improvements. A Stanford University study analysed the impact sleeping 10 hours a night had on basketball players' performances.[27] Players improved their free-throw percentages by 9.0 per cent and their three-point accuracy by 9.2 per cent, as well as improving ratings of physical and mental wellbeing during practices and games after five to seven weeks. A study of tennis players showed that increasing sleep by an average of 1 hour 40 minutes per night, from seven and a half hours to nine, for one week, improved performance.[28]

There is growing evidence that frequent naps can enhance performance by protecting those skills that have just been practised against interference from other activities during napping, particularly for discrete tasks like those carried out on the football field.[29, 30] The optimal duration and frequency of naps has yet to be established – but naps of around 20 minutes are suggested by Genevieve Albouy, a neuroscientist at the University of Utah.

The Portuguese superstar Cristiano Ronaldo, for example, breaks up his sleep every day into six 90-minute periods.[31] He has his own sleep coach: the sort of attention to detail that is still exceptional, but becoming more prevalent among the world's very best athletes. Some teams are already monitoring how much players sleep – using smart technology such as the Oura Ring[32] – which, while controversial from a privacy perspective, has a clear rationale from a skill acquisition perspective.

Teams could even encourage players to nap on site, as Real Madrid is reported to be doing using sleep pods and snooze boxes.[33, 34] 'There is evidence that napping between training sessions in which competing material is learned protects the motor memory traces against one another,' said Albouy. 'Napping has been suggested to accelerate or condense the motor memory consolidation process.' The ideal time for athletes to have a nap, Albouy said, is one to two hours after the learning episode. This finding suggests that there could be benefits for skill acquisition if sports teams organize naps on the training ground for players in between different practice sessions.

Other neuroscientists have explored whether athletes' self-regulation skills can be improved.[35] The function of the autonomic system, which regulates several functions in the body without conscious control, can be measured in the brain using electroencephalogram (EEG) technology – a skull cap with electrodes fitted. This cap tracks activity across regions of the brain and means that strategies to better control or manipulate brain function can be explored. The human brain is never at rest, but EEG activity can be recorded accurately, with activity patterns thought to reflect various mental states.[36]

For instance, skilled athletes demonstrate more activity in the so-called alpha band in the brain, which is associated with reduced cognitive function and greater automaticity; novices show increased activity in the theta band, which is associated with increased mental effort and conscious processing.[37]

In one study in archery, activation in the theta band was shown to have a negative impact on performance. So if athletes can be trained using neurofeedback to reduce or quieten this activity, performance should improve – as it did in the study.[38] Neurofeedback has also been shown to have potential to enhance performance in sports such as dance, golf and gymnastics.[35] If brain activity patterns could be linked to superior performance and interventions could be developed to control such activity, the opportunities to enhance performance would be profound. But, despite the early promise of neurofeedback, research remains sparse.

Injury prevention and nutrition

Injuries used to be thought of as simple bad luck. But in recent years thinking about injuries in sport has evolved. Injuries are very often the difference between which players and teams achieve glory and which do not: when Leicester City won the Premier League title in 2016, its players missed fewer games to injury than those of any other team.[39] In the NBA, the company Kitman Labs has calculated 63 per cent of injuries – equating to $8.1 million per team, per year, in salaries for players stuck in the treatment room – are for avoidable ruptures and strains. An extra $8.1 million a year translates to an average of 20 per cent more wins per season, which points to how significant more effective injury prevention can be.

'The future of athlete performance, injury mitigation and treatment will almost certainly include a synthesis of individualized athlete performance data including workload, biometrics and biologic interventions that will fundamentally improve the ability of athletes and medical staff to mitigate injury risk,' said Travis Maak, the head team physician for the Utah Jazz in the NBA, who is also on the NBA research committee. Individualized early intervention to prevent injuries, and accelerate recovery, could eventually include using stem cells to help repair damaged tissues, Maak explained.

For all these tantalizing possibilities, there remains significant performance potential in a more mundane field: diet.[40] 'Athletes will be looking for specific diets that are personalized,' said James Morton, a scientist from Liverpool John Moores University. It is already common for players to have personal chefs. 'Quite often athletes have the knowledge to know what should be eaten, but they may simply lack the skillsets to cook their own meals. So they're solving the problem by bringing someone in to cook the meals.'

Even in many leading teams, there is still scope for athletes to eat in a way that is more conducive to delivering their best possible performances. 'Teaching or coaching an athlete to self-regulate their own energy intakes day by day, meal by meal, sounds simple but is quite challenging.'

To help their athletes eat smarter, teams are increasingly moving away from the traditional model of three big meals a day. Athletes are being encouraged to adjust their eating pattern depending on the training schedule, which may even mean six feeding points per day. There could be further gains if more teams tailor their nutritional policies to be 'fuel for the work required', Morton said. 'If training is different every day, why should you eat the same every day? Your nutritional plan should be different to adjust for the training load.'

Virtual reality and technology off the field

Nothing can ever quite prepare players for the cauldron of a game – what it is like defending against Lionel Messi, taking a penalty in a shoot-out or facing a cricket bowler or baseball pitcher at 100 miles per hour. This has been the conventional wisdom throughout the history of sport. It could yet be challenged by virtual reality technology – perhaps the most intriguing potential leap forward of all.

Virtual reality in sport is embryonic, but has already shown tantalizing possibilities. For instance, virtual reality allows cricket batters experience of facing bowling at high speeds – training their anticipation and ability to play the ball, without the risk of suffering physical injury. This could be particularly useful in cricket where there are physiological differences between batters and bowlers – batters can practise far longer without getting tired, just like baseball batters can compared with pitchers.

The technology can allow players more repetitions – more deliberate practice. Instead of having to wait around between getting shots to save, virtual reality technology allows football goalkeepers to face two or three times as many shots over, say, an hour-long period, said Cathy Craig, a psychologist at Ulster University who is involved in designing virtual reality for use in cricket, rugby and football.[41] The potential, she said, is for 'giving somebody perfect service every time, the opportunity for quality mental repetitions, accelerating learning'.

The benefits could be particularly great when players are injured or short of game time. The Barcelona Innovation Hub has examined the potential uses of virtual reality. Silvia Ortega, a research project coordinator within the club's sports medicine area, believes that virtual reality may yield benefits in sports rehabilitation: injured players could continue to train their perceptual and cognitive abilities, so when they were back fit they would only have to get up to speed on their physical abilities.

Some Premier League clubs are already using virtual reality in this way. Rezzil, which involves players putting on a headset, standing on a 3 by 3 metre green carpet and being transported to a virtual world, where they move around with their heads, is now used by four of the 'big six' Premier League clubs.[42] When Manchester United's Scott McTominay was injured during the 2019/20 Premier League season, he used Rezzil's virtual reality almost every day to practise making decisions on the pitch. Clubs tweak the software to their personal needs – for instance, changing the formations and styles of play for the team and their opponents. Some injured players have been known to go to the training ground team talk, along with the fit players, and then have a virtual training session afterwards. 'They'll do the same sort of decision-making – the same sort of training but without having to run or move,' said Andy Etches, the founder of Rezzil.

Intriguingly, Barcelona believe that virtual reality could help a player to get a sense of what it was like to have Messi and company as teammates. This could mean that a young player, or a new signing, could be promoted to the first team more quickly.'When a youngster first arrives in the first team, it would be good for him to participate in a virtual match with the players,' Raúl Peláez Blanco, head of sports technology innovation analysis at Barca, has said. 'With the positional data that we have at present, we could reproduce, in detail, how the match would be played out.'[43] Such an approach allows players to be placed back into the context of a recent match to practise their decision-making.

Virtual reality can vary the conditions and constraints from one trial to the next, letting athletes play with and against virtual team-mates and opponents. Crucially, the difficulty of the simulation can be tailored for the individual to create an optimal challenge point for learning. The virtual environment can teach players to detect cues more effectively during real matches – for instance, visual cues can direct an athlete's attention to body areas that are most effective for anticipating an opponent's actions.

The technology allows an athlete to get more practice repetitions for situations that occur relatively infrequently – like batters facing knuckleballs in baseball or cricket, or goalkeepers facing curved free kicks in football. Ultimately, virtual reality could allow players spe-cific practice against exactly the same scenarios they will then face in their next match. In a recent academic paper, Rob Gray from Arizona State University wrote: 'The real return on investment [of virtual reality] is likely to come from the ability to create unique, evidence-based training conditions that are impossible or highly impractical to use in real training.'[44]

'You might come up against a team with a free-kick taker who can cause the ball to bend in specific ways,' Craig said. 'You want to figure out where's the optimal place for the wall, how does the wall itself impact on the goalkeeper's ability to read the trajectory and respond.' Such technology could even pit players from the same team against each other, by giving them identical challenges – goalkeepers could face, say, the same 100 shots each – and see who performed better. While preparing for a knockout match with a potential pen-alty shoot-out at the end, football teams could compare how differ-ent goalkeepers fared against the opponent's penalty kick takers in virtual reality training – informing which goalkeeper they would choose to use in the penalty shoot-out.

Virtual reality is not intended to replace training but simply to be a 'complementary' way of sharpening mental skills, said Etches. Performance on Rezzil may even be predictive of who are the best footballers: in 86 per cent of cases, performances on Rezzil could successfully distinguish between senior professional and academy players in the Premier League. Etches believes that Rezzil cannot just identify those with the most game intelligence, but also develop the skill. 'We're looking to identify and coach better decision-making.'

Researchers have already shown performance benefits to using virtual reality. In 2017, a study divided baseball batters into four groups for a six-week period. The first group undertook adaptive hitting training – which entailed adjusting the pitch speed and location – in a virtual reality environment; the second had extra sessions of batting practice in virtual reality; the third group had extra sessions of batting practice without using virtual reality; and a control group maintained their normal practice regime. On a batting test conducted, the batters who had virtual reality training demonstrated a 117 per cent improvement in a batting test after the training, compared with 36 per cent for the control group. In matches in subsequent seasons, the group who had adaptive hitting training showed the greatest improvements in batting averages. These findings suggest that virtual reality training can lead to meaningful improvements, especially when designers take advantage of simulation to provide training methods – adaptive training – that go beyond the normal demands in training.[45]

In downhill skiing, the US national team used virtual reality before the 2018 Winter Olympics in South Korea.[46] The Jeongseon Alpine Centre hosted the downhill and Super G events; the same venue had been used in the 2016 and 2017 World Cups, which allowed the US team to capture 360-degree video of the courses. Skiers were then immersed in a head-mounted virtual reality system that enabled them to get used to the twists, turns and gate positions of each course. 'Athletes get the opportunity to relive the course over and over again, helping them to develop a mental plan,' said Troy Taylor, the high performance director for US Ski and Snowboard. 'Virtual reality helps athletes learn specific courses, which raises their confidence levels and makes them feel better prepared. It's an added advantage when this preparation can occur away from the slopes when they are travelling in different parts of the world.'

Perhaps most intriguingly, athletes can even use virtual reality to play against themselves. Trevor Bauer, a professional baseball pitcher for the Cincinnati Reds, has used virtual reality to face his own pitches: a new tool to try to improve performance by seeing what cues hitters look for when facing him. 'I've always had this idea that it would be really cool to hit off myself and see how my tunnels look, how my pitches look, how my delivery looks, and try to get some information of how can I further deceive a hitter,' he said. 'I've used VR to do just that – to face myself.'

Not all innovations will deliver what they promise. Indeed, several technologies that are commonly used in elite sport lack a firm scientific basis or, at best, any strong data to substantiate their value. These devices include Dynavision,[47] a 5 by 4 foot board on which are mounted 64 red buttons that can be turned off by touch; Neurotracker,[48, 49] a technology that involves tracking different colour spheres that move randomly around a screen; and stroboscopic glasses,[50] which restrict visual information during play. A fundamental law of science is the notion that learning, and skill transfer, are strongest when practice matches competition as closely as possible. Training aids that focus on developing non-sport-specific, or generic, skills are unlikely to lead to any meaningful transfer to competition.[44, 51]

Whatever works and does not, one change that is already clearly in motion is a more individualized approach to athlete development. Athletes do not play the same, train the same or even sleep the same, and have different needs in all these areas. The smartest sports team will pay increasing heed to this reality, with much training and off-field work being tailored around a player's specific needs.

As with all the areas being explored by innovative players and teams, there is a degree of uncertainty and risk about what will work and what won't. Yet, with science, technology and innovation, sports performance will continue to improve. For the world's best athletes, this is the eternal, never-ending quest.

Epilogue

From how the Murray brothers were raised to the talent goldmine of Wagga Wagga to what athletes see and think during competition, *The Best* has been a journey to understand sporting excellence. With the help of cutting edge science and the tales of athletes themselves, we have tried to deconstruct what makes athletes great. The result, we hope, is an accurate and nuanced account of how athletes reach the pinnacle of sport.

The axiom that every athlete is unique obscures the commonalities in the journeys of many of those who go on to be elite. Some origin tales are a lot more typical than others.

In Part One we showed how sport, often considered society's last bastion of meritocracy, is not really a meritocracy at all. While all athletes are linked by their hard work, the story of who makes it to the top is, to a considerable degree, the story of who gets the right lottery tickets – for instance, who has older siblings and who is born in an area that allows them to maximize their potential. Opportunity is unevenly distributed in sport and beyond; serendipity and environment drive who gets to make good on their talent. Many of the best athletes are born lucky – even if this is in ways they may not understand or that can be detrimental to success in other areas of life.

Of course, talent itself is unevenly distributed – yet, even so, identifying it at an early age is a perilous process. Paradoxically, the most important training for many future elite athletes takes place away from formal sport. The amount of informal play – like the games of *ballon sur bitume* in the Parisian banlieues – that athletes engage in during childhood correlates strikingly with how successful they are in sport later in life. A healthy amount of informal play cultivates creativity, freethinking and technical expertise; a diet of rigid and hyper-serious coaching alone can be detrimental.

Part Two moved from the nursery grounds to elite level competition. We identified how athletes make the adaptations that underpin incredible performance, and accomplish feats impossible to the rest of us. Batters in cricket and baseball learn to pick up information from the opponent's body shape ahead of ball release, helping them anticipate early what will happen next.

Athletes also adapt in remarkable ways to perform other subtler skills. The best athletes are not imbued with extraordinary vision, but instead develop extraordinary brains that allow them to process information much more efficiently and effectively. In sports like football and basketball, leading athletes can identify patterns from both their own team and their opponents to deduce what is likely to happen next; this is how they 'read the game'. Tricksters can use athletes' dexterity in picking up cues against them, by using deception or disguise to lay traps and con their opponents. In competition, elite athletes also use their eyes differently, maintaining a longer focus on the target – the quiet eye – during aiming tasks. The best athletes develop superior perceptual–cognitive skills that enable them to make sense of the world around them more quickly.

Just as the best athletes are distinguished by how they use their brains and eyes in the cauldron of competition, they also stand out for their psychological strengths. Compared with athletes that seem to possess equal sporting talent but do not quite make it to the top, the best athletes tend to have greater levels of passion for the sport, perfectionism, grit, self-confidence and mental toughness. But these mental attributes are not immutable: psychological support can help athletes perform better under pressure and produce 'clutch' performances, like Ian Poulter in the Ryder Cup, and avoid choking.

Part Three showed how the best athletes practise and work to reach and then stay at the top. It explored the art and science of deliberate practice, and how the best athletes don't necessarily train harder – but they do train more smartly, promoting enhanced skill acquisition. Coaches can aid this process too, by creating optimal challenge points which facilitate learning, embracing training methods that ensure variability in practice, and making athletes familiar with confronting unforeseen problems and performing under pressure. Technology holds out the possibility of accelerating skill acquisition too, as our journey to explore the work done by Barcelona Football Club in myriad areas – including artificial intelligence, virtual reality, player tracking and even sleep – showed. While not all technology will deliver on its promise, advancements in these areas could help athletes soar to greater heights.

Our journey has raised some important questions for all those involved in developing talent. For instance, given the profound benefits enjoyed by younger siblings and those born in medium-sized towns, how can sporting federations artificially create these environments for those who do not have these benefits? Encouraging more informal play and exposing more children to playing up a year are methods that prudent talent developers are increasingly exploring. Similarly, athletes and coaches can learn from the type of practice that the best athletes generally engage in, and the importance of practice that is unpredictable, challenging and forces athletes to think for themselves, rather than being told what to do and merely repeating tasks.

No athlete is born great, and no genes bring any guarantees of greatness. Everything we know about genes suggests that several times more athletes have the genes needed to be an elite performer than actually become one. Ultimately, perhaps more than anything else, what defines the best athletes is their adaptability: leading athletes adapt physically, physiologically, technically, tactically and psychologically to the demands they face during practice and competition.

Few can reach this rarefied group. But for all involved in nurturing talent – in sport and beyond – the apex of professional sport provides a laboratory from which to learn. And, we hope, a deeper grasp of what it takes to reach the summit will provide a broader appreciation of the games that we watch and play.

References

Prologue

1 https://www.onlinecasino.ca/odds-of-success
2 Sports and Fitness Industry Association [email]
3 https://www.world.rugby/development/player-numbers?lang=en
4 https://amp.businessinsider.com/michael-calvin-shocking-statistic-why-children-football-academies-will-never-succeed-soccer-sport-2017-6

Chapter 1: We are family

1 www.european-athletics.org/competitions/european-athletics-championships/news/article=filip-and-henrik-ingebrigtsen-bask-jakob-1500m-success-berlin/index.html
2 https://www.espn.com/espnw/culture/feature/story/_/id/17494146/road-23-story-serena-path-greatness
3 www.telegraph.co.uk/cricket/2019/01/18/solving-englands-batting-crisis-younger-brothers-could-key/
4 www.irishtimes.com/sport/other-sports/the-story-behind-the-incredible-ingebrigtsen-brothers-1.3593994
5 www.linkedin.com/pulse/what-do-we-know-talent-identification-england-womens-team-russell/
6 worldathletics.org/news/feature/jakob-ingebrigtsen-european-championships-ber
7 Carette, B., Anseel, F., and Van Yperen, N.W. Born to learn or born to win? Birth order effects on achievement goals. *Journal of Research in Personality*, 45, 5 (2011): 500–3.

8 Collins, D., MacNamara, A., and McCarthy, A. Super champions, champions and almosts: important differences and commonalities on the rocky road. *Frontiers in Psychology*, 6 (2016).

9 https://www.theguardian.com/observer/osm/story/0,, 727737,00.html

10 https://www.espn.com/espnw/culture/feature/story/_/ id/17494146/road-23-story-serena-path-greatness

11 http://sulloway.org/politics.html

12 Sulloway, F.J., and Zweigenhaft, R.L. Birth order and risk taking in athletics: a meta-analysis and study of Major League Baseball. *Personality and Social Psychology Review*, 14, 4 (2011): 402–16.

13 www.telegraph.co.uk/sport/cricket/international/southafrica/ 12062933/South-Africa-v-England-The-making-of-ABde-Villiers.html

14 Hopwood, M.J., Farrow, D., MacMahon, C., and Baker, J. 'Sibling dynamics and sport expertise. *Scandinavian Journal of Science and Medicine in Sport*, 25 (2015): 724–33.

15 Tjelta, L.I. Three Norwegian brothers all European 1500 m champions: what is the secret? *International Journal of Sports Science and Coaching*, 14, 5 (2019): 694–700.

16 Karlinsky, A., and Hodges, N.J. Dyad practice impacts self-directed practice behaviors and motor learning outcomes in a contextual interference paradigm. *Journal of Motor Behavior*, 50, 5 (2015): 579–89.

17 https://www.encyclopedia.com/people/sports-and-games/ sports-biographies/serena-williams

18 Trussell, D.E., and Shaw, S.M. Organized youth sport and parenting in public and private spaces. *Leisure Sciences*, 34, 5 (2012): 377–94.

19 Roca, A., Williams, A.M., and Ford, P. Developmental activities and the acquisition of superior anticipation and decision making in soccer. *Journal of Sports Sciences*, 30, 15 (2012): 1643–52.

20 Weissensteiner, J., Abernethy, B., Farrow, D., and Muller, S. The development of anticipation: a cross sectional examination of the practice experiences contributing to skill in cricket batting. *Journal of Sport and Exercise Psychology*, 30 (2008): 663–84.

21 www.theplayerstribune.com/en-us/articles/raheem-sterlingengland-it-was-all-a-dream

22 Lee, H., Tamminen, K.A., Clark, A.M., Slater, L., Spence, J.C., and Holt, N.L. A meta-study of qualitative research examining determinants of children's independent active free play. *International Journal of Behavioral Nutrition and Physical Activity*, 12, 5 (2015).

23 https://sportspath.typepad.com/files/key_-_the_u.s._womens_youth_national_teams_program_finding_the_next_mia_hamm_and_alex_morgan_2.pdf

24 Cline, F., and Fay, J. *Parenting with Love and Logic: Teaching Children Responsibility*, 2nd edn. Colorado Springs, CO: NavPress, 2006.

25 Janssen, I. Hyper-parenting is negatively associated with physical activity among 7–12 year olds. *Preventive Medicine*, 73 (2005): 55–9.

26 Holt, N.L., Pynn, S., Pankow, K., Neely, K.C., Carson, V., and Ingstrup, M. Family influences on active free play and sport. In T.S. Horn and A.L. Smith (eds), *Advances in Sport and Exercise Psychology*, 4th edn, pp. 117–32. Champaign, IL: Human Kinetics, 2019.

27 Harwood, C.G., and Knight, C.J. Parenting in youth sport: A position paper on parenting expertise. *Psychology of Sport and Exercise*, 16 (2015): 24–35.

Chapter 2: Location, location, location

1 https://en.wikipedia.org/wiki/Pakistan_at_the_2016_Summer_Olympics

2 Culver, D., and Trudel, P. Clarifying the concept of communities of practice in sport. *International Journal of Sports Science and Coaching*, 3, 1 (2008): 1–10.

3 www.suttontrust.com/wp-content/uploads/2019/06/Elitist-Britain-2019.pdf

4 www.theage.com.au/sport/afl/how-private-schools-have-taken-over-the-afl-20191121-p53cso.html

5 Spaaij, R., Farquharson, K., and Marjoribanks, T. Sport and social inequalities. *Sociology Compass* (2015): 400–11.

6 Smith, A., Haycock, D., and Hulme, N. (2013). The class of London 2012: Some sociological reflections on the social backgrounds of Team GB athletes. *Sociological Research Online*, 18, 3 (2013): 15.

7   www.linkedin.com/pulse/background-factors-trying-identity-potentially-talented-robin-russell/

8   Ogden, D.C., and Hilt, M.L. Collective identity and basketball: An explanation for the decreasing number of African-Americans on America's baseball diamonds. *Journal of Leisure Research*, 35, 2 (2003): 213–27.

9   Farah, L., Schorer, J., Baker, J., and Wattie, N. Population density and proximity to junior developmental team affect the development of National Hockey League draftees. *Scandinavian Journal of Science and Medicine in Sport*, 28, 11 (2018): 2427–35.

10 Baker, J., Schorer, J., Cobley, S., Schimmer, G., and Wattie, N. Circumstantial development and athletic excellence: The role of date of birth and birthplace. *European Journal of Sports Sciences*, 9, 6 (2009): 329–39.

11 Imtiaz, F., Hancock, D.J., Vierimaa, M., and Côté, J. Place of development and dropout in youth ice hockey. *International Journal of Sport and Exercise Psychology*, 12, 3 (2014): 234–44.

12 Fraser-Thomas, J., Côté, J., and MacDonald, D.J. Community size in youth sport settings: Examining developmental assets and sport withdrawal. *Physical and Health Education Academic Journal*, 2 (2010): 1–9.

13 Finnegan, L., Richardson, D., Littlewood, M., and McArdle, J. The influence of date and place of birth on youth player selection to a National Football Association elite development programme. *Science and Medicine in Football*, 1, 1 (2017): 30–9.

14 https://www.nytimes.com/2018/02/24/sports/olympics/final-medal-count-norway.html

15 bbc.com/worklife/article/20171211-friluftsliv-the-nordic-concept-of-getting-outdoors

16 Fawver, B., Cowan, R.L., DeCouto, B., Lohse, K.R., Podlog, L., and Williams, A.M. Psychological characteristics, sport engagement, and performance in alpine skiers. *Psychology of Sport and Exercise* [in press].

17 https://idrottsforum.org/aalberg-saether131024/

Chapter 3: Timing is everything

1 telegraph.co.uk/sport/football/teams/england/11996176/ Tottenham-and-England-striker-Harry-Kane-proves-he-is-the-man-for-all-occasions.html

2 http://bbc.co.uk/news/uk-politics-21579484

3 Barnsley, R.H., Thompson, A.H., and Barnsley, P.E. Hockey success and birthdate: The relative age effect. *CAHPER/ACSEPL Journal*, 51, 8 (1985): 23–8.

4 Lovell, R., Towlson, C., Parkin, G., Portas, M., Vaeyens, R., and Cobley, S. Soccer player characteristics in English lower-league development programmes: The relationships between relative age, maturation, anthropometry and physical fitness. *PLoS One* (2015). doi: 10.1371/journal.pone.0137238

5 Fleming, J., and Fleming, S. Relative age effect amongst footballers in the English Premier League and English Football League, 2010–2011. *International Journal of Performance Analysis*, 12, 2 (2012): 361–72.

6 Padron-Cabo, A., Rey, E., Garcia-Soidan, J.L., and Penedo-Jamardo, E. Large scale analysis of relative age effect on professional soccer players in FIFA designated zones. *International Journal of Performance Analysis in Sport*, 16, 1 (2016): 332–46.

7 Salinero, J.J., Perez, B., Burillo, P., and Lesma, M.L. Relative age effect in European professional football: Analysis by position. *Journal of Human Sport and Exercise*, 8, 4 (2013): 966–73.

8 Arrieta, H., Torres-Unda, J., Gil, S.M., and Irazusta, J. Relative age effect and performance in the U16, U18 and U20 European Basketball Championships. *Journal of Sports Sciences*, 34, 16 (2016): 1530–4.

9 Thompson, A., Barnsley, R., and Stebelsky, G. 'Born to play ball': The relative age effect and Major League Baseball. *Sociology of Sport Journal*, 8 (1991): 146–51.

10 Deaner, R., Lowen, A., and Cobley, S. Born at the wrong time: Selection bias in the NHL draft. *PLoS One*, 8 (2013). e57753. 0.1371/journal.pone.0057753.

11 Wattie, N., MacDonald, D.J., and Cobley, S. Birthdate and birthplace effects on expertise attainment. In J. Baker and D. Farrow

(eds), *Routledge Handbook of Sport Expertise*, pp. 373–82. Oxford: Routledge, 2017.

12 Cobley, S., Hanratty, M., O'Connor, D., and Cotton, W. First club location and relative age as influences on being a professional Australian rugby league player. *International Journal of Sports Science and Coaching*, 9 (2014): 335–46.

13 McCarthy, N., Collins, D., and Court, D. Start hard, finish better: further evidence for the reversal of the RAE advantage. *Journal of Sports Sciences*, 34, 15 (2016): 1461–5.

14 Edgar, S., and O'Donoghue, P. Season of birth distribution of elite tennis players. *Journal of Sports Sciences*, 23 (2005): 1013–20.

15 Costa, A.M., Marques, M.C., Louro, H., Ferreira, S.S., and Marinho, D.A. The relative age effect among elite youth competitive swimmers. *European Journal of Sports Sciences*, 13 (2013): 437–44.

16 Schorer, J., Baker, J., Lotz, S., and Büsch, D. Influence of early environmental constraints on achievement motivation in talented young handball players. *International Journal of Sport Psychology*, 41 (2010): 42–57.

17 Safranyos, S., Chittle, L., Horton, S., and Dixon, J.C. Academic timing and the relative age effect among male and female athletes in Canadian interuniversity volleyball. *Perceptual and Motor Skills*, 127, 1 (2019): 182–201.

18 Steidl-Müller, L., Hildebrandt, C., Raschner, C., and Müller, E. Challenges of talent development in alpine ski racing: a narrative review. *Journal of Sports Sciences*, 37, 6 (2019): 601–12.

19 Cobley, S., Baker, J., Wattie, N., and McKenna, J. Annual age-grouping and athlete development: A meta-analytic review of relative age effects in sport. *Sports Medicine*, 39 (2009): 235–56.

20 Smith, K.L., Weier, P.L., Till, K., Romann, M., and Cobley, S. Relative age effects across and within female sport contexts: A systematic review and meta-analysis. *Sports Medicine*, 43 (2008): 1451–78.

21 Towlson, C., Cobley, S., Parkin, G., and Lovell, R. When does the influence of maturation on anthropometric and physical fitness characteristics increase and subside? *Scandinavian Journal of Medicine and Science in Sports*, 28, 8 (2018): 1946–55.

22 Richardson, D., and Stratton, G. Preliminary investigation of the seasonal birth distribution of England World Cup campaign players. *Journal of Sports Sciences*, 10 (1999): 821–2.

23 Baker, J., Janning, C., Wong, H., Cobley, S., and Schorer, J. Variations in relative age effects in individual sports: Skiing, figure skating and gymnastics. *European Journal of Sports Sciences*, 14 (2014): 183–90.

24 Hancock, D., Starkes, J., and Ste-Marie, D. The relative age effect in female gymnastics: A flip-flop phenomenon. *International Journal of Sport Psychology*, 46 (2015): 714–25.

25 Ford, P.R., and Williams, A.M. No relative age effect in the birth dates of award-winning athletes in male professional team sports. *Research Quarterly for Exercise and Sport*, 82 (2011): 373–6.

26 Jones, B.D., Lawrence, G.P., and Hardy, L. New evidence of relative age effects in 'super-elite' sportsmen: A case for the survival and evolution of the fittest. *Journal of Sports Sciences*, 36, 6 (2018): 697–703.

27 Gladwell, M. *Outliers: The Story of Success*. New York: Little, Brown and Company, 2008.

28 Gibbs, B.G., Jarvis, J.A., and Dufur, M.J. The rise of the underdog? The relative age effect reversal among Canadian-born NHL hockey players: A reply to Nolan and Howell. *International Review for the Sociology of Sport*, 47, 5 (2011): 644–9.

29 Fumarco, L., Gibbs, B.J., Jarvis, J.A., and Rossi, G. The relative age effect reversal among the National Hockey League elite. *PLoS One*, 12, 8 (2017): 1–16.

30 www.bbc.com/news/business-32064842

31 www.21stclub.com/

32 Mirwald, R.L., Baxter-Jones, A.D.G., Bailey, D.A., and Beunen, G.P. An assessment of maturity from anthropometric measurements. *Medicine and Science in Sports and Exercise*, 34 (2002): 689–94.

33 Helsen, W.F., Baker, J. Michiels, S., Schorer, J., Van Winckel, J., and Williams, A.M. The relative age effect in European professional soccer: Did ten years of research make any difference? *Journal of Sports Sciences*, 30, 15 (2012): 1665–71.

34 https://talentdevelopmentinirishfootball.com/2019/05/09/relative-age-effect-in-uefa-u17-championships-2019/

35 Steingröver, C., Wattie, N., Baker, J., and Schorer, J. Does relative age affect career length in North American professional sports? *Sports Medicine-Open*, 2, 1 (2016): 18.

36 MacDonald, D.J., Cheung, M., Côté, J., and Abernethy, B. Place but not date of birth influences the development and emergence of athletic talent in American football. *Journal of Applied Sport Psychology*, 21 (2009): 80–90.

37 Unpublished data provided by Brady DeCouto.

38 www.theguardian.com/sport/2015/dec/19/biobanding-scientists-skinny-kids-sporting-superstars

39 Lagestad, P., Steen, I., and Dalen, T. Inevitable relative age effects in different stages of the selection process among male and female youth soccer players. *Sports*, 6, 29 (2018): 1–9.

40 Mann, D.L., and Pleun, J.M.A. van Ginneken. Age-ordered shirt numbering reduces the selection bias associated with the relative age effect. *Journal of Sports Sciences*, 35, 8 (2018): 784–90.

41 Romann, M., and Cobley, S. Relative age effects in athletic sprinting and corrective adjustments as a solution for their removal. *PLoS One*, 10, 4 (2015).

42 Cobley, S., Abbott, S., Eisenhuth, J., Salter, J., McGregor, D., and Romann, M. Removing relative age effects from youth swimming: The development and testing of corrective adjustment procedures. *Journal of Science and Medicine in Sport*, 22, 6 (2019): 735–40.

43 https://www.telegraph.co.uk/cricket/2018/07/29/making-virat-kohli-day-father-died-made-90/

44 https://www.nzherald.co.nz/bay-of-plenty-times/news/article.cfm?c_id=1503343andobjectid=12310141

Chapter 4: Street spirit

1 https://runrepeat.com/most-football-talent-france

2 https://en.wikipedia.org/wiki/Sarcelles#Notable_people

3 www.theguardian.com/football/2016/dec/14/balllon-sur-bitume-street-football-france

4 www.theguardian.com/football/2018/jul/09/world-cup-semi-finals-immigration

5   Memmert, D., Baker, J., and Bertsch, C. Play and practice in the development of sport-specific creativity in team ball sports. *High Ability Studies*, 21, 1 (2010): 3–18.

6   Memmert, D., and Roth, K. The effects of non-specific and specific concepts on tactical creativity in team ball sports. *Journal of Sports Sciences*, 25 (2007): 1423–32.

7   Memmert, D. *Teaching Tactical Creativity in Sport: Research and Practice.* Abingdon: Routledge, 2015.

8   Salmela, J.H., and Moraes, L.C. Development of expertise: The role of coaching, families, and cultural contexts. In J.L. Starkes and K.A. Ericsson (eds), *Expert Performance in Sports: Advances in Research on Sport Expertise*, pp. 275–93. Champaign, IL: Human Kinetics, 2003.

9   Ford, P.R., Carling, C., Garces, M., Marques, M., Miguel, C., Farrant, A., Stenling, A., Moreno, J., Le Gall, F., Holmström, S., Salmela, J.H., and Williams, A.M. The developmental activities of elite soccer players aged under-16 years from Brazil, England, France, Ghana, Mexico, Portugal and Sweden. *Journal of Sports Sciences*, 30 (2012): 1653–63.

10 www.fifa.com/futsalworldcup/news/the-football-greats-forged-futsal-1798909

11 Weigelt, C., Williams, A.M., Wyngrove, T., and Scott, M.A. Transfer and motor skill learning. *Ergonomics*, 43, 10 (2000): 1698–707.

12 Honigstein, R. *Das Reboot: How Germany Reinvented Itself and Conquered the World.* New York: Vintage Digital, 2015.

13 Horning, M., Aust, F., and Gulich, A. Practice and play in the development of German top-level professional football players. *European Journal of Sports Sciences*, 16 (2016): 96–105.

14 Gullich, A. 'Macro-structure' of developmental participation histories and 'mico-structure' of practice of German female world-class and national-class players. *Journal of Sports Sciences*, 37, 12 (2018): 1–9.

15 Ford, P.R., and Williams, A.M. The developmental activities engaged in by elite youth soccer players who progressed to professional status compared to those who did not. *Psychology of Sport and Exercise*, 13 (2012): 349–52.

16 www.dailymail.co.uk/sport/football/article-2305700/Wayne-Rooney--95-cent-game-comes-playing-child-tarmac.html

17 Memmert, D., Baker, J., and Bertsch, C. Play and practice in the development of sport-specific creativity in team ball sports. *High Ability Studies*, 21, 1 (2010): 3–18.

18 Ford, P., Yates, I., and Williams, A.M. An analysis of activities and instructional behaviours used by coaches during practice in English youth soccer: Exploring the link between theory and practice. *Journal of Sports Sciencess*, 28 (2010): 483–95.

19 Williams, A.M., Ward, P., Bell-Walker, J., and Ford, P. Discovering the antecedents of anticipation and decision making skill. *British Journal of Psychology*, 103 (2012): 393–411.

20 Roca, A., Williams, A.M., Ford, P. Developmental activities and the acquisition of superior anticipation and decision making in soccer. *Journal of Sports Sciences*, 30, 15 (2012): 1643–52.

21 Hendry, D.T., Crocker, P.R.E., Williams, A.M., and Hodges, N.J. Tracking and comparing self-determined motivation in elite youth soccer: Influence of development activities, age and skill. *Frontiers in Psychology: Performance Science*, 10 (2019). doi: 10.3389/fpsyg.2019.00304

22 DiFiori, J., Guellich, A., Brenner, J., Côté, J., Hainline, B., Ryan, E., and Malina, R. The NBA and youth basketball: Recommendations for promoting a healthy and positive experience. *Sports Medicine*, 48 (2018).

23 Memmert, A., and König, S. Models of game intelligence and creativity in sport. In N.J. Hodges and A.M. Williams (eds), *Skill Acquisition in Sport*, 3rd edn, pp. 220–36. Abingdon: Routledge, 2019.

24 www.independent.co.uk/sport/football/news-and-comment/south-london-football-gomez-sancho-premier-league-catford-peckham-croydon-a8702541.html

25 https://inews.co.uk/sport/football/champions-league/jadon-sancho-interview-tottenham-vs-borussia-dortmund-champions-league-123394

26 nytimes.com/2018/06/07/sports/soccer/france-world-cup-kylian-mbappe.html

27 Drut, B., and Duhautois, R. *Sciences Sociales Football Club*. Louvain-la-Neuve and Paris: De Boeck Supérieur, 2017 [French].

Chapter 5: In search of excellence

1 www.teambath.com/2012/05/06/helen-glover/

2 www.theguardian.com/sport/2012/aug/01/profiles-helen-glover-heather-stanning?newsfeed=true

3 Gladwell, M. *Outliers: The Story of Success*. New York: Little, Brown & Company, 2008.

4 Sneeru, J., Pinkham, C., Dugas, L., Patrick, B., and LaBella, C. Sports specialization in young athletes: Evidence-based recommendations. *Sports Health: A Multidisciplinary Perspective*, 5, 3 (2013): 25–7.

5 DiFiori, J., Guellich, A., Brenner, J., Côté, J., Hainline, B., Ryan, E., and Malina, R. The NBA and youth basketball: Recommendations for promoting a healthy and positive experience. *Sports Medicine*, 48 (2018). 10.1007/s40279-018-0950-0.

6 Ericsson, K.A. Toward a science of the acquisition of expert performance in sports clarifying the differences between deliberate practice and other types of practice. *Journal of Sports Sciences* [in press].

7 Ford, P.R., Coughlan, E.K., Hodges, N.J., and Williams, A.M. Deliberate practice in sport. In J. Baker and D. Farrow (eds), *Routledge Handbook of Sport Expertise*, pp. 347–62. Abingdon: Routledge, 2015.

8 www.theplayerstribune.com/en-us/articles/joel-embiid-its-story-time

9 http://archive.nba.com/preview2007/journey_nash.html

10 www.wsj.com/articles/the-secret-to-novak-djokovics-success-skiing-1433434695

11 https://www.telegraph.co.uk/sport/sportvideo/footballvideo/9679848/Zlatan-Ibrahimovic-taekwondo-blackbelt-key-to-Swedish-strikers-goalscoring-prowess.html

12 www.telegraph.co.uk/sport/cricket/international/england/9859642/Englands-Jos-Buttler-makes-impact-in-New-Zealand.html

13 Smeeton, N., Ward, P., and Williams, A.M. Transfer of perceptual skill in sport. *Journal of Sports Sciences*, 19, 2 (2004): 3–9.

14 Gabbett, T.J. Physical qualities of experts. In J. Baker and D. Farrow (eds), *Routledge Handbook of Sport Expertise*, pp. 121–9. Abingdon: Routledge, 2017.

15 Müller, S., and Rosalie, S.M. Transfer of expert visual-perceptual-motor skill in sport. In A.M. Williams and R.J. Jackson (eds), *Anticipation and Decision Making in Sport*, pp. 375–93. Abingdon: Routledge, 2019.

16 www.couriermail.com.au/sport/cricket/steve-smiths-ultimate-tale-of-survival-at-the-gabba-forged-under-his-fathers-tutelage/news-story/6fbc43f112351d287192ad24d29114d6

17 Jayanth, N., Pinkham, C., and Dugas, L. Sports specialization in young athletes: evidence-based recommendations. *Sports Health: A Multidisciplinary Journal*, 5, 3 (2012): 251–7.

18 Fleisig, G.S., Andrews, J.R., Cutter, G.R., et al. Risk of serious injury for young baseball pitchers: A 10-year prospective study. *American Journal of Sports Medicine*, 39, 2 (2011): 253–7.

19 Myer, G., Jayanthi, N., DiFiori, J., Faigenbaum, A., Kiefer, A., Logerstedt, D., and Micheli, L. Sports specialization, part II: Alternative solutions to early sport specialization in youth athletes. *Sports Health*, 8 (2015). 10.1177/1941738115614811.

20 Wilhelm, A., Choi, C., and Deitch, J. Early specialization: effectiveness and risk of injury in professional baseball players. *Orthopedic Journal of Sports Medicine*, 5, 9 (2107): 1–5.

21 Kearney, P.E., and Hayes, P.R. Excelling at youth level in competitive track and field athletics is not a prerequisite for later success. *Journal of Sports Sciences*, 36, 21 (2018): 2502–9.

22 Bridge, M.W., and Toms, M.R. The specialising or sampling debate: a retrospective analysis of adolescent sports participation in the UK. *Journal of Sports Sciences*, 31, 1 (2013): 87–96.

23 Güllich, A. Sport-specific and non-specific practice of strong and weak responders in junior and senior elite athletics: A matched-pairs analysis. *Journal of Sports Sciences*, 36, 19 (2018): 2256–64.

24 Moesch, K., Elbe, A.M., Hauge, M.L.T., and Wilkman, J.M. Late specialization: The key to success in centimeters, grams, or seconds (cgs) sports. *Scandinavian Journal of Science and Medicine in Sports* (2011). DOI: 10.1111/j.1600-0838.2010.01280.x

25 Rees, T., Hardy, L., Güllich, A., Abernethy, B., Cote, J., Wood-man, T., Montgomery, H., Lain, S., and Warr, C. The Great British medalists project: A review of current knowledge on the development of the world's best sporting talent. *Sports Medicine*, 46 (2106): 1041–58.

26 www.manchestereveningnews.co.uk/sport/football/foot-ball-news/marcus-rashford-rejected-liverpool-join-10954380

27 Ford, P.R., Carling, C., Garces, M., Marques, M., Miguel, C., Farrant, A., Stenling, A., Moreno, J., Le Gall, F., Holmström, S., Salmela, J.H., and Williams, A.M. The developmental activities of elite soccer players aged under-16 years from Brazil, England, France, Ghana, Mexico, Portugal and Sweden. *Journal of Sports Sciences*, 30 (2012): 1653–63.

28 Helsen, W.F., Starkes, J.L., and Hodges, N.J. Team sports and the theory of deliberate practice. *Journal of Sport and Exercise Psychology*, 20 (1998): 12–34.

29 Ford, P.R., Hodges, N.J., Broadbent, D.P., O'Connor, D., Scott, D., Datson, N., Anderson, H.A., and Williams, A.M. The developmental and professional activities of female international soccer players from five high-performing nations. *Journal of Sports Sciences* [in press].

30 Law, M., Côté, J., and Ericsson, K.A. Characteristics of expert development in rhythmic gymnastics: A retrospective study. *International Journal of Sport and Exercise Psychology*, 5 (2007): 82–103.

31 Baker, J., and Young, B. 20 years later: Deliberate practice and the development of expertise in sport. *International Review of Sport and Exercise Psychology*, 7 (2014): 135–57.

32 Fawver, B., Cowan, R.L., DeCouto, B., Lohse, K.R., Podlog, L., and Williams, A.M. Psychological characteristics, sport engagement, and performance in alpine skiers. *Psychology of Sport and Exercise* [in press].

33 www.espn.co.uk/golf/news/story?id=2432057

34 www.theguardian.com/news/2006/may/05/guardianobituaries.obituaries

35 www.nytimes.com/1997/04/30/sports/earl-woods-looks-out-for-son.html

36 Côté, J., Baker, J., and Abernethy, B. Practice and play in the development of sport expertise. In R.C. Eklund and G. Tenenbaum (eds), *Handbook of Sport Psychology*, 3rd edn, pp. 184–202. Hoboken, NJ: Wiley, 2007.

37 Côté, J., and Erickson, K. Diversification and deliberate play during the sampling years. In J. Baker and D. Farrow (eds), *Routledge Handbook of Sport Expertise*, pp. 305–16. Abingdon: Routledge, 2017.

38 Ford, P.R., Ward, P., Hodges, N.J., and Williams, A.M. The role of deliberate practice and play in career progression: The early engagement hypothesis. *High Ability Studies*, 20 (2009): 5–75.

39 Hendry, D.T., and Hodges, N.J. Early majority engagement pathway best defines transitions from youth to adult elite men's soccer in the UK: A three time-point retrospective and prospective study. *Psychology of Sport and Exercise*, 36 (2018): 81–9.

40 Hendry, D.T., Williams, A.M., Ford, P.R., and Hodges, N.J. Developmental activities and perceptions of challenge for National and Varsity women soccer players in Canada. *Psychology of Sport and Exercise*, 43 (2019): 210–18.

Chapter 6: The X factor

1 Connolly, C. *Enemies of Promise*. Oxford: George Routledge & Sons, 1938.

2 www.si.com/vault/2004/03/29/366282/ready-for-freddy-at-14-freddy-adu-is-already-the-highest-paid-and-most-celebrated-player-in-mls-now-its-time-for-him-to-play-his-first-game – all citations in this section.

3 http://metro.co.uk/2013/11/30/20-month-old-child-becomes-youngest-professional-footballer-in-the-world-4208126/

4 https://trainingground.guru/articles/manchester-city-under-5s-elite squad-described-as-absolute-madness

5 Weisman, A.C., Bracken, N., Horton, S., and Weir, P.L. The difficulty of talent identification: Inconsistency among coaches through skill-based assessment of youth hockey players. *International Journal of Sports Science and Coaching*, 9 (2014): 447–55.

6 www.newyorker.com/sports/sporting-scene/freddy-adu-and-the-children-of-the-beautiful-game

7 Baker, J., Schorer, J., and Wattie, N. (2018). Compromising talent: Issues in identifying and selecting talent in sport. *Quest*, 70, 1 (2018): 48–63.

8 Baker, J., Cobley, S., Scorer, J., and Wattie, N. *The Routledge Handbook of Talent Identification and Development in Sport*. Oxford: Routledge, 2017.

9 https://global.espn.com/football/club/united-states-usa/660/blog/post/3873263/freddy-adu-exclusive-im-not-ready-to-give-it-up

10 bbc.co.uk/news/business-32064842

11 Dugdale, J.H., Sanders, D., Myers, T., Williams, A.M., and Hunter, A.M. Progression from youth to professional soccer: A longitudinal study of successful and unsuccessful academy graduates. *Scandinavian Journal of Science and Medicine in Sport* [in press].

12 Güllich, A., Hardy, L., Kuncheva, L., Laing, S., Barlow, M., Evans, L., Rees, T., Abernethy, B., Cote, J., Warr, C., and Wraith, L. Developmental biographies of Olympic super-elite and elite athletes: A multidisciplinary pattern recognition analysis. *Journal of Expertise*, 19, 2 (2019): 1.

13 Koz, D., Fraser-Thomas, J., and Baker, J. Accuracy of professional sports drafts in predicting career potential. *Scandinavian Journal of Medicine and Science in Sports*, 22 (2012): 64–9.

14 Williams, A.M., and Ericsson, K.A. Perceptual-cognitive expertise in sport: Some considerations when applying the expert performance approach. *Human Movement Science*, 24, 3 (2005): 283–307.

15 Williams, A.M., Ford, P.R., and Brust, B.J. Talent identification and development in soccer since the millennium. *Journal of Sports Sciences* [in press].

16 Williams, A.M., and Reilly, T. Talent identification and development in soccer. *Journal of Sports Sciences*, 18, 9 (2000): 657–67.

17 www.fourfourtwo.com/performance/training/how-catch-wengers-eye

18 Larkin, P., and O'Connor, D. Talent identification and recruitment in youth soccer: Recruiter's perceptions of the key attributes for player recruitment. *PLoS One*, 12, 4 (2017). e0175716.

19 Roberts, S.J., McRobert, A.P., Lewis, C.J., and Reeves, M.J. Establishing consensus of position-specific predictors for elite youth soccer in England. *Science and Medicine in Football*, 3, 3 (2019): 205–13.

20 Ward, P., and Williams, A.M. Perceptual and cognitive skill development in soccer: The multidimensional nature of expert performance. *Journal of Sport and Exercise Psychology*, 25, 1 (2003): 93–111.

21 Van Yperen, N.W. Why some make it and others do not: Identifying psychological factors that predict career success in professional adult soccer. *The Sport Psychologist*, 23 (2009): 317–29.

22 https://global.espn.com/football/club/united-states-usa/660/blog/post/3873263/freddy-adu-exclusive-im-not-ready-to-give-it-up

23 www.cameo.com/friz09

24 www.uksport.gov.uk/our-work/investing-in-sport/historical-funding-figures

25 www.bbc.co.uk/sport/olympics/44146009

26 www.telegraph.co.uk/sport/2019/11/17/system-british-sport-failing-athletes-fault-lies-top

27 Epstein, D. *The Sporting Gene*. London: Penguin Random House, 2013.

28 Tucker, R., and Collins, M. What makes champions? A review of the relative contribution of genes and training to sporting success. *British Journal of Sports Medicine*, 46 (2012): 555–61.

29 Sapolsky, R. *Behave: The Biology of Humans at Our Best and Worst*, p. 265. London: Penguin Books, 2017.

30 Doerfler, W., and Böhm, P. (eds), *BoEpigenetics: A Different Way of Looking at Genetics*. New York: Springer International Publishing, 2016.

31 Baker, J., Wattie, N., and Schorer, J. (2019). A proposed conceptualization of talent in sport: The first step in a long and winding road. *Psychology of Sport and Exercise*, 43 (2019): 27–33.

32 Deans, C., and Maggert, K.A. What do you mean, 'epigenetic'? *Genetics*, 1, 199 (2015): 887–96.

33 Taniasawa, K., Wang, J., et al. Sport and exercise genetics: the FIMS 2019 consensus statement update. *British Journal of Sports Medicine* (2019). Doi:10.1136/bjsports-2019-101532.

34   Pitsiladis, Y.P., and Wang, G. Genomics of elite sporting performance. In J. Baker and D. Farrow (eds), *Routledge Handbook of Sports Expertise*, pp. 295–304. Abingdon: Routledge, 2017.

35   Norton, K., and Olds, T. Morphological evolution of athletes over the 20th century. *Sports Medicine*, 31 (2001): 763–83.

Chapter 7: How to hit a ball in under 0.5 seconds

1   Ward, P., Williams, A.M., and Bennett, S. Visual search and biological motion perception in tennis. *Research Quarterly for Exercise and Sport*, 73, 1 (2002): 107–12.

2   Triolet, C., Benguigui, N., Le Runigo, C., and Williams, A.M. Quantifying the nature of anticipation in tennis. *Journal of Sports Sciences*, 31, 8 (2013): 820–30.

3   Dicks, M., Araujo, D., and van der Kamp, J. Perception-action for the study of anticipation and decision making. In A.M. Williams and R.J. Jackson (eds), *Anticipation and Decision Making in Sport*, pp. 181–200. Oxford: Routledge, 2019.

4   Murphy, C.P., Jackson, R.C., Cooke, K., Roca, A., Benguigui, N., and Williams, A.M. Contextual information and perceptual-cognitive expertise in a dynamic, temporally-constrained task. *Journal of Experimental Psychology: Applied*, 22 (2016): 455–70.

5   Murphy, C.P., Jackson, R.C., and Williams, A.M. The role of contextual information during skilled anticipation. *Quarterly Journal of Experimental Psychology*, 71, 10 (2018): 2070–87.

6   Mann, D.L., Spratford, W., and Abernethy, B. The head tracks and gaze predicts: How the world's best batters hit a ball. *PloS One*, 8, 3 (2013). e58289.

7   Singer, R.N., Williams, A.M., Janelle, C., Frehlich, S., Barber, D., and Boutchard, L. Visual search during 'live' on-court situations in tennis. *Research Quarterly for Exercise and Sport*, 69, 3 (1998): 109–16.

8   www.youtube.com/watch?v=ja6HeLB3kwY

9   Williams, A.M., Davids, K., and Williams, J.G. *Visual Perception and Action in Sport*. London: E. & F.N. Spon, 1999.

10   www.easv.org/bauschlomb-olympic-vision-centre-findings/

11 Mann, D.L., Ho, N.Y., De Souza, N.J., Watson, D.R., and Taylor, S.J. Is optimal vision required for the successful execution of an interceptive task? *Human Movement Science*, 26 (2007): 343–56.

12 Mann, D.L., Abernethy, B., and Farrow, D. The resilience of natural interceptive actions in refractive blur. *Human Movement Science*, 29, 3 (2010): 386–400.

13 Ward, P., and Williams, A.M. Perceptual and cognitive skill development in soccer: The multidimensional nature of expert performance. *Journal of Sport and Exercise Psychology*, 25, 1 (2003): 93–111.

14 www.cricket365.com/oli-fisher/the-seven-fastest-balls-ever-bowled-in-international-cricket/

15 Land, M.F., and McLeod, P. From eye movements to actions: How batsmen hit the ball. *Nature Neuroscience*, 3 (2000): 1340–5.

16 McRobert, A., Williams, A.M., Ward, P., and Eccles, D. Perceptual-cognitive mechanisms underpinning expertise: The effects of task constraints. *Ergonomics*, 52, 4 (2009): 474–83.

17 McRobert, A., Ward, P., Eccles, D., and Williams, A.M. The effect of manipulating context-specific information on perceptual–cognitive processes during a simulated anticipation task. *British Journal of Psychology*, 102 (2011): 519–34.

18 Runswick, O., Roca, A., McRobert, A., Williams, A.M., and North, J. The impact of context on cognitive load and anticipation. *Applied Cognitive Psychology*, 32, 2 (2018): 49.

19 Kato, T., and Fukuda, T. Visual search strategies of baseball batters: Eye movements during the preparatory phase of batting. *Perceptual & Motor Skills*, 94 (2002): 380–6.

20 Williams, A.M., and Weigelt, C. Vision and proprioception in interceptive actions. In K. Davids, G. Savelsbergh, S. Bennett and J. Van der Kamp (eds), *Vision and Interceptive Actions in Sport*, pp. 90–108. London: Routledge, 2002.

21 Higuich, T., Nagami, T., Nakata, H., Watanabe, M., Isaka, T., and Kanosue, K. Contribution of visual information about ball trajectory to baseball hitting accuracy. *PLoS One* (2016). doi: 10.1371/journal.pone.0148498

22 Sherwin, J., Muraskin, J., and Sajda, P. You can't think and hit at the same time: Neural correlates of baseball pitch classification. *Frontiers in Neuroscience*, 6, 177 (2012): 1–11.

23 Muraskin, J., Sherwin, J., and Sajda, P. Knowing when not to swing: EEG evidence that enhanced perception-action coupling underlies baseball batter expertise. *NeuroImage*, 123 (2015): 1–10.

24 www.nytimes.com/2018/04/13/sports/sports-science.html

25 www.washingtonpost.com/national/health-science/scientists-examine-what-happens-in-the-brain-when-bat-tries-to-meet-ball/2016/08/29/d32e9d4e-4d14-11e6-a7d8-13d06b37f256_story.html

Chapter 8: Superintelligence

1 www.thefa.com/news/2014/oct/29/jamie-carraghers-the-fas-developing-defenders-course-291014

2 https://liverpoolfc.fandom.com/wiki/100_Players_Who_Shook_The_Kop_(2013)

3 Williams, A.M., Davids, K., Burwitz, L., and Williams, J.G. Visual search strategies of experienced and inexperienced soccer players. *Research Quarterly for Exercise and Sport*, 65, 2 (1994): 127–35.

4 Williams, A.M., and Davids, K. Visual search strategy, selective attention, and expertise in soccer. *Research Quarterly for Exercise and Sport*, 69, 2 (1998): 111–28.

5 Ward, P., Ericsson, K.A., and Williams, A.M. Complex perceptual-cognitive expertise in a simulated task environment. *Journal of Cognitive Engineering and Decision Making*, 7, 3 (2013): 231–54.

6 Information from Geir Jordet.

7 www.sofoot.com/xavi-clearing-the-ball-is-an-intellectual-defeat-453815.html

8 McGuckian, T.B., Cole, M.H., Jordet, G., Chalkley, D., and Pepping, G.-J. Don't turn blind! The relationship between exploration before ball possession and on-ball performance in Association Football. *Frontiers in Psychology*, 9 (2018). doi: 10.3389/fpsyg.2018.02520

9 Roca, A., Ford, P.R., McRobert, A., and Williams, A.M. Perceptual-cognitive skills and their interaction as a function of task constraint in soccer. *Journal of Sport and Exercise Psychology*, 35 (2013): 144–55.

10 Vater, C., Williams, A.M., and Hossner, E. What do we see out of the corner of our eye? The role of visual pivots and gaze anchors in sport. *International Reviews of Sport and Exercise Psychology*, (2019): 1–23

11 Casanaova, F., Gargante, J., Silva, G., Alves, A.J., Oliveira, J., and Williams, A.M. The effects of prolonged intermittent exercise on perceptual–cognitive processes. *Medicine and Science in Sport and Exercise*, 45, 8 (2013): 1610–17.

12 Williams, A.M., and Elliott, D. Anxiety and visual search strategy in karate. *Journal of Sport and Exercise Psychology*, 21, 4 (1999): 362–75.

13 North, J., Williams, A.M., Ward, P., and Ericsson, A. Identifying the critical information sources to skilled anticipation and recognition using retrospective verbal reports. *Memory*, 2 (2011): 155–68.

14 Gobert, F., Lane, P.C.R., Crocker, S., Cheng, P.D.H., Jones, G., Oliver, I., Pine, S.M. Chunking mechanisms in human learning. *Trends in Cognitive Sciences*, 5, 6 (2001): 236–43.

15 Williams, A.M., Hodges, N.J., North, J., and Barton, G. Perceiving patterns of play in dynamic sport tasks: Investigating the essential information underlying skilled performance. *Perception*, 35 (2006): 317–32.

16 Williams, A.M., Janelle, C.J., and Davids, K. Constraints on visual behavior in sport. *International Journal of Sport and Exercise Psychology*, 2 (2004): 301–18.

17 https://www.pro-football-reference.com/leaders/pass_rating_career.htm

18 Garland, D.J., and Barry, J.R. Cognitive advantage in sport: The nature of perceptual structures. *American Journal of Psychology*, 2 (1991): 211–28.

19 http://www.sloansportsconference.com/wp-content/uploads/2013/Live%20by%20the%20Three,%20Die%20by%20the%20Three%20The%20Price%20of%20Risk%20in%20the%20NBA.pdf

20 Kahenman, D. *Thinking Fast, Thinking Slow*. New York: Farrar, Straus & Giroux, 2011.

Chapter 9: The art of the con

1 https://www.baseballprospectus.com/news/article/31030/prospectus-feature-introducing-pitch-tunnels/

2 Bahill, T.A., and LaRitz, T. Why can't batters keep their eyes on the ball? *American Scientist*, 72, 3 (1984): 249–53.

3 Mann, D.L., Spratford, W., and Abernethy, B. The head tracks and gaze predicts: How the world's best batters hit a ball. *PLoS One*, 8, 3 (2013): e58289.

4 Higuchi, T., Nagami, T., Nakata, H., Watanabe, M., Isaka, T., and Kanosue, K. Contribution of visual information about ball trajectory to baseball hitting accuracy. *PLoS ONE*, 11, 2 (2016). e0148498. doi: 10.1371/journal.pone.0148498

5 Cañal-Bruland, R., Filius, M.A., and Oudejans, R.R.D. Sitting on a fastball. *Journal of Motor Behavior*, 47, 4 (2015): 267–70.

6 https://www.baseballprospectus.com/news/article/31030/prospectus-feature-introducing-pitch-tunnels/

7 https://www.washingtonpost.com/sports/nationals/greg-maddux-a-hall-of-fame-approach-that-carried-an-average-arm-to-cooperstown/2014/01/07/fdd7ae82-77d3-11e3-af7f-13bf0e9965f6_story.html

8 https://www.washingtonpost.com/sports/nationals/greg-maddux-a-hall-of-fame-approach-that-carried-an-average-arm-to-cooperstown/2014/01/07/fdd7ae82-77d3-11e3-af7f-13bf0e9965f6_story.html

9 http://www.perceptionaction.com/pitchtunnels/

10 Jackson, R.C., and Cañal-Bruland, R. Deception in sport. In A.M. Williams and R.C. Jackson (eds), *Anticipation and Decision Making in Sport*, pp. 99–116. Abingdon: Routledge, 2019.

11 Gray, R. 'Markov at the bat': A model of cognitive processing in baseball batters. *Psychological Science*, 13 (2002): 542–7.

12 Loffing, F., Stern, R., and Hagemann, N. Pattern-induced expectation bias in visual anticipation of action outcomes. *Acta Psychologica*, 161 (2015): 45–53.

13 Sinnett, S., and Kingstone, A. A preliminary investigation regarding the effect of tennis grunting: Does white noise during

a tennis shot have a negative impact on shot perception? *PLoS ONE* 5, 10 (2010): e13148.

14 www.theguardian.com/sport/2011/oct/25/caroline-wozniacki-wta-maria-sharapova

15 Muller, F., Jauernig, L., and Cañal-Bruland, R. The sound of speed: How grunting affects opponents' anticipation in tennis. *PLoS ONE*, 14, 4 (2019): e0214819.

16 www.independent.co.uk/sport/tennis-wimbledon-92-grunt-and-graf-in-way-of-seles-dream-the-determination-of-monica-seles-came-over-1530972.html

17 https://metro.co.uk/2017/07/12/why-do-players-grunt-in-tennis-6774211/

18 www.the42.ie/wozniacki-fury-over-opponents-unfair-grunting-3854706-Feb2018/

19 www.youtube.com/watch?v=zjLgoReDBGw

20 Brault, S., Bideau, B., Kulpa, R., and Craig, C.M. Detecting deception in movement: The case of the side-step in rugby. *PLoS ONE*, 7, 6 (2012): e37494.

21 Brault, S., Bideau, B., Craig, C., and Kulpa, R. Balancing deceit and disguise: How to successfully fool the defender in a 1 vs. 1 situation in rugby. *Human Movement Science*, 29 (2010): 412–25.

22 Mori, S., and Shimada, T. Expert anticipation from deceptive action. *Attention, Perception, & Psychophysics*, 75 (2013): 751–70.

23 Kuhn, G., and Findlay, J.M. Misdirection, attention and awareness: inattentional blindness reveals temporal relationship between eye movements and visual awareness. *Quarterly Journal of Experimental Psychology*, 63 (2010): 136–46.

24 Kunde, W., Skirde, S., and Weigelt, M. Trust my face: cognitive factors of head fakes in sports. *Journal of Experimental Psychology: Applied*, 17 (2011): 110–27.

25 Güldenpenning, I., Weigelt, M., and Kunde, W. Processing head fakes in basketball: Are there ironic effects of instructions on the head-fake effect in basketball? *Human Movement Science* (2019). doi: 10.1016/j.humov.2019.102499

26 www.stitcher.com/podcast/the-wharton-moneyball-post-game-podcast/wharton-moneyball/e/61757252

27 www.espncricinfo.com/ci/content/story/339437.html

28 Runswick, O., Roca, A., McRobert, A., Williams, A.M., and North, J. Why bad balls get wickets. The role of congruent and incongruent information in anticipation. *Journal of Sports Sciences*, 35, 5 (2019): 537–43.

Chapter 10: The quiet eye

1 Retief Broodryk. Unpublished PhD thesis, North-West University, South Africa, 2019.

2 Vickers, J.N. Visual control while aiming at a far target. *Journal of Experimental Psychology: Human Perception and Performance*, 22 (1996): 342–54.

3 Gonzalez, C., Causer, J., Miall, R.C., Grey, M.J., Humphreys, G., and Williams, A.M. Identifying the causal mechanisms of the quiet eye period. *European Journal of Sports Sciences*, 17, 1 (2015): 74–84.

4 Causer, J., Bennett, S.J., Holmes, P.S., Janelle, C., and Williams, A.M. Quiet eye duration and gun motion in elite shotgun shooting. *Medicine and Science in Sports and Exercise*, 42, 8 (2009): 1599–608.

5 Vickers, J., Rodrigues, S., and Edworthy, G. Quiet eye and accuracy in the dart throw. *International Journal of Sports Vision*, 6 (2000).

6 Gonzalez, C., Causer, J., Miall, R.C., Grey, M.J., Humphreys, G., and Williams, A.M. Exploring the quiet eye in archery using field- and laboratory-based tasks. *Experimental Brain Research* (2017): 1–13.

7 Adolphe, R., Vickers, J.N., and Laplante, G. The effects of training visual attention on gaze behaviour and accuracy: A pilot study. *International Journal of Sports Vision*, 4 (1997): 28–33.

8 Vickers, J.N., and Lewinski, W. Performing under pressure: Gaze control, decision making, and shooting performance of elite and rookie officers. *Human Movement Science*, 31 (2012): 101–17.

9 Wilson, M.R., McGrath, J., Vine, S.J., Brewer, J., Defriend, D., and Masters, R.S.W. Perceptual impairment and visuomotor control in virtual laparoscopic surgery. *Surgical Endoscopy*, 25 (2011): 2268–74.

10 Harvey, A., Vickers, J.N., Snelgrove, R., Scott, M.F., and Morrison, S. Expert surgeon's quiet eye and slowing down: Expertise differences in performance and quiet eye duration during identification and dissection of the recurrent laryngeal nerve. *American Journal of Surgery*, 207 (2014): 187–93.

11 Williams, A.M., Singer, R.N., and Frehlich, S.G. Quiet eye duration, expertise, and task complexity in near and far aiming tasks. *Journal of Motor Behavior*, 34 (2002): 197–207.

12 Causer, J., Holmes, P.S., Smith, N.C., and Williams, A.M. Anxiety, movement kinematics and visual attention in elite-level performers. *Emotion*, 11, 3 (2011): 595–602.

13 Carey, L.M., Jackson, R.C., Fairweather, M.M., Causer, J., and Williams, A.M. Perceptual–cognitive expertise in golf putting: Capturing and enhancing performance on the greens. In M. Toms (ed.), *Handbook of Golf Science*, pp. 161–72. London: Routledge, 2018.

14 Wilson, M.R., Vine, S.J., and Wood, G. The influence of anxiety on visual attentional control in basketball free-throw shooting. *Journal of Sport and Exercise Psychology*, 28 (2009): 937–46.

15 Beilock, S.L., and Carr, T.H. On the fragility of skilled performance: What governs choking under pressure? *Journal of Experimental Psychology: General*, 130 (2001): 701–25.

16 Vickers, J.N. Gaze control in putting. *Perception*, 21 (1992): 117–32.

17 Vickers, J.N. Neuroscience of the quiet eye in golf putting. *International Journal of Golf Science*, 1 (2012): 2–9.

18 Carey, L.M., Jackson, R.C., Fairweather, M.M., Causer, J., and Williams, A.M. Perceptual–cognitive expertise in golf putting: Capturing and enhancing performance on the greens. In M. Toms (ed.), *Handbook of Golf Science*, pp. 161–72. London: Routledge, 2018.

19 Vickers, J., and Williams, A.M. Why some choke and others don't! *Journal of Motor Behavior*, 39, 5 (2007): 381–94.

20 Causer, J., Holmes, P.S., and Williams, A.M. Quiet eye training in a visuomotor control task. *Medicine and Science in Sport and Exercise*, 43, 6 (2011): 1042–9.

21 Wilson, M.R., Causer, J., and Vickers, J.N. Aiming for excellence: the quiet eye as a characteristic of expertise. In J. Baker and D. Farrow (eds), *Routledge Handbook of Sport Expertise*, pp. 22–37. Abingdon: Routledge, 2017.

22 Harle, S., and Vickers, J.N. Training quiet eye improves accuracy in basketball free throw. *The Sport Psychologist*, 15 (2001): 289–305.

23 Vine, S.J., Moore, L.J., Wilson, M. Quiet eye training facilitates competitive putting performance in elite golfers. *Frontiers in Psychology*, 2, 8 (2011). doi: 10.3389/fpsyg.2011.00008

24 Wood, G., and Wilson, M.R. Quiet-eye training for soccer penalty kicks. *Cognitive Processing*, 12 (2011): 257–66.

25 https://royalsocietypublishing.org/doi/10.1098/rsos.170136

26 Vickers, J.N., Causer, J., and Vanhooren, D. The role of quiet eye timing and location in the basketball three-point shot: A new research paradigm. *Frontiers in Psychology* (2019): https://doi.org/10.3389/fpsyg.2019.02424

Chapter 11: Southpaw advantage

1 http://stats.espncricinfo.com/ci/engine/records/batting/most_runs_career.html?class=1;id=2;type=team

2 Mann, D.L., Runswick, O.R., and Allen, P.M. Hand and eye dominance in sport: Are cricket batters taught to bat back-to-front? *Sports Medicine*, 46 (2016): 1355–63.

3 http://stats.espncricinfo.com/ci/engine/records/batting/most_runs_career.html?class=1;id=2;type=team This is an updated version of a fact previously noted by the Australian cricket writer S.B. Tang.

4 Mann, D.L., Runswick, O.R., and Allen, P.M. Hand and eye dominance in sport: Are cricket batters taught to bat back-to-front? *Sports Medicine*, 46 (2016): 1355–63.

5 Mann, D.L., Loffing, F., and Allen, P.M. The success of sinister right-handers in baseball. *The New England Journal of Medicine*, 377 (2017): 1688–90.

6 Brown, D.M., Poucher, Z.A., Myers, M., Graham, J.D., and Cairney, J. Sinister right-handedness provides Canadian-born Major League Baseball players with an offensive advantage: A further test of the hockey influence on batting hypothesis. *PLoS ONE*, 14, 8 (2019): e0221501.

7 Loffing, F. Left-handedness and time pressure in elite interactive ball games. *Biology Letters*, 13 (2017): 0446.

8 Faurie, C., and Raymond, M. Handedness frequency over more than ten thousand years. *Proceedings of the Royal Society of London B*, 271 (2004): 43–5.

9 Statistics from ESPNCricinfo via Jarrod Kimber.

10 Loffing, F., and Hagemann, N. Performance differences between left- and right-sided athletes in one-on-one interactive sports. In F. Loffing, N. Hagemann and B. Strausse (eds), *Laterality in Sports*, pp. 249–77. San Diego, CA: Academic Press, 2016.

11 Hagemann, N. The advantage of being left-handed in interactive sports. *Attention, Perception, and Psychophysics*, 71 (2009): 1641–8.

12 Loffing, F., Hagemann, N., Schorer, J., and Baker, J. Skilled players' and novices' difficulty anticipating left- vs. right-handed opponents' action intentions varies across different points in time. *Human Movement Science*, 40 (2015): 410–4.

13 Schorer, J., Loffing, F., Hagemann, N., and Baker, J. Human handedness in interactive situations: negative perceptual frequency effects can be reversed! *Journal of Sports Sciences*, 30 (2012): 507–13.

14 McMorris, T., and Colenso, S. Anticipation of professional soccer goalkeepers when facing right- and left-footed penalty kicks. *Perceptual and Motor Skills*, 82 (1996): 931–4.

15 Loffing, F., and Hagemann, N. Performance differences between left- and right-sided athletes in one-on-one interactive sports. In Loffing, F., Hagemann, N., and Strausse, B. (eds), *Laterality in Sports*, pp. 249–77. San Diego, CA: Academic Press, 2016.

16 Faurie, C., and Raymond, M. Handedness, homicide and negative frequency-dependent selection. *Proceedings of the Royal Society B: Biological Sciences*, 272, 1558 (2005): 25–28.

17 www.latimes.com/archives/la-xpm-1989-07-08-sp-2489-story.html

18 www.golfdigest.com/story/built-to-last

19 Allen, P., Mann, D., Runswick, O., Mann, S., and Fletcher, A. Eye and hand dominance in golf. Paper presented at European Academy of Optometry and Optics, Rome, 2019.

20 http://news.bbc.co.uk/sportacademy/hi/sa/golf/features/newsid_2946000/2946513.stm

Chapter 12: The psychology of greatness

1 www.bbc.co.uk/sport/rugby-union/50233481

2 Renninger, K.A., and Hidi, S. *The Power of Interest for Motivation and Learning*. New York: Routledge, 2016.

3 Weissensteiner, J., Abernethy, B., Farrow, D., and Gross, J. Distinguished psychological characteristics of expert cricket batsmen. *Journal of Science and Medicine in Sport*, 15 (2012): 74–9.

4 Duckworth, A.L., Peterson, C., Matthews, M.D., and Kelly, D.R. Grit: Perseverance and passion for long-term goals. *Journal of Personality and Social Psychology*, 92, 6 (2007): 1087–101.

5 Hodges, N.J., Ford, P.R., Hendry, D.T., and Williams, A.M. Getting gritty about practice and success: Motivational characteristics of great performers. *Progress in Brain Research*, 232 (2017): 167–73.

6 B.B., Markgraf, K.M., and Gnacinski, S.L. Examining the merit of grit in women's soccer: questions of theory, measurement, and application. *Journal of Applied Sport Psychology*, 29, 3 (2017): 353–66.

7 Duckworth, A.L., and Quinn, P.D. Development and validation of the short grit scale (Grit-S). *Journal of Personality Assessment*, 91, 2 (2009): 166–74.

8 Larkin, P., O'Connor, D., and Williams, A.M. Perfectionism and sport specific engagement in elite youth soccer players. *Journal of Sports Sciences*, 34, 14 (2016): 1305–10.

9 Larkin, P., O'Connor, D., and Williams, A.M. Does grit influence sport specific engagement and perceptual-cognitive expertise in elite youth soccer? *Journal of Applied Sport Psychology*, 28, 2 (2016): 129–38.

10 Credé, M., Tynan, M.C., and Harms, P.D. Much ado about grit: A meta-analytic synthesis of the grit literature. *Journal of Personality and Social Psychology*, 113, 3 (2017): 492–511.

11 Gullich, A., Hardy, L., Kuncheva, L., Lain, S., Barlow, M., Evans, L., Rees, T., Abernethy, B., Cote, J., Warr, C., and Wraith, L. Developmental biographies of Olympic super-elite and elite athletes: A multidisciplinary pattern recognition analysis. *Journal of Expertise*, 2, 1 (2019): 23–46.

12 Fawver, B., Cowan, R.L., DeCouto, B., Lohse, K.R., Podlog, L., and Williams, A.M. Psychological characteristics, sport engagement, and performance in alpine skiers. *Psychology of Sport and Exercise* [in press].

13 Roberts, G.C. Motivation in sport and exercise from an achievement goal theory perspective: After 30 years where we are? In G.C. Roberts and D.C. Treasure (eds), *Advances in Motivation in Sport and Exercise*, 3rd edn, pp. 5–58. Champaign, IL: Human Kinetics, 2012.

14 Jordet, G. Psychological characteristics of expert performers. In J. Baker and D. Farrow (eds), *Routledge Handbook of Sport Expertise*, pp. 106–20. Abingdon: Routledge, 2017.

15 Collins, D., MacNamara, A., and McCarthy, A. Super champions, champions, and almosts: Important differences and commonalities on the rocky road. *Frontiers in Psychology*, 6 (2016).

16 www.theguardian.com/football/2006/oct/27/newsstory.sport8

17 https://web.archive.org/web/20070929103222/http://www.soccerway.com/news/2006/October/16/doctors-cech-out-for-rest-of-season

18 Fletcher, D., and Mustafa, S. A grounded theory of psychological resilience in Olympic champions. *Psychology of Sport and Exercise*, 13 (2012): 669–78.

19 Wadey, R., Podlog, L., Galli, N., and Mallellieu, S.D. Stress-related growth following sport injury: Examining the applicability of the organismic valuing theory. *Scandinavian Journal of Medicine and Science in Sports*, 26 (2016): 1132–9.

20 Brewer, B.W. The role of psychological factors in sport injury rehabilitation outcomes. *International Review of Sport and Exercise Psychology*, 3 (2010): 40–62.

21 Fawver, B., Beatty, G.F., Mann, D.T.Y., and Janelle, C.M. Staying cool under pressure: Developing and maintaining emotional expertise in sport. In N.J. Hodges and A.M. Williams (eds), *Skill Acquisition in Sport: Research, Theory and Practice*, 3rd edn, pp. 271–90. Abingdon: Routledge, 2019.

22 Moran, A., and O'Shea, H. Motor imagery practice and skilled performance in sport: From efficacy to mechanisms. In N.J.

Hodges and A.M. Williams (eds), *Skill Acquisition in Sport: Research, Theory and Practice*, 3rd edn, pp. 61–76. Abingdon: Routledge, 2019.

23 MacNamara, A., Button, A., and Collins, D. The role of psychological characteristics in facilitating the pathway to elite performance. Part I: Identifying mental skills and behaviors. *The Sport Psychologist*, 24 (2010): 52–73.

24 https://www.mlb.com/player/joey-votto-458015?stats= splits-r-hitting-mlbandyear=2106

25 Crust, L., and Clough, P.J. Relationship between mental toughness and physical endurance. *Perceptual and Motor Skills*, 100, 1 (2005): 192–4.

26 Clough, P., Earle, K., and Sewell, D. Mental toughness: The concept and its measurement. In I. Cockerill (ed.), *Solutions in Sport Psychology*, pp. 32–45. Andover: Cengage Learning EMEA, 2002.

27 Golby, J., and Sheard, M. Mental toughness and hardiness at different levels of rugby league. *Personality and Individual Differences*, 37, 5 (2004): 933–42.

28 Nichols, A.R., Holt, N.L., Polman, R.C.J., and Bloomfield, J. Stressors, coping, and coping effectiveness amongst professional rugby union players. *The Sport Psychologist*, 17 (2006): 333–40.

29 Thomas, P.R., Schlinker, P.J., and Over, R. Psychological and psychomotor skills associated with prowess at ten-pin bowling. *Journal of Sports Sciences*, 14, 3 (1996): 255–68.

30 Mahoney, J.W., Gucciardi, D.F., Ntoumanis, N., and Mallett, C.J. Mental toughness in sport: Motivational antecedents and associations with performance and psychological health. *Journal of Sport and Exercise Psychology*, 36, 3 (2014): 281–92.

31 Nichols, A.R., Holt, N.L., Polman, R.C.J., and Bloomfield, J. Stressors, coping, and coping effectiveness amongst professional rugby union players. *The Sport Psychologist*, 17 (2006): 333–40.

32 Van Yperen, N.W. Why some make it and others do not: Identifying psychological factors that predict career success in professional adult soccer. *The Sport Psychologist*, 23 (2009): 317–29.

33 Nichols, A.R. A longitudinal phenomenological analysis of coping effectiveness amongst Scottish international adolescent golfers. *European Journal of Sports Sciences*, 7 (2007): 169–78.

34 Ntoumanis, N., and Jones, G. Interpretation of competitive trait anxiety symptoms as a function of locus of control beliefs. *International Journal of Sport Psychology*, 29 (1998): 99–114.

35 Hanton, S., O'Brien, M., and Mellalieu, S. Individual differences, perceived control and competitive anxiety. *Journal of Sports Sciences*, 26, 1 (2003): 39–55.

36 Toering, T.T., and Jordet, G. Self-control in professional soccer players. *Journal of Applied Sport Psychology*, 27, 3 (2015): 335–50.

37 Smith, E., Hill, A.P., and Hall, H.K. The relationship between ism, depressive symptoms and burnout in academy footballers. Paper presented at the 3rd Perfectionism Networks Meeting. University of Kent, England, 2016.

38 www.independent.co.uk/news/uk/home-news/british-people-depression-west-mental-health-uk-oecd-europe-scandinavia-women-more-men-a7945321.html

39 Gulliver, A., Griffiths, K.M., Mackinnon, A., Batterham, P.J., and Stanimirovic, R. The mental health of Australian elite athletes. *Journal of Science and Medicine in Sport*, 18, 3 (2015): 255–61.

40 https://apnews.com/9bcb7f4e073447bb9573a217802ce05b/Survey:-Athletes-feel-pressure-of-win-at-all-costs-culture

41 Ulrich, R., Pope, H.G., Cléret, L. et al. Doping in two elite athletics competitions assessed by randomized-response surveys. *Sports Medicine*, 48 (2018): 211–219.

42 https://www.bbc.co.uk/sport/42871491

43 https://www.nytimes.com/2018/04/17/sports/soccer/liverpool-legends-bayern-masters-football.html

44 www.mind.org.uk/media/1085139/Mental-Health-and-Elite-Sport.pdf

Chapter 13: Why athletes choke

1 https://www.metro.news/would-someone-kindly-give-him-a-large-brandy-hes-gone-gaga/1147759/

2 https://edition.cnn.com/2018/07/17/sport/jean-van-de-velde-sporting-disaster-carnoustie-spt-intl/index.html]

3 http://news.bbc.co.uk/1/hi/sport/golf/397813.stm

4 Freakonomics podcast.

5 Netflix Losers documentary.

6 www.youtube.com/watch?v=mZtLJbC42e4

7 Neil, R., and Woodman, T. Performance anxiety, arousal and coping in sport. In T.S. Horn and A.L. Smith (eds), *Advances in Sport and Exercise Psychology*, pp. 211–28. Champaign, IL: Human Kinetics, 2019.

8 Eysenck, M.W., Deraksham, N., Santos, R., and Calvo, M.G. Anxiety and cognitive performance: Attentional control theory. *Emotion*, 7 (2007): 336–53.

9 Beilock, S.L., and Carr, T.H. On the fragility of skilled performance: What governs choking under pressure? *Journal of Experimental Psychology: General*, 130 (2001): 701–25.

10 Beilock, S.L. *Choke: What the Secrets of the Brain Reveal about Getting It Right When You Have To.* New York: Simon & Schuster, 2010.

11 https://hbr.org/2019/06/why-talented-people-fail-under-pressure

12 Toma, M. Missed shots at the free-throw line: Analyzing the determinants of choking under pressure. *Journal of Sports Economics*, 18, 6 (2015): 539–59.

13 http://ftp.iza.org/dp11761.pdf

14 Otten, M. Choking vs. clutch performance: A study of sport performance under pressure. *Journal of Sport and Exercise Psychology*, 31 (2009): 583–601.

15 Mellalieu, S.D., Neil, R., and Hanton, S. An investigation of mediating effects of self-confidence between anxiety intensity and direction. *Research Quarterly for Exercise and Sport*, 77 (2006): 263–70.

16 Hayslip, B., Jr, Petrie, T., MacIntire, M.M., and Jones, G.M. The influences of skill level, anxiety and psychological skills use on amateur golfers' performances. *Journal of Applied Sport Psychology*, 22 (2010): 123–33.

17 Gray, R., Allsop, J., and Williams, S. Changes in putting kinematics associated with choking and excelling under pressure. *International Journal of Sport Psychology*, 44 (2013): 387–407.

18 Gray, R., Orm, A., and Woodman, T. Ironic and reinvestment effects in baseball pitching: How information about an opponent can influence performance under pressure. *Journal of Sport and Exercise Psychology*, 39 (2017): 3–12.

19 Williams, A.M., Vickers, J., and Rodrigues, S. The effects of anxiety on visual search, movement kinematics and performance in table tennis: A test of Eysenck and Calvo's processing efficiency theory. *Journal of Sport and Exercise Psychology*, 24, 4 (2002): 438–55.

20 Cocks, A.J., Jackson, R.C., Bishop, D.T., and Williams, A.M. Anxiety, anticipation and contextual information: A test of attentional control theory. *Cognition and Emotion*, 30, 6 (2016): 1037–48.

21 Wilson, M.R., Kinrade, N.P., and Walsh, V. High-stakes decision-making: anxiety and cognition. In A.M. Williams and R.J. Jackson (eds), pp. 232–49. *Anticipation and Decision-making in Sport*. Abingdon: Routledge, 2019.

22 www.thecricketmonthly.com/story/1176611/the-unimprovable-game

23 www.thetimes.co.uk/article/anatomy-of-heartbreak-nkj8d-9vbhhm?shareToken=9d31c686c822918360d632df9cd1b969

24 Spencer, S.J., Steele, C.M., and Quinn, O.M. Stereotype threat and women's math performance. *Journal of Experimental Social Psychology*, 35, 1 (1998): 4–28.

25 www.espncricinfo.com/story/_/id/21896922/gary-kirsten-accepts-south-africa-choked

26 www.telegraph.co.uk/sport/rugbyunion/international/new-zealand/23230

27 Mahoney, J.W., Gucciardi, D.F., Ntoumanis, N., and Mallett, C.J. Mental toughness in sport: motivational antecedents and associations with performance and psychological health. *Journal of Sport and Exercise Psychology*, 36, 3 (2014): 281–92.

28 Bell, J.J., Hardy, L., and Beattie, S. Enhancing mental toughness and performance under pressure in elite young cricketers: A 2-year longitudinal intervention. *Sport, Exercise, and Performance Psychology*, 2, 4 (2013): 281–97.

29 Hanton, S., Neil, R., Mellalieu, S., and Fletcher, D. Competitive experience and performance status: An investigation into multidimensional anxiety and coping. *European Journal of Sports Sciences*, 8 (2008): 143–52.

30 Smeeton, N.J., Williams, A.M., Hodges, N.J., and Ward, P. The relative effectiveness of explicit instruction, guided-discovery and discovery learning techniques in enhancing perceptual skill in sport. *Journal of Experimental Psychology: Applied*, 11, 2 (2005): 98–110.

31 Alder, D., Ford, P.R., Causer, J., and Williams, A.M. The effects of high- and low-anxiety training on the anticipation judgments of elite performers. *Journal of Sport and Exercise Psychology*, 38, 1 (2018): 93–104.

32 www.reuters.com/article/us-golf-ryder-poulter/poulters-five-birdie-finish-lifts-europe-hopes-idUSBRE88T00S20120930

33 www.theguardian.com/sport/2012/sep/30/ryder-cup-2012-poulter-mcilroy

34 telegraph.co.uk/sport/golf/rydercup/9764959/Miracle-of-Medinah-How-Europe-turned-the-2012-Ryder-Cup-on-its-head.html

35 Jackman, P.C., Crust, L., and Swann, C. The role of mental toughness in the occurrence of flow and clutch states in sport. *International Journal of Sport Psychology* (in press).

36 Swann, C., Crust, L., Jackman, P., Vella, S.A., Allen, M.S., and Keegan, R. Psychological states underlying excellent performance in sport: Toward an integrated model of flow and clutch states. *Journal of Applied Sport Psychology*, 29, 4 (2017): 375–401.

37 Walton, G.M., and Cohen, G.L. Stereotype lift. *Journal of Experimental Social Psychology*, 39 (2002): 456–67.

Chapter 14: How to lead

1 www.rugbyworldcup.com/match/final#stats

2 Cotterill, S.T., and Fransen, K. Athlete leadership in sport teams: Current understanding and future directions. *International Review of Sport and Exercise Psychology*, 9, 1 (2016): 116–33.

3 Fransen, K., Vanbeselaere, N., De Cuyper, B., Vande Broek, G., and Boen, F. Perceived sources of team confidence in soccer and basketball. *Medicine and Science in Sports and Exercise*, 47, 7 (2015): 1470–84.

4 Fransen, K., Vanbeselaere, N., De Cuyper, B., Vande Broek, G., and Boen, F. The myth of the team captain as principal leader: Extending the athlete leadership classification within sport teams. *Journal of Sports Sciences*, 32, 14 (2014): 1389–97.

5 www.iol.co.za/sport/rugby/super-rugby/stormers-choose-a-draw-in-newlands-thriller-against-crusaders-23477943

6 www.youtube.com/watch?v=Fr26b5D2rj8

7 www.landofbasketball.com/statistics/winning_streaks.htm

8 www.nytimes.com/2009/02/15/magazine/15Battier-t.html

9 www.foxsports.com/other/story/heats-battier-has-brains-talent-and-heart-020212

10 Carron, A.V., Colman, M.M., and Wheeler, J. Cohesion and performance in sport: A meta-analysis. *Journal of Sport and Exercise Psychology*, 24 (2002): 168–88.

11 www.independent.co.uk/sport/football/news-and-comment/the-andy-cole-column-the-real-reason-ive-hated-shering-ham-for-15-years-he-refused-to-shake-my-hand-1915658.html

12 Filho, E., Tennenbaum, G., and Yanyun, Y. Cohesion, team mental models, and collective efficacy: Towards an integrated framework of team dynamics in sport. *Journal of Sports Sciences*, 33, 6 (2015): 641–53.

13 https://mol.im/a/7842549

14 Filho, E., and Tenenbaum, G. Team mental models in sports: An overview. In R. Schinke (ed.), *Athletic Insight's Writings in Sport Psychology*. Hauppauge, NY: Nova Science Publishers, Inc, 2012.

15 North, J., and Williams, A.M. Familiarity detection and pattern perception. In A.M. Williams and R.J. Jackson (eds), *Anticipation and Decision-Making in Sport*. London: Routledge, 2019.

16 Eys, M., and Evans, M.B. Group dynamics in sport, exercise, and physical activity contexts. In T.S. Horn and A.L. Smith (eds),

Advances in Sport and Exercise Psychology, pp. 171–88. Champaign, IL: Human Kinetics, 2019.

17 Lausic, D., Tenenbaum, G., Eccles, D., Joeng, A., and Johnston, T. Interteam communication and performance in doubles tennis. *Research Quarterly for Exercise and Sport*, 80, 2 (2009): 281–90.

18 Berman, S.L., Down, J., and Hill, C.W. Tacit knowledge as a source of competitive advantage in the National Basketball Association. *Academy of Management Journal*, 45 (2002): 13–31.

19 Lindenberger, U., Li, S.C., Gruber, W., and Müller, V. Brains swinging in concert: cortical phase synchronization while playing guitar. *BMC Neuroscience*, 10 (2009): 1–12.

20 Sänger, J., Müller, V., and Lindenberger, U. Intra- and interbrain synchronization and network properties when playing guitar in duets. *Frontiers in Human Neuroscience*, 6 (2012): 1–19.

21 Sänger, J., Müller, V., and Lindenberger, U. Directionality in hyperbrain networks discriminates between leaders and followers in guitar duets. *Frontiers in Human Neuroscience*, 7 (2013): 1–14.

22 Astolfi, L., Toppi J., Borghini G., Vecchiato G., He, E.J., Roy A., and Babiloni, F. Cortical activity and functional hyperconnectivity by simultaneous EEG recordings from interacting couples of professional pilots. Paper presented at the IEEE Engineering in Medicine and Biology Society Annual Conference, 2012 (pp. 4752–5). doi: 10.1109/EMBC.2012.6347029.

23 Filho, E., and Tenenbaum, G. Team mental models: Theory, empirical evidence, and applied implications. In G. Tenenbaum and R.C. Eklund (eds), *Handbook of Sport Psychology*, 4th edn. Hoboken, NJ: John Wiley & Sons [in press].

24 Filho, E., Gershgoren, L., Basevitch, I., Schinke, R., and Tenenbaum, G. Peer leadership and shared mental models in a college volleyball team: A season long case study. *Journal of Clinical Sport Psychology*, 8 (2014): 184–203.

25 Cotterill, S.T., and Fransen, K. Athlete leadership in sport teams: Current understanding and future directions. *International Review of Sport and Exercise Psychology*, 9, 1 (2016): 116–33.

26 Lausic, D., Tenenbaum, G., Eccles, D., Joeng, A., and Johnston, T. Interteam communication and performance in doubles tennis. *Research Quarterly for Exercise and Sport*, 80, 2 (2009): 281–90.

27 Pain, M., and Harwood, C. Team building through mutual sharing and open discussion of team functioning. *The Sport Psychologist*, 23 (2009): 523–42.

28 Kerr was interviewed in December 2018, six months before Golden State reached their fifth straight final.

29 Gearity, B.T., and Murray, M.A. Athletes' experiences of the psychological effects of poor coaching. *Psychology of Sport and Exercise*, 12, 3 (2011): 213–21.

30 Turman, P.D. Coaches and cohesion: The impact of coaching techniques on team cohesion in the small group sport setting. *Journal of Sport Behaviour*, 23, 1 (2003): 86–103.

31 www.espn.co.uk/nba/story/_/id/26524600/secret-team-dinners-built-spurs-dynasty

32 https://art19.com/shows/the-book-of-basketball-podcast/episodes/77ebcbaa-b12e-423a-a678-73088a8994e6\

33 Eccles, D.W., and Kazmier, A.W. The psychology of rest in athletes: An empirical study and initial model. *Psychology of Sport and Exercise*, 44 (2019): 90–8.

Chapter 15: How to win a penalty shoot-out

1 www.theguardian.com/football/blog/2017/jun/28/england-penalty-shootouts-european-under-21-championship

2 www.theguardian.com/football/2018/jul/04/garethsouthgate-england-reason-to-believe-daniel-taylor

3 www.theguardian.com/football/2018/jul/05/englandgareth-southgate-penalties-overcome-hoodoo

4 https://uk.reuters.com/article/uk-soccer-worldcup-col-eng-penalty/this-time-england-left-nothing-to-chance-in-shoot-out-idUKKBN1JU1T6

5 Jordet, G., Eferink-Gemser, M.T., Lemmink, K.A.P.M, and Vischer, C. The 'Russian roulette' of soccer: Perceived control and anxiety in a major tournament penalty shootout. *International Journal of Sport Psychology*, 37 (2006): 281–98.

6   Jordet, G., Hartman, E., and Vuijk, P.J. Team history and choking under pressure in major soccer penalty shootouts. *British Journal of Sport Psychology*, 103 (2012): 268–83.

7   Timmis, M.A., Piras, A., and van Paridon, K.N. Keep your eye on the ball; the impact of an anticipatory fixation during successful and unsuccessful soccer penalty kicks. *Frontiers in Psychology*, 9 (2018): 2058.

8   www.skysports.com/football/news/12023/11388401/germany-in-world-cup-penalty-shoot-outs-every-kick-in-history-analysed

9   Jordet, G. Why do English players fail in soccer penalty shootouts? A study of team status, self-regulation, and choking under pressure, *Journal of Sports Sciences*, 27, 2 (2009): 97–106.

10 www.thetimes.co.uk/article/england-have-finally-learnt-to-spot-the-difference-rdbtbt60d

11 www.theguardian.com/football/2006/dec/24/worldcup2006.sport1

12 Lyttleton, B. *Twelve Yards: The Art and Psychology of the Perfect Penalty Kick*. London: Penguin Publishing, 2015.

13 www.laliga.com/en-GB/news/what-became-of-gaizka-mendieta

14 Van der Kamp, J. A field simulation study of the effectiveness of penalty kick strategies in soccer: Late alterations of kick direction increase errors and reduce accuracy. *Journal of Sports Sciences*, 24, 5 (2005): 467–77.

15 Palacios-Huerta, I. *Beautiful Game Theory: How Soccer Can Help Economics*. Princeton, NJ: Princeton University Press, 2016.

16 http://palacios-huerta.com/docs/aer100Dec2010.pdf

17 Moll, T., Jordet, G., and Pepping, G.J. Emotional contagion in soccer penalty shootouts: Celebration of individual success is associated with ultimate team success. *Journal of Sports Sciences*, 28, 9 (2010): 983–92.

18 Navia Manzano, J.A., and Ruiz Perez, L.M. On the use of situation and body information in goalkeeper actions during a soccer penalty kick. *International Journal of Sport Psychology*, 44, 3 (2013): 234–51.

19 Savelsbergh, G.J.P., Williams, A.M., van der Kamp, J., and Ward, P. Visual search, anticipation and expertise in soccer goalkeepers. *Journal of Sports Sciences*, 20 (2002): 279–87.

20 Piras, A., and Vickers, J.N. The effect of fixation transitions on quiet eye duration and performance in the soccer penalty kick: Instep versus inside kicks. *Cognitive Processing* 12 (2011): 245–55.

21 Williams, A.M., and Burwitz, L. Advance cue utilisation in soccer. In T. Reilly, J. Clarys, and A. Stibbe (eds), *Science and Football II*, pp. 239–44. London: E. & F.N. Spon, 1993.

22 Dicks, M., Button, C., and Davids, K. Availability of advance visual information constrains association football goalkeeping performance during penalty-kicks. *Perception*, 39 (2010): 1111–24.

23 Dicks, M., Button, C., and Davids, K. Individual differences in the visual control of intercepting a penalty kick in association football. *Human Movement Science*, 29, 3 (2010): 401–11.

24 Wimshurst, Z.L., Sowden, P.T., and Wright, M. Expert-novice differences in brain function of field hockey players. *Neuroscience*, 315 (2016): 31–44.

Chapter 16: Practising smarter

1 https://www.basketball-reference.com/wnba/leaders/ft_pct_career.html

2 https://www.basketball-reference.com/leaders/ft_pct_career.html

3 https://www.wnba.com/news/elena-delle-donne-free-throw-foul-shooting/

4 https://www.basketballreference.com/wnba/players/d/delleel01w.html

5 https://www.basketball-reference.com/wnba/players/d/delleel01w.html

6 Orwell, G. *Animal Farm*. New York: The New American Library, 1946.

7 Ericsson, K.A., Krampe, R.T., and Tesch-Römer, C. The role of deliberate practice in the acquisition of expert performance. *Psychological Review*, 100 (1993): 363–406.

8   Ericsson, K.A., and Lehmann, A.C. Expert and exceptional per-
    formance: Evidence of maximal adaptation to task constraints.
    Annual Review of Psychology, 47, 1 (1996): 273–305.

9   Ford, P.R., Coughlan, E.K., Hodges, N.J., and Williams, A.M.
    Deliberate practice in sport. In J. Baker and D. Farrow (eds),
    Routledge Handbook of Sport Expertise, pp. 347–62. Abingdon:
    Routledge, 2015.

10 Ericsson, K.A. Toward a science of acquisition of great performance
    in sports: Clarifying the differences between deliberate practice
    and other types of practice. *Journal of Sports Sciences* [in press].

11 Macnamara, B.N., Moreau, D., and Hambrick, D.Z. The rela-
    tionship between deliberate practice and performance in sports:
    A meta-analysis. *Perspectives on Psychological Science*, 11, 3 (2016):
    333–50.

12 Ericsson, K.A. Summing up hours of any type of practice versus
    identifying optimal practice activities: Commentary on Macna-
    mara, Moreau, and Hambrick (2016). *Perspectives on Psychological
    Science*, 11, 3 (2016): 351–4.

13 Ericsson, K.A., and Pool, R. *Peak: Secrets of the New Science of
    Success*. Boston, MA: Houghton Mifflin Harcourt, 2016.

14 www.basketball-reference.com/wnba/players/d/delleel01w.html

15 Ford, P.R., and Coughlan, E.K. Operationalizing deliber-
    ate practice for performance improvements in sport. In N.J.
    Hodges and A.M. Williams (eds), *Skill Acquisition in Sport*, 3rd
    edn, pp. 183–290. Oxford: Routledge, 2019.

16 Ericsson, K.A. Deliberate practice and the modifiability of
    body and mind: Toward a science of structure and acquisition
    of expert and elite performance. *International Journal of Sport
    Psychology*, 38 (2007): 4–34.

17 Guadagnoli, M., and Lee, T. Challenge point: Framework for
    conceptualizing the effects of various practice conditions on
    motor learning. *Journal of Motor Behavior*, 39, 2 (2004): 212–24.

18 Yan, V.X., Guadagnoli, M.A., and Haycocks, N. Appropriate
    failure to create effective learning. In N.J. Hodges and A.M.
    Williams (eds), *Skill Acquisition in Sport*, 3rd edn, pp. 313–29.
    Abingdon: Routledge, 2019.

19 Deakin, J.M., and Cobley, S. A search for deliberate practice: An examination of the practice environments in figure skating and volleyball. In J.L. Starkes and K.A. Ericsson (eds), *Expert Performance in Sports: Advances in Research on Sport Expertise*, pp. 115–35. Champaign, IL: Human Kinetics, 2003.

20 Coughlan, E.K., Williams, A.M., McRobert, A.P., and Ford, P.R. How experts practice: A novel test of deliberate practice theory. *Journal of Experimental Psychology: Learning, Memory and Cognition*, 40 (2013): 449–58.

21 Coughlan, E., Ford, P.R., and Williams, A.M. Lessons from the experts: The effect of increasing engagement in deliberate practice and cognitive processing on intermediate skill level performers. *Journal of Sport and Exercise Psychology* [in press].

22 Williams, A.M., and Weigelt, C. Vision and proprioception in interceptive actions. In K. Davids, G. Savelsbergh, S. Bennett, and J. Van der Kamp (eds), *Vision and Interceptive Actions in Sport*, pp. 90–108. London: Routledge, 2002.

23 www.chinupgoggles.com/

24 Dunton, A., O'Neill, C., and Coughlan, E.K. The impact of a training intervention with spatial occlusion goggles on controlling and passing a football. *Science and Medicine in Football*, 3, 4 (2019): 281–6.

25 www.wnba.com/news/wnba-stats-50-40-90-is-the-icing-on-edds-historic-season/

Chapter 17: The power of coaching

1 Anderson, D.I., Magill, R.A., Mayoa, A.M., and Steel, K.A. Enhancing motor skill acquisition with augmented feedback. In N.J. Hodges and A.M. Williams (eds), *Skill Acquisition in Sport*, 3rd edn, pp. 3–19. Abingdon: Routledge, 2019.

2 Magill, R.A., and Anderson, D.I. *Motor Learning and Control: Concepts and Applications*, 11th edn. New York: McGraw-Hill, 2017.

3 Shea, J.B., and Morgan, R.L. Contextual interference effects on acquisition, retention, and transfer of a motor skill. *Journal of Experimental Psychology: Human Learning and Memory*, 5, 2 (1979): 179–87.

4 Roca, A., Williams, A.M., and Ford, P. Developmental activities and the acquisition of superior anticipation and decision making in soccer. *Journal of Sports Sciences*, 30, 15 (2012): 1643–52.

5 Chow, J.Y., Shuttleworth, R., Davids, K., and Araujo, D. Ecological dynamics and transfer from practice to performance in sport. In N.J. Hodges and A.M. Williams (eds), *Skill Acquisition in Sport*, 3rd edn, pp. 330–44. Abingdon: Routledge, 2019.

6 Ford, P.R., and O'Connor, D. Practice and sports activities in the acquisition of anticipation and decision making. In A.M. Williams and R.J. Jackson (eds), *Anticipation and Decision-Making in Sport*, pp. 269–85. Abingdon: Routledge, 2019.

7 Renshaw, I., Headrick, J., Maloney, M., Moy, B., and Pinder, R. Constraints-led learning in practice: designing effective learning environments. In N.J. Hodges and A.M. Williams (eds), *Skill Acquisition in Sport*, 3rd edn, pp. 63–82. Abingdon: Routledge, 2019.

8 Kantak, S.S., and Winstein, C.J. Learning–performance distinction and memory processes for motor skills: A focused review and perspective. *Behavioural Brain Research*, 228, 1 (2012): 219–31.

9 Magill, R.A., and Anderson, D.I. *Motor Learning and Control: Concepts and Applications*, 11th edn. New York: McGraw-Hill, 2017.

10 Williams, A.M., and Hodges, N.J. Practice, instruction and skill acquisition: Challenging tradition. *Journal of Sports Sciences*, 23, 6 (2005): 637–50.

11 Hodges, N.J., and Williams, A.M. (eds), *Skill Acquisition in Sport*, 3rd edn. Abingdon: Routledge, 2019.

12 Wright, D., and Kim, T. Contextual interference: New findings, insights, and implications for skill acquisition. In N.J. Hodges and A.M. Williams (eds), *Skill Acquisition in Sport*, 3rd edn, pp. 99–118. Abingdon: Routledge (2019).

13 Hall, K.A., Domingues, D., and Cavazos, R. Contextual interference effects with skilled basketball players. *Perceptual and Motor Skills*, 78 (1994): 835–41.

14 Goode, S., and Magill, R.A. Contextual interference effects in learning 3 badminton serves. *Research Quarterly for Exercise and Sport*, 57, 4 (1986): 308–14.

15 Porter, J.M., and Magill, R.A. Systematically increasing contextual interference is beneficial for learning sport skills. *Journal of Sports Sciences*, 28 (2010): 1277–85.

16 Farrow, D., and Buszard, T. Exploring the applicability of the contextual interference effect in sport practice. *Progress in Brain Research*, 234 (2017): 69–83.

17 Buszard, T., Reid, M., Krause, L., Kovalchik, S., and Farrow, D. Quantifying contextual interference and its effect on skill transfer in skilled youth tennis players. *Frontiers in Psychology* 8 (2017). doi: 10.3389/fpsyg.2017.01931

18 Schmidt, R.A. A schema theory of discrete motor skill learning. *Psychological Review*, 82, 4 (1975): 225–60.

19 Schmidt, R.A., Lee, T.D., Winstein, C.J., Wulf, G., and Zelaznik, H.N. *Motor Control and Learning: A Behavioural Emphasis.* Champaign, IL: Human Kinetics, 2018.

20 Fazeli, D., Taheri, H.R., and Kakhki, A.S. Random versus blocked practice to enhance mental representation in golf putting. *Perceptual and Motor Skills* 124, 3 (2017): 674–88.

21 Porter, J.M., and Magill, R.A. Systematically increasing contextual interference is beneficial for learning sport skills. *Journal of Sports Sciences*, 28, 12 (2010): 1277–85.

22 Dias, G., Couceiro, M.S., Barreiros, J., Clemente, F.M., Mendes, R., and Martins, F.M.L. Distance and slope constraints: Adaptation and variability in golf putting. *Motor Control*, 18 (2014): 221–43.

23 Porter, J.M., Landin, D., Hebert, E.P., and Baum, B. The effects of three levels of contextual interference on performance outcomes and movement patterns in golf skills. *International Journal of Sports Science and Coaching*, 2, 3 (2007): 243–56.

24 www.thecricketmonthly.com/story/1027027/batting-3-0

25 Ste-Marie, D.M., Carter, M.J., and Yantha, Z.D. Self-controlled learning: Current findings, theoretical perspectives, and future directions. In N.J. Hodges and A.M. Williams (eds), *Skill Acquisition in Sport*, 3rd edn, pp. 119–40. Abingdon: Routledge, 2019.

26 Masters, R.S.W., Duijn, T.V., and Uiga, L. Advances in implicit motor learning. In N.J. Hodges and A.M. Williams (eds), *Skill Acquisition in Sport*, 3rd edn, pp. 77–96. Abingdon: Routledge, 2019.

27 Wulf, G. Attentional focus and motor learning: A review of 15 years. *International Review of Sport and Exercise Psychology*, 6, 1 (2013): 77–104.

28 Fairbrother, J.T. Skill acquisition: The science and practice of teaching sport skills. In M.H. Anshel, E.E. Labbe, T.A. Petrie, S.J. Petruzzello, and J.A. Steinfeldt (eds), *APA Handbook of Sport and Exercise Psychology*, vol. 1. Washington, DC: American Psychological Association, 2019.

29 Couvillion, K.F., and Fairbrother, J.T. Expert and novice performers respond differently to attentional focus cues for speed jump roping. *Frontiers in Psychology*, 9 (2018). doi: 10.3389/fpsyg.2018.02370

30 Ford, P., Yates, I., and Williams, A.M. An analysis of activities and instructional behaviours used by coaches during practice in English youth soccer: exploring the link between theory and practice. *Journal of Sports Sciences*, 28 (2010): 483–95.

31 www.sofoot.com/xavi-clearing-the-ball-is-an-intellectual-defeat-453815.html

Chapter 18: The next frontier

1 https://barcainnovationhub.com/acerca-de/

2 https://youtu.be/d32b8rgfrwg

3 https://www.sporttechie.com/fc-barcelona-realtrack-systems-wearable-technology-wimu/

4 https://www.orbisresearch.com/reports/index/global-real-time-location-systems-in-sports-rtls-market-2019-by-company-regions-type-and-application-forecast-to-2024

5 Ric, A., and Peláez, R. *Football Analytics: Now and beyond – A Deep Dive into the Current State of Advanced Data Analysis.* Barcelona: Barça Innovation Hub, 2019.

6 https://twitter.com/braingametennis/status/1175519162938155013

7 https://content.iospress.com/articles/journal-of-sports-analytics/jsa190294

8   https://cafefutebol.files.wordpress.com/2013/12/substitution_timing.pdf

9   https://papers.ssrn.com/sol3/papers.cfm?abstract_id= 3132563

10 www.forbes.com/sites/shaneyoung/2019/11/30/the-nbas-three-point-revolution-continues-to-take-over/#6b-6c7e4056b8

11 www.forbes.com/sites/shaneyoung/2019/11/30/the-nbas-three-point-revolution-continues-to-take-over/#6b-6c7e4056b8

12 www.statsperform.com/

13 www.homecourt.ai/

14 www.secondspectrum.com/index.html

15 www.nbastuffer.com/analytics101/nba-teams-that-have-analytics-department/

16 https://metrica-sports.com/

17 Alamar, B.J. *Sports Analytics: A Guide for Coaches, Managers, and Other Decision Makers.* New York: Columbia University Press, 2013.

18 irishtimes.com/sport/other-sports/the-super-global-sports-star-of-2019-the-nike-vaporfly-1.4114640

19 irishtimes.com/sport/other-sports/nike-vaporflys-won-t-be-banned-but-regulations-will-tighten-1.4154918

20 nytimes.com/interactive/2019/12/13/upshot/nike-vapor-fly-next-percent-shoe-estimates.html

21 vice.com/en_uk/article/bmqdad/chasing-marginal-gains-sports-grey-area-between-innovation-and-cheating

22 www.bbc.com/sport/olympics/19089259

23 www.cyclingplus.com/articles/hope-technology-unveils-stunning-new-gb-track-bike/

24 Mang, C.S., Borich, M.R., Wadden, K.P., Boyd, L.A., and Siengsukon. Motor learning and its neurophysiology. In N.J. Hodges and A.M. Williams (eds), *Skill Acquisition in Sport*, 3rd edn, pp. 293–312. Abingdon: Routledge, 2019.

25 Copenhaver, E.A., and Diamond, A.B. The value of sleep on athletic performance, injury, and recovery in the young athlete. *Pediatric Annals*, 46, 3 (2017): 106–11.

26 Gupta, L., Morgan, K., and Gilchrist, S. Does elite sport degrade sleep quality? A systematic review. *Sports Medicine*, 47, 7 (2017): 1317–33.

27 Mah, C.D., Mah, K.E., Kezirian, E.J., and Dement, W.C. The effects of sleep extension on the athletic performance of collegiate basketball players. *SLEEP*, 34, 7 (2011): 943–50.

28 Schwartz, J., and Simon, R.D. Sleep extension improves serving accuracy: A study with college varsity tennis players. *Physiology and Behavior*, 151, 1 (2015): 541–4.

29 Albouy, G., King, B.R., Schmidt, C., Desseilles, M., Dang-Vu, T.T., Balteau, E., Phillips, C., Degueldre, C., Orban, P., Benali, H., Peigneux, P., Luxen, A., Karni, A., Doyon, J., Maquet, P., and Korman, M. Cerebral activity associated with transient sleep-facilitated reduction in motor memory vulnerability to interference. *Scientific Reports*, 11, 6 (2016): 34948. doi: 10.1038/srep34948.

30 Nishida, M., and Walker, M.P. Daytime naps, motor memory consolidation and regionally specific sleep spindles. *PLoS One*, 2, 4 (2007): e341.

31 www.independent.co.uk/sport/football/news-and-comment/cristiano-ronaldo-secret-laura-trott-jason-kenny-sex-sleep-expert-team-gb-chris-hoy-a7932146.html

32 https://ouraring.com/

33 www.bbc.co.uk/sport/football/32276547

34 https://bleacherreport.com/articles/2720313-footballs-secret-sports-science-the-power-of-sleep

35 Beckmann, J., and Elbe, A.M. *Sport psychological interventions in competitive sports*. Cambridge: Cambridge Scholars Publishing, 2015.

36 Mirifar, A., Beckmann, J., and Ehrlenspiel, F. Neurofeedback as supplementary training for optimizing athletes' performance: A systematic review with implications for future research. *Neuroscience and Biobehavioral Reviews*, 75 (2017): 419–32.

37 Dyke, F. et al. Cerebral cortical activity associated with non-experts' most accurate motor performance. *Human Movement Science*, 37 (2014): 21–31.

38 Landers, D.M., Petruzzello, S.J., Salazar, W., Crews, D.J., Kubitz, K.A., Gannon, T., and Han, M. The influence of electrocortical biofeedback on performance in pre-elite archers. *Medicine and Science in Sports and Exercise*, 23 (1991): 123–9.

39 www.bbc.co.uk/sport/football/36189778

40 Jeukendrup, A., and Gleesen, M. *Sport Nutrition: An Introduction to Energy Production and Performance*, 2nd edn. Champaign, IL: Human Kinetics, 2020.

41 www.incisiv.tech

42 https://rezzil.com/home-us/

43 https://barcainnovationhub.com/the-use-of-vr-ar-mr-to-improved-performance-in-sports

44 Gray, R. Sports training technologies: achieving and assessing transfer. In N.J. Hodges and A.M. Williams (eds), *Skill Acquisition in Sport*, 3rd edn, pp. 203–19. Abingdon: Routledge, 2019.

45 Gray, R. Transfer of training from virtual to real baseball batting. *Frontiers in Psychology*, 8 (2017). doi: 10.3389/fpsyg.2017.02183

46 www.bbc.com/sport/winter-olympics/42572433

47 https://info.dynavisioninternational.com/

48 https://neurotracker.net/

49 www.nytimes.com/2017/01/04/sports/neurotracker-athletic-performance.html

50 www.extremetech.com/extreme/133529-nikes-stroboscopic-eyewear-improves-visual-memory-hand-eye-coordination

51 Broadbent, D.P., Causer, J., Williams, A.M., and Ford, P.R. Perceptual-cognitive skill training and its transfer to expert performance in the field: Future research directions. *European Journal of Sports Sciences*, 15, 4 (2014): 322–31.

Index

Would you like your people to read this book?

If you would like to discuss how you could bring these ideas to your team, we would love to hear from you. Our titles are available at competitive discounts when purchased in bulk across both physical and digital formats. We can offer bespoke editions featuring corporate logos, customized covers, or letters from company directors in the front matter can also be created in line with your special requirements.

We work closely with leading experts and organizations to bring forward-thinking ideas to a global audience. Our books are designed to help you be more successful in work and life.

For further information, or to request a catalogue, please contact:
business@johnmurrays.co.uk
sales-US@nicholasbrealey.com (North America only)

Nicholas Brealey Publishing is an imprint of
John Murray Press.